Teamwork in Human Services

□ □ □
□ □ □
□ □ □

Teamwork in Human Services

Models and Applications Across the Life Span

Edited by

HOWARD G. GARNER, PH.D.

Professor, School of Education
Virginia Commonwealth University
Richmond, Virginia

FRED P. ORELOVE, PH.D.

Executive Director
Virginia Institute for Developmental Disabilities
Virginia Commonwealth University
Richmond, Virginia

WITH ELEVEN CONTRIBUTING AUTHORS

Butterworth–Heinemann

Boston London Oxford Singapore Sydney Toronto Wellington

Every effort has been made to ensure that the information in this text is accurate and conforms to standards accepted at the time of publication. However, as treatment recommendations vary, the reader is advised to verify all suggested programs.

Recognizing the importance of preserving what has been written, it is the policy of Butterworth–Heinemann to have the books it publishes printed on acid-free paper, and we exert our best efforts to that end.

Library of Congress Cataloging-in-Publication Data

Teamwork in human services : models and applications across the life span / edited by Howard G. Garner, Fred Orelove : with 11 contributing authors.
    p.   cm.
    Includes bibliographical references and index.
    ISBN 0-7506-9519-6 (acid-free paper)
    1. Social service—Team work. 2. Health care teams. 3. Human services.   I. Garner, Howard G. II. Orelove, Fred P.
HV41.T43   1994
361'.0068'4--dc20

            94-9103
            CIP

British Library Cataloguing-in-Publication Data

A catalogue record for this book is available from the British Library.

Butterworth–Heinemann
313 Washington Street
Newton, MA 02158

10 9 8 7 6 5 4 3 2 1

Printed in the United States of America

Contents

Contributors

Christine A. Ameen, Ed.D
Director of Program Evaluation and Planning
Starr Commonwealth Schools
Albion, MI 49224

Maité deLamerens-Pratt, M.D. FAAP
Pediatric Consultants, P.C.
777 Washington Avenue, Suite 400
Memphis, TN 38105

Corinne Welt Garland, M.Ed.
Executive Director
Child Development Resources
Lightfoot, VA 23090

Howard G. Garner, Ph.D.
Professor of Education
Division of Teacher Education
Virginia Commonwealth University
Richmond, VA 23284-2020

Gerald S. Golden, M.D.
Adjunct Professor of Neurology
University of Pennsylvania School of Medicine
and Consultant
Children's Seashore House
Philadelphia, PA 19104

Judith Hernan, MSN, RN, NHA
Administrator
York Lutheran Retirement Community and Center
1801 Folkemer Circle
York, PA 17404

Joyce G. Losen, Ed.M.
Assistant to the Superintendent
Westport Public Schools
Westport, CT 06880

Stuart M.Losen, Ph.D.
Adjunct Professor
Graduate School of Education and Applied Professions
Fairfield University, Fairfield, CT
and Licensed Clinical Psychologist
260 Riverside Avenue
Westport, CT 06880

Martin L. Mitchell, Ed.D.
Vice President of Program Evaluation and Planning
Starr Commonwealth Schools
Albion, MI 49224

Fred P. Orelove, Ph.D.
Executive Director
Virginia Institute for Developmental Disabilities
Virginia Commonwealth University
Richmond, VA 23284-3020

Vicki C. Pappas, Ph.D.
Director, Planning and Policy Studies Program
Institute for the Study of Developmental Disabilities
Indiana University
Bloomington, IN 47405

Tawara D. Taylor, MA
Director of Community Services Division
University Affiliated Program
Georgetown University
3800 Reservoir Road, NW
Washington, DC 20007-2197

Virginia J. Williams, MA
Senior Advisor
University Affiliated Program
Georgetown University
3800 Reservoir Road, NW
Washington, DC 20007-2197

□ □ □
□ □ □
□ □ □

Preface

In the 1990s teamwork has become a major goal of almost all organizations—from small businesses to large corporations, from clinics to hospitals, from schools to school divisions, from day-care centers to residential programs. Teams in human services programs across the life span provide high-quality services that are individualized and carefully coordinated. In a work world of restricted resources, complex problems, renewed focus on quality, and increased competition, the need to work together in pursuit of common goals has become both evident and imperative.

No longer can organizations afford to have small groups of specialists organized in departments and working in isolation on narrow aspects of multifaceted issues and problems. The old way of doing business produced distrust and competition among professionals who were serving the same patient, student, or client. Today, teams are being formed to include professionals with different knowledge and skills who are expected to work together, communicate, collaborate, analyze and solve problems, make collective decisions, and monitor the delivery and coordination of services. The person receiving services and the family are often viewed as important members of the team because of their special interest, vital information, and perspective.

In hospitals, schools, community agencies, and other human services programs, everyone seems to favor teamwork and to desire its many benefits, but, unfortunately, not everyone engages in behavior that promotes teamwork. Sharing the values and goals of teamwork is not the same as actually participating as a member of an ongoing team in which stress and conflict are inevitable. Put simply, teamwork is not as easy to achieve as one might think. Teamwork in health and human services, as in the world of sports, requires a detailed knowledge of the rules, skill development, a great deal of practice, and success. Thus, education and training in teamwork have become a new priority in many programs within universities, continuing education, and human resource development.

In addition to learning and practicing the knowledge and skills of their highly specialized disciplines, all professionals now need to learn how to be a member of a team, which involves skills such as communicating effectively with others, collaborating in problem solving and decision making, and maximizing the benefits of the overlap among the helping professions. These are complex skills that require a strong knowledge base, including an in-depth understanding of different types of teamwork and the various settings in which teams work.

The goal of *Teamwork in Human Services: Models and Applications Across the Life Span* is to provide the knowledge base for the development of teamwork skills in health and human services across the life span of the persons receiving those services. This book is designed for both graduate students and practicing professionals. It can serve as a textbook for interdisciplinary courses in both university and in-service training experiences. It provides both theory and practice— the theoretical bases for teamwork in human services, an analysis of the different models of teamwork, and discussion by practicing professionals of how teamwork actually works in early intervention programs, special education, residential child care, medical settings, community services, and programs for older persons.

Working together in teams has brought a new level of effectiveness, excitement, and satisfaction to professionals in health and human services. Those with experience, who are now enjoying these benefits, have an obligation to share their understanding of teamwork and its processes with those who are just beginning. *Teamwork in Human Services* represents such an effort.

Acknowledgments

We would like to acknowledge our colleagues who work daily with infants, children, and adults with special needs and who have contributed to our knowledge of and experience in teamwork and the helping process. We also recognize the work of professionals in University Affiliated Programs for People with Developmental Disabilities across the country who have been pioneers in developing interdisciplinary training programs in teamwork. We especially want to acknowledge the teamwork we have enjoyed with our wives, Ann Sarratt Garner and Irene Carney, in helping to rear our children and building our respective families.

MODELS OF
TEAMWORK

1

□ □ □
□ □ □
□ □ □

Critical Issues in Teamwork

Howard G. Garner

INTRODUCTION

The Need for Teamwork

Today it is widely accepted that professionals need to work together in teams to meet the complex needs of their students, clients, and patients across the life span. In schools, hospitals, clinics, and community-based programs, professionals from different disciplines are working together in teams, communicating information, making shared decisions, and pursuing common goals. Depending on the setting and the services provided, teams vary in size, membership, and scope of responsibilities. Some of these differences are based on the model of teamwork being employed: multidisciplinary, interdisciplinary, transdisciplinary, or inter-agency. Across all models teamwork is valued as the best means of ensuring that decisions regarding people who are receiving services will be based on complete information and that services will be coordinated, consistent, and goal directed. Most teams work to include the person receiving services and the person's family in the process of establishing goals and implementing a plan determined through consensus.

Teams have been used in some areas of health care for several decades (Ducanis & Golin, 1979). Garrett (1955) observed that in the fields of treating chronic illness and rehabilitation, "the team approach" was then so widely used that its validity had been accepted unconsciously, and the term had become a platitude almost without meaning. Today teamwork is more than a value and a philosophy of service delivery—it is now embedded in the structure of many organizations. Medical centers include specialized teams in trauma centers, operating rooms, transplant units, and cancer rehabilitation. In the growing field of gerontology, where the complex needs of the elderly involve all aspects of a person's life, teams are used in both assessment and treatment planning (Campbell & Cole, 1987).

In some settings teamwork is required by federal and state laws. For example, early intervention teams serving infants with special needs are mandated by the federal Public Law 99–457. This law explicitly directs teams to work with the infant's family in planning and providing services (McGonigel & Garland, 1988). Since 1978, when P.L. 94–142 went into effect, multidisciplinary teams have been required of all public schools in assessing students for special education, determining eligibility for services, and planning individualized educational programs (Losen & Losen, 1985).

Interagency teams are now being used to plan and assist persons in making important life transitions from hospital to home–based care (Katz, Pokorni, & Long, 1989), from infant intervention programs to preschool programs (Kilgo, Richard, & Noonan, 1989), and from school programs for students with severe disabilities to the world of work and independent living (Everson, Barcus, Moon, & Morton, 1987). Families of persons with disabilities report the greatest stress occurs when their family member has to make significant changes in their status, program, location, and the professionals from whom services are received (Turnbull & Turnbull, 1986). Interagency teams of professionals work with the families and the person with a disability to prevent the phenomenon of clients "falling through the cracks" in the service delivery system.

Most human problems, occurring from early childhood to old age, result from the interaction of a number of physical, psychological, spiritual, and environmental factors, and thus cross the traditional boundaries of the helping disciplines (Mariano, 1989). As a result, most professionals today acknowledge that no discipline has "the answer" to the problems being faced. Most acknowledge, further, that only when the knowledge and skill of all disciplines and professionals serving an individual are combined and coordinated, can the needs of the whole person be met.

Consequences When Teamwork Does Not Occur

When teamwork is absent, the consequences for clients, students, and patients are frustration, inefficiency, inconsistency, and even serious mistakes. When communication does not occur among helping professionals working with the same individual, important decisions are made without complete information regarding the nature of the problems, the person's strengths and needs, and the resources and supports available. When communication among professionals serving the same individual is absent or incomplete, mistakes are made. The most common excuse for errors in human services is captured in the statement, "If I had known *then* what I know *now*, I would have made another decision and acted differently."

When interventions and treatment strategies are not jointly planned and carefully coordinated by teams, the individuals receiving services too often are confused, because specialists, who have different insights and priorities, sometimes give inconsistent and contradictory advice. This often leads to failure on the part of the client or patient to comply with the professional prescriptions. As a result, the client or patient is often blamed for the failure of the treatment plan to effect change. In this situation responsibility and accountability for the effectiveness of the treatment plan are diffused.

Competition and conflict among the professionals frequently result as well. In too many settings professional turf is carefully guarded, and distrusting camps plot against one another beneath a veneer of professionalism. The human services disciplines may be called "the helping professions," but they can be extremely competitive and even vicious with one another under certain conditions.

BASIC TENETS OF TEAMWORK

"Teamwork in the helping professions" means different things to different people, depending on the model of teamwork being used, the setting, and the persons being served by the team. There are, however, a few basic tenets to which most advocates of teamwork seem to be committed.

Communication Is Essential

Communication among the professionals serving the same individual is viewed as fundamental and essential for teamwork to occur. Each discipline has important information to communicate regarding the nature of problems and needs of the person being served. This information is based on formal and informal assessment procedures, observation, research, and professional experience. Each discipline has a somewhat different and sometimes unique perspective regarding the effects of these problems on the client and the family. Only when complete information from all disciplines is brought together can one understand the complexity of the problems being faced (Garner, 1988).

Collaboration in Treatment Planning and Service Delivery

A second tenet of teamwork is that collaboration in both planning and implementing a course of action in pursuit of common goals is necessary to achieve coordination, consistency, and a positive outcome (Spencer & Coye, 1988). Each helping discipline employs a variety of strategies, treatments, and techniques that can be used in response to specific problems and needs. Only when these interventions are carefully selected and coordinated can they achieve their promise.

Conflict Prevention and Resolution

A third tenet of teamwork is that functioning teams provide a mechanism for both preventing and resolving conflicts. Conflict is viewed as inevitable in human organizations, especially when several people work independently in pursuit of different goals.Unresolved conflict is viewed as a major barrier to effective services and a source of stress for both professionals and those being served. Teams provide a forum in which different values and priorities can be discussed and reconciled prior to their being acted out. In those situations where conflict does occur, teams provide a process through which frustration and misunderstanding can be expressed and resolution and a renewed sense of common purpose can be achieved.

Personal and Professional Development

A final tenet of teamwork, subscribed to by most advocates, is that teamwork promotes personal and professional development, facilitates reliable feedback among colleagues, and provides emotional support for professionals working in demanding and stressful situations. Where teams are functioning effectively, professionals report high levels of satisfaction with their jobs, high morale, and a reduction of stress (Varney, 1989).

In summary, teamwork in the helping professions is based on communication, collaboration, shared decision making, cooperation, consistency, conflict resolution, and mutual support. The advocates of teamwork state that functioning teams provide higher quality services for clients and high levels of satisfaction and morale for the professionals.

IMPEDIMENTS TO TEAMWORK

As early as 1955, Garrett noted that teamwork was widely accepted as best practice. Today everyone continues to be in favor of teamwork, and yet, so many programs and professionals continue to encounter a variety of barriers and impediments that seem to get in the way of colleagues from different disciplines working together effectively. These barriers include specialization, organizational structure, role ambiguity and incongruent expectations, and authority and power structures.

Specialization in the Helping Professions

Increased specialization in the various helping disciplines has resulted in professionals with high levels of knowledge and competence in narrow fields of study (McMahon, 1989). Each part of the human body and human development, system and subsystem of human functioning, and aspect of daily living has become the focus of analysis, research, and prescriptions for improvement by specialists in a variety of disciplines.

Today, for example, the American Board of Medical Specialties (1991) includes 24 boards, awarding 34 general certificates and 50 subspecialty certificates. The same pattern exists in the field of nursing. The American Nurses' Association has published practice standards in 22 specialty areas. The Nursing Organization Liaison Forum is made up of 44 participating special interest organizations (Styles, 1989).

A similar pattern exists in other helping professions. The Council for Exceptional Children includes 18 divisions for special education teachers of students with different disabilities, related services professionals, and a variety of specialized roles in schools from diagnosticians to administrators. The pattern of specialization also is seen among psychologists, physical therapists, and occupational therapists who receive specialized training to work with clients of specific ages, with specific disorders, and in specific settings.

Specialization has increased the knowledge and skill level of professionals in relatively narrow fields of study. Training in these specialties most often occurs in isolation from other disciplines that have interest and concern for the same disorders and disabilities. Specialization also tends to overlook the needs and functioning of the whole person and their individual life experience.

Organizational Structure

Many human services organizations continue to be organized according to the hierarchical, departmental model (Garner, 1988). This model organizes personnel in homogeneous units, usually called departments or services, based on the discipline, title, and role of the various professionals. The departmental model in hospitals, for example, usually includes a separate department for medicine, nursing, physical therapy, occupational therapy, social work, and psychology. In large hospitals each specialization, such as surgery, radiology, and pediatrics, has its own administrative unit as well. Each department has a director or chairperson who supervises the activities of department members and pursues the best interests of the department in the ongoing competition with other departments for resources, space, control, and recognition.

Garner (1982) identifies seven major weaknesses of the departmental model in a human services organization. These weaknesses include the following:

1. Departmental loyalties create a "we vs. they" perception and attitude among members of different departments. Comparisons are made in departmental treatment philosophies, professional work habits, and attitudes toward those who receive services. "Our" position is almost always superior to "theirs."
2. Departments compete with one another for influence, power, control, space, and financial resources. Departments with fewer resources and less status resent those with more. Clients, students, and patients are sometimes caught in this competition.
3. Physical separation of departments leads to isolation and the absence of communication. Interdisciplinary support, encouragement, and shared insight do not occur routinely as professionals who serve the same individuals retreat to their departmental offices and colleagues.
4. A shared philosophy, common goals, and compatible intervention techniques often are not established, pursued, and utilized by professionals in different departments who serve the same individuals.
5. Professionals who have the most direct interaction with the clients, students, and patients are often left out of the decision-making process regarding treatment plans and therapeutic interventions. Thus, decisions are made without adequate information, increasing the probability that the plans will not completely match the person's needs and condition.
6. Opportunities for interdisciplinary communication, problem solving, and planning are infrequent. Each discipline does what it thinks is best practice given the information available at the time. Conflict occurs when the decisions of one department interfere with or contradict those of another.
7. Significant decisions are made by those at the top of the departmental hierarchy. The staff responsible for implementation often view these decisions as inappropriate and thus feel little or no commitment to execute them. Inconsistency is a major problem when this occurs, leading to accusations and resentment.

Role Ambiguity and Incongruent Expectations

Varney (1989) states that a team's problems are more often than not due to a lack of clearly defined roles. He identifies two basic types of roles and responsibilities that need to be evaluated and clarified: those involving the tasks to be completed and those involving the management of the team's processes. Varney's analysis of team functioning focuses on the world of business, but his concepts apply equally to the helping professions.

Role ambiguity and conflict occur within teams in the helping professions due to a variety of factors. One is the paradox of a significant amount of overlap in the knowledge and skill of many disciplines and the high degree of specialization. In addition, most helping professionals are trained in isolation from one another and therefore have a poor understanding and little appreciation of one another's knowledge and skill. In medical settings role ambiguity and conflict occur between doctors and nurses, between occupational therapists and physical therapists, and between psychiatrists and psychologists. Similar issues regarding role arise in school settings between special education teachers and therapists, between social workers and psychologists, and between administrators and direct service personnel.

Varney recommends a process of role clarification when a new team is being formed and when role conflict occurs within an existing team. He advocates open discussion during team meetings to establish role definitions that all team members can understand and support. He recommends the use of a third party, such as a process consultant, to assist teams in resolving some of the difficult decisions regarding role and responsibility. This person also can assist teams in clarifying their roles during team communication and decision-making processes.

Authority and Power Structures

Team decision making is often described as both participatory and democratic. A common issue in teams, however, is the authority and power of individual team members. An impediment to effective team functioning is confusion or rigidity regarding authority and power structures within the team.

Authority comes from the mandates of the organization and is associated with a specific position. Power, on the other hand, resides with an individual and is bestowed by the group. Given and Simmons (1977) discussed these issues as they affect health care teams. They stated:

> The physician's traditional role as head of the health-care team requires that the holder be decisive, authoritarian, and assertive. Deferring to others is to acknowledge limitations. . . . Therefore, if there is a true team approach to

patient care, the physician may have to relinquish some authority to other team members. This may create both personal and professional conflict. (pp. 171–172)

Certain individuals (physicians in hospitals or psychologists in schools) are given power by other team members who defer to their expertise, even though they may resent their dependence on the individual and aspire to a more equal and collaborative relationship.

In summary, in spite of a broad base of philosophical support for the team concept, a number of impediments have prevented teams from succeeding. In the search for key ingredients to effective teams, the remainder of this chapter is devoted to an analysis of effective teams in a variety of organizational settings and the stages through which teams go in their development.

EIGHT CHARACTERISTICS OF EFFECTIVELY FUNCTIONING TEAMS

Larson and LaFasto (1989) conducted extensive research over a three-year period to identify the characteristics of effectively functioning teams. They interviewed the members of a wide range of teams, including those in cardiac surgery, Centers for Disease Control, sports, and geographic expeditions. Across all areas, they found consistent patterns and characteristics that distinguished successful from unsuccessful teams. They then tested their findings with a relatively homogeneous group of executive management and project teams in the world of business. In a third phase, they sampled unusual teams in unique settings that were functioning effectively to assess if the findings from the first two phases could be generalized. Eight characteristics emerged with an amazing degree of consistency across all of the successful teams studied. These characteristics are discussed below.

A Clear, Elevating Goal

When an effectively functioning team was identified, Larson and LaFasto (1989) found that the team members who were interviewed always described the team as having a clear understanding of its objective.

Conversely, in ineffective teams Larson and LaFasto found, "the goal had become unfocused; the goal had become politicized; the team had lost a sense of urgency or significance about its object; the team's efforts had become diluted by too many other competing goals; individual goals had taken priority over team goals; and so on" (p. 27).

A second aspect of how a team's goals influence team functioning was the potential elevating effect of goals on its members. Elevating goals were perceived as challenging to both individuals and to the collective effort. Also, effective teams experienced a sense of urgency and of making a real difference in pursuing their goals.

A Results-Driven Structure

Larson and LaFasto (1989) conclude that a team's success is dependent on a structure designed around the results to be achieved, not around preexisting conditions or assumptions. They identified three different types of teams that require unique structures: problem resolution teams, creative teams, and tactical teams. The structure of a problem resolution team needs to promote trust. The structure of a creative team needs to allow autonomy. The structure of a tactical team needs to reinforce clarity.

Competent Members

It is not surprising to find "competent members" as a characteristic of successful teams. Larson and LaFasto (1989), however, identify specific types of competence that are needed in different types of teams. The first finding in this area was that a successful team needs members who have both the technical skills to achieve the team's objectives and the personal skills to work in collaboration with others. The research showed, however, that each of the three types of teams requires members with somewhat different personal characteristics. For example, problem-solving teams require members who have a high degree of integrity and who engender trust and can trust others, while creative teams need members who are more independent thinkers who are "self starters" with a high degree of confidence and tenacity. Members of tactical teams, such as a cardiac surgery team, report a need for members who are highly responsive and action oriented with a sense of urgency and precision.

Unified Commitment

The members of effective teams experience a high level of team spirit with a strong sense of loyalty and dedication to the team. A unified commitment results in a loss of self in pursuit of the team's goals. As Larson and LaFasto (1989) state:

> Group spirit and teamwork come about as a result of identification with a team. In that identification there is a relinquishing of the self—not a denial of the self, but a voluntary redefinition of the self to include membership in the team as an important aspect of the self. (pp. 76–77)

A unified commitment can be increased and achieved through active participation by all team members in the planning and decision-making processes (Dyer, 1987). Participation increases motivation, effort, and a sense of shared ownership for the goals and the means of reaching them. Also, in effective teams a delicate balance exists between the seemingly incompatible needs of individuals to be integrated as members of the team and to stand out as different and special.

A Collaborative Climate

A climate in which people work well together was viewed as essential for teamwork (Larson & LaFasto, 1989). This climate was defined as including clear roles, responsibilities, and lines of communication. But it also included a feeling of trust among the team members.

Trust fosters teamwork by allowing team members to stay focused on the problem. Trust promotes more efficient communication and coordination. When a deep level of trust exists within a team, the members are able to confront problems and deal openly with negative factors affecting the team's function. It also improves the quality of collaborative outcomes and allows team members to compensate for one another's deficiencies.

Standards of Excellence

Standards of excellence are expectations and values regarding individual work and teamwork including such things as quantity, quality, and how people work together. Standards of excellence provide pressure to perform in a certain manner with rewards for success and consequences for failure. In their analysis of effective teams, Larson and LaFasto (1989) discovered that standards of excellence come from several different sources: (1) from within the individual, (2) from team pressure, (3) from consequences of success and failure, and (4) from external pressures such as a regulatory or funding source.

Also, the *team leader* is a source of pressure to perform. Team leadership may be elected, appointed, or rotated. Team leaders have different styles of inspiring, demanding, facilitating, and encouraging different levels of performance.

External Support and Recognition

Larson and LaFasto (1989) observe that teams need the resources to accomplish their tasks, support from key individuals and agencies outside the team who can affect the team's success, and recognition and rewards for their performance. They note, however, that "external support and recognition" tend to be mentioned by teams that are doing either very poorly or very well. Ineffective teams tend to attribute their failure to the absence of support and resources over which the team has no control. Outstanding teams believe the support and recognition being given do not match their high level of accomplishment.

Some organizations advocate teamwork but lack the organizational structures to create and support teams (Eubanks, 1990). Teams members are particularly sensitive to the perception that leaders at the top of the organization do not value and support the work of their team. Mazur, Beeston, and Yerxa (1979) report the difficulties encountered in gaining support for interdisciplinary training for physicians. They state, "No progress was apparent. This failure probably reflects the low priority placed upon interdisciplinary teamwork in the face of other demands on students" (p. 712).

Principled Leadership

Summarizing the extensive research on leadership in the management literature, Larson and LaFasto (1989) identify three consistent characteristics of leadership: "Effective leaders (1) establish a vision; (2) create change; and (3) unleash talent" (p. 121).

The research on team leadership revealed two "blind spots" of ineffective leaders. The most significant complaint involved leaders who were unwilling to confront and resolve issues related to the deficient performance of team members. The second blind spot was the tendency of the ineffective leader to dilute the team's efforts with too many priorities. Often this behavior was accompanied by the leader's seeing all goals as critical and driving the team in pursuit of the personal success of the leader rather than the team.

The eight characteristics of effectively functioning teams can serve as a guide for analyzing teams in various settings. It is important to note that teamwork does not occur immediately on the formation of groups of professionals around groups of students, clients, and patients. It takes time, effort, and understanding for teams to develop to the point where they truly achieve their promise. When a team has all eight characteristics of an effective team, it will have gone through a number of stages of team development.

STAGES OF TEAM DEVELOPMENT

Various team analysts and social psychologists believe team functioning is greatly influenced by each team's stage of development (Brill, 1976; Francis & Young, 1979; Tuckman, 1965). It is obvious that all teams do not perform equally. This is easily seen by anyone who has ever served on one team and observed another. Even in the same organization, operating with identical structures, goals, and leadership, teams can differ greatly in their effectiveness. Some teams are efficient in gathering information, making decisions, implementing their plans, resolving conflicts, and promoting the professional development of their members. Other teams seem to become stuck in negative processes with team members not trusting one another, not communicating, feeling left out, having divided loyalties, competing for control, and pursuing independent goals. When this happens, team members and administrators attempt to figure out what is going wrong and often attribute the problems to a variety of factors, including personality conflicts, lack of ample time, inadequate leadership, and insufficient organizational support. Although these factors can influence teamwork, the stages of team development seem to provide a more comprehensive explanation of the differences among teams—especially those in the same organization.

The number of stages of team development varies from four to seven, depending on the theoretical model being used. Each stage is characterized by patterns of communication, group interaction, group process, and focus. Across theoretical models, the stages are presented in a similar order; however, most analysts believe that teams do not have to progress through the stages in the same sequence. Also, it is possible for teams to regress to lower stages of development under certain conditions, such as when turnover in team membership occurs. In the following discussion, concepts from several models of the stages of team development will be integrated.

Tuckman (1965) identifies four stages of team development: forming, storming, norming, and performing. During the *forming* stage, the team develops a sense of its purpose and its identity. The trust level in the team is low at this point and communication is guarded, constricted, and topic centered (Stanford & Roark, 1974). Interaction is usually leader centered or among subgroups within the team. Francis and Young (1979) observe that this early stage also involves "testing" by team members as they attempt to seek their place in the group. Brill (1976) refers to this as the orientation phase of team development. Team members are getting to know one another, developing relationships, and seeking clarification regarding the team's goals and their respective roles.

The second stage of team development involves some *storming*—the beginning of the search for group values, procedures, and norms. This search usually leads to conflict in a variety of forms. In some teams this stage is characterized by confusion on the part of some team members as they attempt to understand the team's legitimate role in the process of making decisions. In other teams different members of the team compete with one another for control and influence. Francis and Young (1979) refer to this behavior as "infighting." In the face of this conflict, some team members begin to withdraw or feel stuck and question the team's direction. The interaction pattern is erratic during this stage and communication can be distorted, angry, and confrontive (Stanford & Roark, 1974). The open expression of differences, however, serves to increase the level of trust among members.

Fortunately, teams mature and move through a transition period leading to the more productive *norming* stage. Here, teams develop a shared sense of their values, expectations, procedures, and traditions. A greater openness in communication leads to increased sharing of perceptions and the giving and receiving of feedback. Issues are confronted more easily with an improved balance between the group task and group maintenance concerns.

The *performing* stage is characterized by a strong sense of "we" and of team cohesiveness. Collaboration, coordination, and consistency become realities instead of goals. The team becomes efficient in making decisions and resolving conflict. Interaction patterns within the team are usually group centered but are flexible, moving from task to person to team as appropriate. Higher levels of the performing stage include the expression of affection and the willingness to take risks. The mature team in this stage provides a supportive environment in which all team members can actualize their personal and professional potential.

Summary

Teamwork is advocated by professionals and used in hospitals, schools, and community agencies that serve persons across the life span. Teamwork seeks to serve the whole person and to integrate the knowledge and skill of professionals with training in a variety of disciplines. Advocates of teamwork believe that students, patients, and clients receive inferior services when various helping professionals make decisions based on incomplete information and implement interventions in isolation from others who are serving the same individuals.

There are different models of teamwork (multidisciplinary, interdisciplinary, transdisciplinary, and interagency) and these are applied in different settings. In spite of these differences, those who support the team concept believe in four basic tenets:

1. Communication is essential for teamwork to occur;
2. Effective treatment planning and service delivery require collaboration among all who work with the same individuals or groups;
3. Conflicts among professionals can be prevented and resolved through teamwork;
4. Teams promote the personal and professional growth of their members.

Teamwork is not easily achieved due to a number of significant impediments. These include the specialization in the helping professions, the departmental structure of most human services organizations, role ambiguity and incongruent expectations among team members, and authority and power structures.

Recent research has established eight characteristics of effectively functioning teams. Effective teams have a clear goal that inspires and challenges their members. Successful achievement of these goals is dependent on a results-driven structure, appropriate to the type of team. The members of the teams must be competent and have skills and qualities that also match the team's mission. A unified commitment within the team is achieved through active participation in planning and decision making by all team members. This can occur when a collaborative climate exists in which the trust level is high and members can take risks. Successful teams also have high standards of excellence that are concrete and clear and supported through discipline. Effective teams require external support to provide the resources and recognition to give reinforcement for the team's achievements. Finally, effective teams require principled leaders who establish a vision, create change, and unleash the talent of the team members.

Teams improve their skills in communication, decision making, conflict resolution, and performance as they progress through various stages of development. Over time teams members develop higher levels of trust, become more team centered, and achieve greater flexibility in responding to the needs of both the persons being served and the members of the team.

Helping professionals are faced with patients, students, and clients with complex needs. Many organizations are now trying to meet these needs and to provide quality programs through the use of teams of professionals from different disciplines. The challenge for the members of teams and the administrators of programs is to assess the degree to which their teams incorporate the eight characteristics of effective teams and the degree to which the organization provides the structure, resources, and supports necessary for effective team functioning.

REFERENCES

American Board of Medical Specialties (1991). *ABMS compendium of certified medical specialists*. Evanston, IL.

Brill, N. I. (1976). *Teamwork: Working together in the human services*. Philadelphia, PA: Lippincott.

Campbell, L. J., & Cole, K. D. (1987). Geriatric assessment teams. *Clinical Geriatric Medicine, 3,* 99-110.

Ducanis, A. J., & Golin, A. K. (1979). *The interdisciplinary health care team: A handbook.* Germantown, MD: Aspen.

Dyer, W. G. (1987). *Teambuilding: Issues and alternatives* (2d ed.). Reading, MA: Addison-Wesley.

Eubanks, P. (1990). Teambuilding: It starts at the top—of a tree? *Hospitals, 64,* 56-57.

Everson, J. M., Barcus, M., Moon, S., & Morton, M. V. (1987). *Achieving outcomes: A guide to interagency training in transition and supported employment.* Richmond, VA: Rehabilitation Research Training Center, Virginia Commonwealth University.

Francis, D., & Young, D. (1979). *Improving work groups: A practical manual for team building.* San Diego, CA: University Associates.

Garner, H. G. (1982). *Teamwork in programs for children and youth: A handbook for administrators.* Springfield, IL: Charles C Thomas.

Garner, H. G. (1988). *Helping others through teamwork.* Washington, DC: Child Welfare League of America.

Garrett, J. G. (1955). Social psychology of teamwork. In M. R. Harrower (Ed.), *Medical and psychological teamwork in the care of the chronically ill* (pp. 67-70). Springfield, IL: Charles C Thomas.

Given, B., & Simmons, S. (1977). The interdisciplinary health care team: Fact or fiction? *Nursing Forum, 25,* 165-184.

Katz, K., Pokorni, J., & Long, T. (1989). *Chronically ill and at-risk infants: Family-centered intervention from hospital to home.* Palo Alto, CA: VORT Corporation.

Kilgo, J. L., Richard, N., & Noonan, M. J. (1989). Teaming for the future: Integrating transition planning with early intervention services for young children with special needs and their families. *Infants and Young Children, 2*(2), 37-48.

Larson, C. E., & LaFasto, F. M. (1989). *Teamwork: What must go right/what can go wrong.* Newbury Park, CA: Sage.

Losen, S., & Losen, J. (1985). *The special education team.* Boston: Allyn and Bacon.

Mariano, C. (1989). The case for interdisciplinary collaboration. *Nursing Outlook, 37,* 285-288.

Mazur, H., Beeston, J., & Yerxa, E. (1979). Clinical interdisciplinary health team care: An educational experiment. *Journal of Medical Education, 54,* 703-713.

McGonigel, M. J., & Garland, C. W. (1988). The individualized family service plan and the early intervention team: Team and family issues and recommended practices. *Infants and Young Children, 1*(1), 10-21.

McMahon, B. (1989). Teamwork: A complete service with specialist skills. *Professional Nurse*, 4, 433-435.

Spencer, P. E., & Coye, R. W. (1988). Project bridge: A team approach to decision-making for early services. *Infants and Young Children*, 1(1), 82-92.

Stanford, G., & Roark, A. (1974). *Human interaction in teaching*. Boston, MA: Allyn and Bacon.

Styles, M. M. (1989). *On specialization in nursing: Toward a new empowerment*. Kansas City, MO: American Nurses' Foundation.

Tuckman, B. W. (1965). Developmental sequences in small groups. *Psychological Bulletin*, 63, 384-399.

Turnbull, A. P., & Turnbull, H. R. (1986). *Families, professionals, and exceptionality: A special partnership*. Columbus, OH: Merrill.

Varney, G. H. (1989). *Building productive teams: An action guide and resource book*. San Francisco: Jossey-Bass.

2

□ □ □
□ □ □
□ □ □

Multidisciplinary versus Interdisciplinary Teamwork

Howard G. Garner

INTRODUCTION

Everyone seems to be in favor of the "team concept." It is difficult to oppose values such as communication, cooperation, and coordination of services, especially when your vocation is devoted to helping others. With the almost universal acceptance of teamwork as a goal worth pursuing, the term *team* is now being used somewhat indiscriminately. In some organizations today, for example, every group, committee, or task force that is formed is referred to as a "team." Teamwork is clearly in vogue both in the business world and in health and human services. However, one does not have to look very far to discover that "teamwork" means different things to different people.

To some people teamwork means having positive attitudes toward professionals from other disciplines, sharing information periodically, and cooperating—but at a comfortable distance. To others teamwork means a collaborative working relationship in which daily communication ensures consistency, major decisions are made through consensus, and a sense of equal partnership prevails. It is not surprising, therefore, that two professionals from the very same discipline who work on different teams may have dissimilar expectations and experiences regarding their interactions with persons from other disciplines and departments. Teams differ in their purpose, size, structure, leadership, and power. Teams differ in the amount of independence the team members have. In some teams decisions are reached through a consensus decision-making process, and all team members are expected to implement the decision. In other teams the members communicate their knowledge, insights, and observations, but the team is not expected to make any major decisions.

The independence of each discipline in a multidisciplinary team was illustrated in research evaluating the effects of multidisciplinary conferences on the therapy plans of the professionals who participated in weekly case conferences (Spiegel & Spiegel, 1984). In a rheumatology rehabilitation unit several physicians in subspecialties, a nurse, a physical therapist, an occupational therapist, and a social worker, met weekly to discuss and review their patients. The researchers collected quantitative and qualitative data on the therapy plans of each professional for each of the patients before and after the multidisciplinary team meeting. Spiegel and Spiegel (1984) state:

> The study . . . demonstrated that multidisciplinary conferences can produce substantial changes in the formulation of patient problems and management plans. Following a multidisciplinary conference on a rehabilitation unit, the health team altered therapy plans by 38 percent, problems by 15 percent, goals for hospitalization by 59 percent, and discharge date by 18 percent. (p. 437)

In comparing the different disciplines the researchers found the changes in the physician and nursing plans exceeded the other disciplines. What seems most relevant for this discussion is the assumption that each member of the multidisciplinary team was able to act independently following the case conference. The team did not make decisions that all team members were expected to follow but only shared information and recommendations. The decision to use the team's input to change plans and goals was left to each team member and discipline.

Prompted by the observation that all teams do not function in the same manner, Shalinsky (1989) analyzes the differences among what he called *polidisciplinary groups* in human service organizations. His analysis reveals that many professionals and teams are frustrated by problems in the areas of leadership, communication, decision making, and conflict resolution. He concludes that one aspect of the problem was the lack of understanding regarding the different types of teams and how they function.

Jantsch (1971) previously identified six levels of what he calls *disciplinarity* in organizations:

1. The single discipline operating in isolation;
2. The multidisciplinary group, which includes various disciplines but lacks cooperation—each discipline functioning independently;
3. The pluridisciplinary group, where cooperation occurs but without coordination of services or activities (e.g., a multiservice center where facilities are shared but not programs);
4. The cross-disciplinary group, which includes cooperation and coordination but is dominated by one discipline (e.g., a surgical team);
5. The interdisciplinary group, which has cooperation, coordination, and equality in pursuit of goals chosen by the group;
6. The transdisciplinary group, in which the differences among the disciplines are transcended and individuals are able to assume roles and functions of disciplines other than their own.

The goal of this chapter is to compare and contrast two of these levels that occur frequently in human services organizations: multidisciplinary and interdisciplinary teams. Chapter 3 is devoted to the transdisciplinary model. Chapter 4 focuses on interagency teamwork, which involves both cross-discipline and cross-agency issues.

MULTIDISCIPLINARY TEAMWORK

The multidisciplinary teamwork model is, as its name implies, based on the inclusion of professionals from multiple disciplines or agencies who share a common task or are working with the same individuals. The multidisciplinary approach to teamwork originally developed from the medical model of patient care in which the physician received information from professionals from different disciplines who served the same patients (Hart, 1977). In some multidisciplinary teams, the physician met with the team members individually, received their assessment information and consultations, and then made decisions independently regarding prescriptions for treatment. More recently, multidisciplinary teams meet on a regular basis, share information, and, in some cases, coordinate their activities. However, in a multidisciplinary team each discipline remains relatively autonomous and can make many decisions independently regarding how best to serve the client, patient, or student. Two examples of multidisciplinary teams will help demonstrate the essential features that distinguish them from interdisciplinary teams.

Multidisciplinary Teams in Child Development Clinics

Child development clinics frequently use the multidisciplinary team model. These clinics are designed to provide intensive and comprehensive assessments of individual children's development and to recommend plans of action to remediate and treat identified deficits, delays, and disorders. These clinics are most often under the direction of a pediatrician. Children are referred to the clinic by pediatricians, schools, and other community agencies. The reasons for referral usually span the areas of physical, cognitive, emotional, and social development.

When the parents bring their child to the clinic, they usually meet first with the physician who explains what the day's activities may include and introduces other key members of the clinic staff. The physician then reviews the child's medical history. Following this, the parents meet with a social worker who conducts a detailed interview to develop a social and family history. At this same time, the physician gives the child a thorough medical examination. In addition to the pediatric examination, some children are evaluated by other medical specialists such as neurologists and orthopedists. Then, depending on the child's areas of weakness, the child is evaluated by a variety of other professionals. Some of these professionals are full-time members of the child development clinic, and others may be members of other departments and used on an as-needed basis.

A psychologist administers an age-appropriate intelligence test plus other assessment procedures to determine the child's level of social skill, cognitive, and affective development. Depending on the child's age, an educational diagnostician might test the child's achievement in basic academic areas and evaluate how the child receives, processes, and expresses information. A speech and language pathologist may evaluate the child's articulation and language development. A physical therapist would evaluate the child if there were any indications of developmental delay in the areas of gross motor development. An occupational therapist would provide an assessment if the child had difficulties in the areas of fine motor development, self-care, and the use of adaptive equipment.

The number of professionals providing assessments would vary depending of the child's areas of strength and special needs. Some clinics conduct these assessments in one day while others might spread the process over two or more days to avoid exhausting the child and the parents. The evaluation process is intensive and thorough, producing a great deal of information about the child and the family. Following the assessment, each professional writes a report on the child's levels of functioning, including test results, analyses, and recommendations. The social worker develops a written social and family history. In some clinics these reports are sent to the pediatrician for analysis and integration. In most clinics, the professionals on the multidisciplinary team meet to share their respective reports and to compare their findings. The physician usually chairs this meeting and takes the lead in developing a comprehensive picture of the child. Inconsistencies in the test results may require extended discussion and further assessments. In some clinics the parents are invited to this meeting where they can hear the report of each discipline directly. Other clinics view this participation as potentially overwhelming to the parents and have the physician or another team member meet later with the parents to provide a condensed report with specific recommendations for next steps.

Child development clinics may or may not provide any direct services to children and families other than the comprehensive assessment. Some clinics provide only assessments and make their recommendations to other professionals regarding the best course of treatment. Clinics that are associated with medical centers often provide treatment services as well. When this occurs, the members of the team providing treatment may function as an interdisciplinary team rather than a multidisciplinary one. This transition from multidisciplinary to interdisciplinary will be discussed more extensively later in this chapter.

Multidisciplinary Teams in Case Management

A similar pattern of disciplines working together but operating independently can be seen in the field of case management of child sexual abuse. Wagner (1987) describes the need to bring all of the professions involved together, including those who gather information regarding child abuse cases, who prosecute perpetrators, and who treat the victims. He recommends a multidisciplinary team that includes a prosecutor from the district attorney's office who would provide the leadership for the team, a physician, a law enforcement officer, a social worker, and a mental health professional. He states, "Membership is open to all professionals who are actively involved in the management of child sexual abuse cases so it is not unusual for attendance at meetings to exceed 15 members" (p. 435). These teams are designed to "overcome the isolation of working in their individual agencies so they can work cooperatively with others in the coordination of services for molestation victims" (p. 438).

This is an excellent example of a multidisciplinary team. The various disciplines represented are distinctive and have specialized knowledge and skills. Very little overlap occurs among the roles of the various team members. Each member brings specific information and expertise to the team meeting and represents an agency that provides unique services. The goal of the team is case management and the coordination of their respective activities and services. In his description of this team, Wagner makes only a passing reference to the team as a decision-making group. Their activities are limited primarily to information sharing and coordination.

Key Elements of Multidisciplinary Teams

In developing a basis for distinguishing between multidisciplinary and interdisciplinary teams, it is helpful to note the key elements of the multidisciplinary team in the two examples discussed above. These key elements include team membership, the primary loyalty of team members, the physical and psychological distance between team members, independence, team leadership, and decision making.

Team Membership

The membership of these teams varies based on the special needs of each child who is assessed in the clinic and on the agencies and professionals involved in each child abuse case. The number of professionals who participate in a particular case may range from as few as four to as many as fifteen. Moreover, multidisciplinary teams frequently experience changing team membership with different professionals attending team meetings to represent their respective discipline, department, or agency. This factor results in the selection of the multidisciplinary model over the interdisciplinary model in some settings. Lowe and Herranen (1981) state: "As a result of the constantly changing personnel and patients, the integrative (interdisciplinary) approach is not applicable or congruent to the acute care setting" (p. 8). Without consistent membership the team cannot be expected to achieve a strong sense of its own identity, power, and responsibilities, or to develop a very high level of trust and openness necessary to make consensus decisions.

Primary Loyalty of Team Members

The members of the multidisciplinary team serving a specific child may or may not be members of the clinic staff and thus their primary loyalty may be to other departments or units within a larger organization such as a medical center. In the child abuse case management team, most team members work for different agencies and thus have primary loyalty and responsibility to those organizations—not to the team. Territoriality is a major barrier to effective team functioning, and divided loyalties within the team maintain a level of tension and competition that impedes interdisciplinary sharing and cooperation.

Distance between Team Members

Multidisciplinary team members most often experience varying degrees of physical and psychological distance between their respective work spaces and one another. In the case of the interagency child abuse team, the physical distance separating offices of the team members obviously is determined by the location of their respective agencies. Opportunities for informal and frequent communications are decreased when team members do not share the same general space. Psychological factors are seen as well when the meeting location is rotated among the participating agencies and the team members are aware of whose turf the meeting is being held on. In the case of the child development clinic, a few core members may have their offices relatively close together while other specialists may have their offices in other areas of the medical center. Even those located in close proximity to one another may not share space and equipment. In clinics based on the multidisciplinary model, the psychological distance between work areas is often guarded as each discipline respects and protects one another's independence.

Independence of Team Members

In the child development team the team members function relatively independently, seeing the child or parents alone, administering discipline-specific assessments, and developing recommendations within their respective areas of expertise. Similarly, the members of the case management team in child abuse function independently with little overlap in their knowledge, skills, or activities. Communication and sharing of information are highly valued in multidisciplinary teams, but the team seldom makes a decision that all team members are expected to follow.

Team Leadership

Multidisciplinary teams frequently have a strong leader who calls and presides over meetings, who feels primary responsibility for collecting and analyzing information from all team members, and who ultimately makes final decisions. In the child development clinic this person is usually a pediatrician. In the case management team this person is often the prosecutor from the district attorney's office. In some multidisciplinary teams that meet over an extended period of time with stable membership, this pattern may change as a high level of trust is developed and the team begins to function in a more interdisciplinary manner. When this occurs, team leadership may actually be shared, and various members may take turns chairing the meetings.

Team Decision Making

The multidisciplinary team exists to bring together people who are working with the same students, clients, or patients. The team allows its members to communicate information that the other professionals may need to do their jobs. Through communication some coordination of activities is often achieved. Multidisciplinary teams are, however, usually limited in their power to make decisions that have major effects on the members. Multidisciplinary teams often make recommendations rather than final decisions. One exception to this would be an interagency team in which interagency agreements are worked out by the heads of those agencies who have the power to negotiate changes in policy or funding. Another exception is special education eligibility committees in public schools that have the responsibility and power to determine which children are eligible to receive special education services. This summary of key elements in the multidisciplinary model raises a number questions regarding alternative models. The remainder of this chapter is devoted to a discussion of the interdisciplinary model and a comparison with the multidisciplinary approach.

INTERDISCIPLINARY TEAMWORK

Interdisciplinary teamwork occurs when two or more professionals from different disciplines work together in planning and delivering services to the same patient, client, or student. As in the multidisciplinary model, interdisciplinary teamwork values the contributions of each discipline and works to ensure regular and systematic communication. Interdisciplinary teamwork, however, uses a team decision-making process, rather than the decision of one individual, to establish a plan for the individuals being served. The team members are then expected to cooperate, collaborate, and coordinate their activities to implement the team's plan and to achieve its goals. Interdisciplinary teams accept the fact that the knowledge, skills, roles, and responsibilities of its members often overlap, which requires routine discussion and clarification of these issues to prevent role conflicts and to use effectively all of the professional resources within the team.

When they are functioning well, interdisciplinary teams provide a supportive work environment for their members. Team members often enjoy a level of interpersonal closeness that allows the expression of appreciation for one another's contributions and of concern for experiences of stress and frustration. In addition, interdisciplinary teams can provide a form of peer supervision in which team members receive helpful feedback from one another, leading to improved job performance.

It is clear from this brief description that much more is expected of interdisciplinary teams than of multidisciplinary teams. Although these two types of teamwork may appear similar on the surface, they differ significantly when observed in action. Whereas a multidisciplinary team brings professionals together from different disciplines to share information, make recommendations, and coordinate activities, the interdisciplinary process empowers the team to make and implement decisions, increases the interdependence of team members, and has more potential for effecting change. It should not be surprising that interdisciplinary teamwork is more difficult to achieve and, consequently, much more has been written about the factors contributing to successful interdisciplinary teamwork.

"Everyone is in favor of teamwork, but it is not easy to achieve." This paradox indicates that professionals do not work well together just because they belong to a "team." But what is required to achieve this goal that everyone supports in principle? The answers to this question focus on two major areas: (1) the organizational context within which teams function, and (2) the internal processes within teams themselves.

Organizational Context

Garner (1982) analyzes the negative effects of departmentalized organizations on interdisciplinary teams, citing the strong human tendency to defend and retreat to one's primary place in an organization rather than invest in a collaborative effort on neutral turf. He argues for a "total team model" in which professionals would be assigned to teams devoted to serving groups of patients, clients, and students rather than to departments. In this model the persons receiving services become the basis of the organization's structure rather than the various professional disciplines. This new structure would also have all team members report to the same administrator who had skills in delegating power and responsibility to teams and in supporting and monitoring team functioning.

McClane (1992) discusses five related features of an organizational context that support interdisciplinary teamwork. These include the organizational culture, team rewards, external relationships, team goals and objectives, and performance feedback.

Organizational Culture

Within every organization one can gain a sense of "how things are done here" and what is really important. The culture of an organization sets the tone for and prompts certain behaviors on the part of the employees. In reference to organizations that profess a commitment to teamwork, McClane (1992) stated,

A key indicator of this quality comes from analyzing where important decisions are being made. If teams are used primarily as a means to disseminate information or to conduct trivial work, it will be difficult for team-based therapy to be taken seriously. By contrast, if major decisions are made in team settings or team-therapy is used extensively, there is a greater likelihood that therapy teams will be successful. (p. 29)

McClane also emphasizes the importance of both administrative support for team-based therapy and the administration using teams to make major decisions that affect everyone in the organization.

Team Rewards

Regarding team rewards, McClane (1992) wrote, "Potentially, working as part of a therapeutic team can contribute to members' performance in other areas of work, overall job satisfaction, formal performance appraisal ratings, and career development" (p. 30). McClane saw the need for the organization's performance appraisal system to include appraisal of team performance as an integral part of each person's individual performance. Garner (1988) concurs with McClane's suggestion that team members contribute to one another's annual performance review.

External Relationships

Another aspect of the organizational context affecting teams is their external relationships with other units in the hospital, school, or agency. These include other teams providing services to individuals as well as units that support the teams' work. Team members need to develop a clear understanding of and sensitivity to these relationships in order to maintain positive communication and reduce the likelihood of conflict that can consume important time and energy.

Goals and Objectives

Given the complex needs of the persons being served and the wide range of potential interventions to meet these needs, the organization, the administration, and the teams need clarity regarding the goals and objectives of the teams (Locke & Latham, 1990). Everyone concerned needs a clear and shared understanding of the persons who are to be served, the services that are to be provided, and the expected outcomes. McClane notes that teams should expect leadership from organizational leaders in defining these issues, but he emphasized that teams need to take a proactive stance in clarifying their responsibilities.

Performance Feedback

Finally, performance feedback is needed from outside the team to help the team gauge its effectiveness in meeting its goals. Teams need to know when they have been successful and have made a difference in the lives of those they serve and in the larger organization. Regular feedback sessions with administrators, representatives from other teams or units, and surveys of those who have received services from the team are some ways of gaining routine and reliable performance feedback.

Comparison of the Two Models of Teamwork

The issues regarding organizational context affect both multidisciplinary and interdisciplinary teams but in differing degrees. Multidisciplinary teams frequently are formed in the effort to overcome the negative effects of organizational fragmentation and competition. These teams attempt to bring together professionals who have their primary loyalty to different disciplines, departments, and agencies. Often these teams lack administrative direction and support, clear goals and objectives, and well-defined relationships to other groups and agencies. These deficiencies result in lowered expectations regarding what can be achieved by the multidisciplinary team.

Interdisciplinary teams, on the other hand, are most often created to deliver services to patients, clients, and students. The reality of these people's needs raises expectations regarding what can and should be achieved if everyone works together toward common goals. Yet, in many organizations that provide direct services, the environmental supports essential to effective functioning are missing, and, thus, teams function in a manner that is more multidisciplinary than interdisciplinary.

The organizational context in which teams are asked to function clearly is a major factor in determining whether teams are effective, efficient, and satisfying or whether they become the battleground for unresolved departmental and interpersonal tensions. Organizational change is possible as evidenced by the move to the team model in a large number of American businesses and in many schools, hospitals, and community-based services. Many administrators and professionals, however, still desire the benefits of teamwork without having to make the organizational changes necessary to structure, empower, and support interdisciplinary teams.

Internal Processes of Teams

A great deal has been written about the internal processes of interdisciplinary teams, covering topics such as the stages of team development (discussed in Chapter 1), team leadership, communication, problem solving and decision making, conflict resolution, feedback, team members' knowledge of teamwork theory and values, and their understanding of the roles and skills of team members (Campbell, 1992; Frank & Elliott, 1992; Garner, 1988; Lowe & Herranen, 1981; Mariano, 1989; Saltz, 1992). Because this literature is quite extensive, it is not possible to provide a complete discussion of all of the important issues in this chapter. For the purpose of contrasting interdisciplinary teamwork and multidisciplinary teamwork, however, several of the internal processes of teams will be discussed and comparisons made between the two models.

Knowledge and Understanding of Other Disciplines

A major factor affecting the internal processes of teams and causing conflict when team members attempt to reach and implement decisions is the general lack of knowledge and understanding regarding the roles, responsibilities, and skills of their team colleagues. Newberger (1976) discusses the ignorance of the conceptual basis for practice of each other's discipline as a cause of the confusion between disciplines regarding who should take what responsibilities and for chauvinistic attitudes and lack of confidence in other disciplines.

To help overcome this barrier Mariano (1989) argues for "pre-professional and professional team training where students come together with various disciplines to learn principles and skills of collaboration; explore role specificity and role generality; examine the unity of knowledge and connections among disciplines; and develop flexibility" (p. 287). Lowe and Herranen (1981) state that all professionals need to develop a strong identity with their respective disciplines but also an in-depth understanding and appreciation of one another's roles and functions. It is interesting to note that this perceived need for better education in both teamwork principles and the roles and responsibilities of the various disciplines crosses all models of teamwork and is not unique to the interdisciplinary model.

Team Leadership

In interdisciplinary teams leadership is considered a responsibility to be shared by all team members and one that shifts from member to member depending on the issue being discussed and how the team is functioning. In this context leadership means more than chairing the team meeting. Campbell (1992) analyzed the different leadership roles and functions that teams need to operate effectively. She identified two clusters of positive leadership behaviors: task-oriented acts and maintenance-oriented acts. Task-oriented behaviors include initiating discussion, seeking and sharing information or opinions, pulling ideas together, and stating possible conclusions in the search for group consensus. Maintenance-oriented behaviors include suggesting procedures for facilitating team discussions, mediating differences between team members, and praising the contributions of others. Obviously, these leadership behaviors can come from any member of a team. For this to occur, all members need to see themselves as equally responsible for the success of the team process.

To ensure a sense of equal ownership and responsibility, Garner (1988) suggested that teams systematically rotate the responsibility of chairing team meetings. This position requires skills such as organizing and conducting the meeting, helping to keep the team on track, ensuring maximum participation in discussions and decisions, and facilitating other teams members in assuming leadership roles during the team meeting. Garner stated that assigning these responsibilities to one team member over an extended period of time creates an imbalance in the team and inhibits all team members from experiencing their full responsibility for the team's success or failure.

Team Problem Solving and Decision Making

As with team leadership, successful interdisciplinary problem-solving and decision-making processes are dependent on participation by all members of the team. The assumption is that professionals working together in teams will make better decisions and implement them with greater consistency and enthusiasm when they actively participate in collecting information, analyzing the problem, identifying possible alternatives, and choosing a specific course of action. In reference to the effects of participation on the implementation of a decision, Garner (1992) stated:

> Consistency is achieved when teams are able to make consensus decisions regarding treatment goals and daily plans for each patient. Consensus decisions incorporate the values, perspectives, and expertise of all who must execute the decisions in working with the patient and family. Thus, in order to achieve commitment to common goals and, thereby, consistency, effective teams become proficient in problem identification, communication, problem solving, negotiation, compromise, and consensus decision making. (p. 131)

Consensus decision making requires a high trust level in which team members can openly express their ideas, concerns, and feelings. Strongly held values sometimes come into conflict, especially when compromise is required to achieve a decision all team members can support. This process can be time consuming, but the benefits to those receiving services from the team are significant and worth the time and effort.

Comparison of the Two Models of Teamwork

This limited discussion of the leadership and decision-making issues in interdisciplinary teams provides a contrast with the multidisciplinary model. The expectation that all interdisciplinary team members share responsibility for team leadership and the chairing of team meetings is one obvious difference. As noted earlier, multidisciplinary teams often are led by one person from a particular discipline who feels, and in reality has, more responsibility for the decisions and outcomes. It should be acknowledged, however, that even in a multidisciplinary team with a designated leader, other team members with knowledge and skills in small group processes will periodically engage in some of the task-oriented and maintenance-oriented leadership behaviors discussed above. In interdisciplinary teams these behaviors are expected of all team members, and training and reinforcement are provided to ensure their occurrence.

The emphasis on team process in decision making in interdisciplinary teams is not as prominent in multidisciplinary teams. As noted earlier, many multidisciplinary teams are not given the authority to make major decisions. More often these teams are asked to present recommendations to other groups or individuals who make the final decisions. In many multidisciplinary teams, such as the child development clinic, final decisions often are not made by the whole team but by the head of the team, based on input from all of the members. In the case of special education eligibility committees, which are sometimes called teams, final decisions are made by formal voting on whether a child is eligible for services or not. Interdisciplinary teams try to avoid votes that create winners and losers. Consensus is the goal in interdisciplinary teams since all members of the team will need to implement the team's decision for it to succeed.

SUMMARY

Teamwork is a common goal of most health, education, and human services organizations. It takes many different forms, however, depending on a number of important variables, including the model of teamwork employed, tasks of the team, its membership, organizational structure and support, and the processes teams use in accomplishing their tasks. Different models of teamwork have been developed to meet different needs, and an understanding of these models can assist team members in making their teams more effective.

The multidisciplinary model is used most often when the level of involvement and interaction among the professionals and disciplines is limited. Multidisciplinary teams frequently involve individuals from different departments within the same organization or from different agencies. When working on a team, each discipline maintains a high degree of independence and plays a unique role.

Many multidisciplinary teams experience changing membership from one meeting to the next, with attendance dependent on the cases being considered or who is representing a particular discipline or organizational unit. This factor alone affects the dynamics of the multidisciplinary team meeting. For without stable membership, open and trusting relationships among team members cannot develop, and the team does not share a common identity and cannot progress to more advanced stages of team development. As a result, the team has difficulty solving problems and making decisions about complex issues.

Multidisciplinary teams frequently have a permanent leader and chairperson who has more power and status than the other members. In some situations the other team members function as consultants to this leader, who integrates the contributions from the team members and makes final decisions.

In contrast, interdisciplinary teams usually are formed to provide direct services to groups of patients, clients, or students, depending on the setting. These teams function best when they operate within an organizational context that values and rewards teamwork, whose structure encourages loyalty to the team rather than discipline specific units, where administrative leadership empowers teams to take responsibility and make decisions, and where the external relationships between teams and other units are supportive. Interdisciplinary team members work closely with one another in sharing information, evaluating individual needs, developing integrated treatment and intervention plans, and implementing these plans in a coordinated and consistent manner. Overlap between various disciplines is acknowledged and role clarification is an ongoing part of the team's responsibilities. Leadership within the team is shared, and consensus decisions are sought whenever the issue deserves the time required. The members of interdisciplinary teams are interdependent and experience a good deal of support from their team colleagues.

These differences between the multidisciplinary and interdisciplinary models of teamwork may help explain some of the conflict that occurs when teams are formed but do not function as expected. Conflict is a normal part of people working together. It occurs in all groups and all teams. However, a certain amount of conflict and frustration that occurs within teams may be due not to usual differences in values, style, and philosophy, but to incompatible expectations by team members regarding the team itself—its role and how it should function. If some members of a team expect their team to be multidisciplinary and others expect the team to be interdisciplinary, one would anticipate a good deal of conflict for some of the members, depending on how the team functioned in reality. Also, one would anticipate conflict if all members of a team desired to function as an interdisciplinary team, but the organizational context did not support their achieving this level of functioning.

It is important for professionals who wish to gain the promised benefits of teamwork to understand the different models of teamwork, to choose the model that matches their organizational and programmatic needs, and to ensure that the members of the teams that are formed receive training in both the models and the skills necessary to make each model work. In closing, this discussion will become even more relevant as the reader explores two other models of teamwork—transdisciplinary and interagency in Chapters 3 and 4.

References

Campbell, L. J. (1992). Team leadership. In *Guide to interdisciplinary practice in rehabilitation settings* (pp. 93-112). Skokie, IL: American Congress of Rehabilitation Medicine.

Frank, R. G., & Elliott, T. R. (1992). Conflict resolution and feedback. In *Guide to interdisciplinary practice in rehabilitation settings* (pp. 143-157). Skokie, IL: American Congress of Rehabilitation Medicine.

Garner, H. G. (1982). *Teamwork in programs for children and youth: A handbook for administrators.* Springfield, IL: Charles C Thomas.

Garner, H. G. (1988). *Helping others through teamwork.* Washington, DC: Child Welfare League of America.

Garner, H. G. (1992). Team problem solving and decision making. In *Guide to interdisciplinary practice in rehabilitation settings* (pp. 131-142). Skokie, IL: American Congress of Rehabilitation Medicine.

Hart, V. (1977). The use of many disciplines with the severely and profoundly handicapped. In E. Sontag, J. Smith, & N. Certo (Eds.), *Educational programming for the severely and profoundly handicapped* (pp. 391-396). Reston, VA: The Council for Exceptional Children, Division on Mental Retardation.

Jantsch, E. (1971). Inter- and transdisciplinary university: A systems approach to education and innovation. *Ikistics, 32,* 430-437.

Locke, E. A., & Latham, G. P. (1990). *A theory of goal setting and task performance.* Englewood Cliffs, NJ: Prentice-Hall.

Lowe, J. I., & Herranen, M. (1981). Understanding teamwork: Another look at the concepts. *Social Work in Health Care, 7*(2), 1-11.

Mariano, C. (1989). The case for interdisciplinary collaboration. *Nursing Outlook, 37,* 285-288.

McClane, W. E. (1992). The context for teamwork. In *Guide to interdisciplinary practice in rehabilitation settings* (pp. 28-43). Skokie, IL: American Congress of Rehabilitation Medicine.

Newberger, E.A. (1976). A physician's perspective on the interdisciplinary management of child abuse. *Psychiatric Opinion, 2,* 13-18.

Saltz, C. C. (1992). Stages and structure in team development. In *Guide to interdisciplinary practice in rehabilitation settings* (pp. 72-92). Skokie, IL: American Congress of Rehabilitation Medicine.

Shalinsky, W. (1989). Polydisciplinary groups in the human services. *Small Group Behavior, 20*(2), 203-219.

Spiegel, J. S., & Spiegel, T. M. (1984). An objective examination of multidisciplinary patient conferences. *Journal of Medical Education, 59,* 436-438.

Wagner, W. G. (1987). Child sexual abuse: A multidisciplinary approach to case management. *Journal of Counseling and Development, 65,* 435-439.

3

□ □ □
□ □ □
□ □ □

Transdisciplinary Teamwork

Fred P. Orelove

ORIGINS OF THE MODEL

Professionals in the helping professions who work with individuals with disabilities have long ago recognized that no one discipline can do the job alone. Whitehouse succinctly captured this need for interdependence over 40 years ago:

> We must understand that there are no discrete categories of scientific endeavors. Professions are only cross-sections of the over-all continuum of human thought. Fundamentally no treatment is medical, social, psychological, or vocational—all treatment is total. Yet members of each profession within the narrowness of their own training and experience will attempt to treat the whole person. Obviously, no one profession can do this adequately under present conditions. (1951, p. 45)

It was not until relatively recently, however, that a model of service delivery formally emerged in which a team of professionals worked not only on a common problem, but used common—indeed, *shared*—techniques. As such, the transdisciplinary model represents a higher degree of development in the evolution of team models. Whereas the multidisciplinary and interdisciplinary approaches are characterized by discipline-specific assessment and implementation, for example, the transdisciplinary model espouses activities that are planned and implemented by the entire team (Orelove & Sobsey, 1991; Woodruff & McGonigel, 1988).

The term *transdisciplinary* and the description of the model typically are credited to Dorothy Hutchison of the Nationally Organized Collaborative Project to Provide Comprehensive Services for Atypical Infants and Their Families (affiliated with United Cerebral Palsy Associations, Inc.). Professor Hutchison, a nurse, defined transdisciplinary as being "of, or relating to a transfer of information, knowledge, or skills across disciplinary boundaries" (United Cerebral Palsy, 1976, p. 1). The concept of *transferring across boundaries*, typically termed *role release*, best epitomizes the transdisciplinary model and distinguishes it from its counterparts. (The concept and execution of role release will be explored in greater detail later in this chapter.) The transdisciplinary model has been implemented most comprehensively in two primary areas. Given the origins of the model, the first area—early intervention for infants and toddlers—should not be surprising. The second area is education for students with severe disabilities. The model seems especially well suited to both groups. In both early intervention and education for learners with severe disabilities, the children have multiple, interrelated needs that practically demand a high degree of collaboration for success (Orelove & Sobsey, 1991; Rainforth, York, & Macdonald, 1992). Moreover, the model has a strong element of family participation, which is in keeping with family involvement in programs in early intervention and in severe disabilities.

The principles underpinning the transdisciplinary model also serve to anchor *collaborative teams*, which are increasingly being developed to work within *inclusive educational systems*. That is, some or all school divisions in virtually every state are educating students with disabilities—including those with severe disabilities—in general education classrooms (see, for example, Giangreco, Cloninger, & Iverson, 1993; Stainback & Stainback, 1990, 1992; Villa, Thousand, Stainback, & Stainback, 1992). The successful development and implementation of assessment, curriculum, and instruction in inclusive settings depend on the successful collaboration of instructional and related services personnel, in coordination with parents.

Although the transdisciplinary model formally began in nursing and received significant impetus from special education, it is noteworthy that major components of the model have been embraced by other disciplines, as well (see, for example, Bird, 1990; Dunn, 1988; Ottenbacher, 1982, 1983; Szymanski, Hanley-Maxwell, & Asselin, 1990; York, Rainforth, & Dunn, 1990; York, Rainforth, & Giangreco, 1990). In school settings, for example, therapists assume a variety of roles under the model, extending beyond the traditional direct therapy to include monitoring and consultation (Dunn, 1991). Three professional organizations—the American Physical Therapy Association, the American Occupational Therapy Association, and the American Speech–Language–Hearing Association—have issued guidelines on the provision of related services that support collaborative teamwork in educational settings (see Table 3.1).

ESSENTIAL COMPONENTS OF THE MODEL

Role Release

It was suggested earlier that the notion of sharing, or transferring, information and knowledge across disciplines is the keystone of the transdisciplinary model. From the inception of the transdisciplinary concept, this sharing was viewed as essential to enhancing both services to individuals with disabilities and the skills of the individual team members.

> The Transdisciplinary Team Approach is a teaching–learning activity that is preliminary to—and concurrent with—the delivery of professional services. As a result, the practice of each staff member and the contribution of each discipline is enriched, and each team member becomes capable of assuming the role of a program facilitator. (United Cerebral Palsy, 1976, p. 2)

This sharing or exchange of certain roles and responsibilities with other team members has most commonly been known as role release (Lyon & Lyon, 1980). The word *release* in the term refers to a "releasing" of some functions of one's primary discipline to other team members.

Although the concept of releasing some of one's functions to another may be rather straightforward and appealing, the application can be more complex and threatening. In fact, most teams need to work up to engaging in role release. Woodruff and McGonigel (1988) describe a transition process for accomplishing this. According to Woodruff and McGonigel,

TABLE 3.1   *Excerpts from Professional Policies and Guidelines on the Provision of Related Services*

Source	Major Provisions in Support of Collaborative Teamwork
American Physical Therapy *Association (1990). Physical therapy practice in educational environments.*	Physical Therapy traditionally has been considered something that occurs in a specially equipped and private room during a scheduled block of time. The LRE requirement means that physical therapists need to: (a) emphasize intervention strategies rather than places and (b) make every effort to identify strategies that team members can use in the course of the child's daily routines, when postural control, mobility, and sensory processing are really required. When related services focus first on the natural opportunities for children to develop and practice motor competence in routine activities in integrated environments, there is greater assurance that the related services will fulfill their mandated purpose: "to assist a handicapped child to benefit from special education."
American Occupational Therapy Association (1989). *Guidelines for occupational therapy services.*	Intervention refers to all activities performed by occupational therapy personnel to carry out IEP. In the educational setting, intervention includes direct therapy, monitoring, and several types of consultation. "Occupational therapy treatment refers to the use of specific activities or methods to develop, improve, and/or restore the performance of necessary functions; compensate for dysfunction; and/or minimize debilitation." The intervention must be planned and provided within the child's least restrictive environment.
American Speech–Language–Hearing Association (1991). *A model for collaborative service delivery for students with language learning disorders.*	The collaborative service delivery model affords the speech-language pathologist the opportunity to: (a) observe and assess how the student functions communicatively and socially in the regular classroom, (b) describe the student's communicative strengths and weaknesses in varied educational contexts, and (c) identify which curricular demands enhance or interfere with the student's ability to function communicatively, linguistically, and socially.

role transition consists of six separate but related processes, organized sequentially:

1. Role extension: Self-directed study and other staff development efforts to increase one's depth of understanding, theoretical knowledge, and clinical skills in one's own discipline.
2. Role enrichment: Team members being well versed in their own disciplines and developing a general awareness and understanding of the terminology and basic practices of other disciplines.
3. Role expansion: Acquiring sufficient information from disciplines represented on the team to allow a team member to make knowledgeable observations and program recommendations outside his or her own discipline.
4. Role exchange: Learning the theory, methods, and procedures of other disciplines and beginning to implement the techniques learned by practicing them under the observation of the team member from the relevant discipline.
5. Role release: Putting newly acquired techniques into practice with consultation from the team member from the discipline that is accountable for those practices.
6. Role support: Informal encouragement from other team members and, when necessary, backup support and help by the team member from the appropriate discipline.

A cursory analysis of these processes reveals at least two important observations. First, the deeper a team engages in role transition, the more personal control an individual team member gives up to the group. Second, to be able to give up some control and to be an effective team member, the individual must first feel comfortable and competent within his or her own discipline. Garland, McGonigel, Frank, and Buck (1989) suggest some questions that transdisciplinary teams ask themselves to determine potential or actual problems with engaging in the role transition process. These questions are described in Table 3.2.

A common misunderstanding of the transdisciplinary model and of role release, in particular, is that it flows in only one direction, typically with the therapist giving up control to the teacher. It is true that the teacher usually plays the role of coordinator or *synthesizer* (Bricker, 1976) simply because he or she often is the only professional hired to work full-time with the learner. The most effective transdisciplinary teams, however, owe their success in part to a fluid, multidirectional sharing of responsibilities. Table 3.3 provides examples of role release that demonstrate this point.

TABLE 3.2   *Key Role Transition Questions for Teams*

Am I committed to the role transition process? Are all the team members? How does our behavior reflect our commitment?

How well do I work at learning from other team members? At sharing my expertise?

To what extent does the administrative structure of the program allow adequate time for the team meetings necessary for successful role transition?

How is time scheduled and how are resources committed for the formal and informal staff development activities that are crucial to role transition?

To what extent do I really believe that families are team members? Does my behavior match my belief?

Do I feel that I must handle every child personally before I am comfortable that an assessment is done properly? If yes, what would make me feel differently?

How do I currently keep up with the latest techniques in my discipline? Does the program support these efforts? How?

What do I see as the single greatest barrier to successful role transition in my program? For me personally?

From Garland et al. (1989).

Finally, it should be stressed that releasing one's role does not entail relinquishing one's accountability. The original description of the transdisciplinary model captured this most succinctly: "The [transdisciplinary approach] is not preparing 'unitherapists' who can be all things to all people. . . . Each team member remains accountable for what is taught, to whom it is taught, how well it is learned, and the resulting child and family centered benefits of the teaching" (United Cerebral Palsy, 1976, p. 3).

Integrated Therapy

One criticism of the multidisciplinary and the interdisciplinary models within educational settings is that all therapy services are provided directly by therapists, typically apart from other team members (Orelove & Sobsey, 1991). There are at least two problems with relying strictly on such an isolated therapy model. First, the needs of students with disabilities—particularly those with more severe disabilities—cannot be addressed in isolation. Most children with cerebral palsy, for example, have communication and sensorimotor needs (as well as

TABLE 3.3   *Role Release Examples*

Role extension: An occupational therapist who is an expert on mealtime skills attends a workshop on new feeding techniques.

Role enrichment: The pediatrician conducts an in-service session on medical terminology.

Role expansion: The special education teacher determines that a child needs her visual acuity tested and makes a referral to the vision specialist.

Role exchange: A parent demonstrates to the physical therapist an activity to increase a child's capacity to bear weight on his arms.

Role release: The social worker teaches a father a simple carrying technique for a child for whom he is the primary service provider.

Role support: The audiologist tests the child's hearing.

social–emotional, academic, and other needs) that require the knowledge and skills across multiple disciplines. Second, requiring therapists to provide direct therapy at all times incorrectly assumes that a therapist will be available to teach learners during natural learning opportunities (Rainforth, York, & Macdonald, 1992).

An alternative approach is to integrate therapy services into the context of instruction across the day. Rainforth, York, and Macdonald (1992) provide this example: "A student who is developing mobility skills . . . receives instruction during the times of the day when he or she needs to make transitions, such as when moving between activities in the classroom or when traveling to and from the bus or cafeteria" (p. 14). The goal of integrated therapy is to create services that enhance the learner's participation in daily life. Thus, the important matter is not necessarily the *location* where services are provided—therapy can be just as isolated within the classroom itself—but rather that the techniques are integrated into the instruction across the day.

The concept of integrated therapy often is misunderstood—some think it means that all services are provided indirectly and that therapists cease working directly with learners. While it is true that the transdisciplinary model does rely more heavily on consultative and indirect approaches, it would be a serious mistake for therapists to stop engaging in hands-on interaction with students (Giangreco, York, & Rainforth, 1989; York, Rainforth, & Giangreco, 1990). Dunn (1988, 1991) does a good job clarifying the distinctions among three major models of service provisions for occupational therapists: direct service, monitoring, and consultation. She argues persuasively for a role for all three models:

> Direct service is time consuming and therefore costly, but can address very complex problems and be quickly adapted to meet the student's changing needs. Monitoring is more time efficient, since others carry out the programs, but the student's health and safety must be considered. Consultation is an effective mechanism for providing ongoing environmental support, but requires special skills to be administered properly. (Dunn, 1988, p. 721)

Another common misconception is that an integrated therapy approach leads to loss of professional identity and possible loss of employment, especially for therapists. The reality, however, is that loss of identity does not happen in transdisciplinary teams that work well together. York, Rainforth, and Giangreco (1990), in fact, make the opposite case:

> Appreciation for the contributions of a therapist does not rise from selective sharing of information and skills and a territorial posture. When therapists share, teach, contribute, and become integrally involved in educational programs, their teammates repeatedly comment about how much they value such therapists, how therapy input and therapist collaboration has benefited students and families, as well as how much they have learned through involvement with such fully participating therapists. (p. 78)

As for the concern about losing one's job, the rationale for implementing an indirect therapy approach should not be to reduce the number of therapists in a given setting. As York, Rainforth, and Giangreco (1990) note: "Learners for whom a transdisciplinary model is appropriate usually have intense and comprehensive related service needs. . . . Caseloads of 60 students across three counties or schedules that allow one hour of consultation per student per month are unlikely to be effective in any service delivery model!" (p. 78).

BENEFITS OF THE MODEL

The transdisciplinary model benefits the consumer, the family, and the professionals who work with both. Because the vast majority of applications have been in early intervention and school programs, this section will describe benefits in those contexts.

For Consumers

As suggested earlier, children and youth with significant disabilities typically require a broad array of educational and related services. Whereas traditional models of service delivery tend to view the child along disciplinary lines (e.g., the language therapist is responsible for the oral region, the occupational therapist is responsible for the upper extremities), the transdisciplinary model views the learner wholistically. Thus, the learner's entire educational program is more cohesive, more unified, and, accordingly, more beneficial to the child's specific needs.

For students with the most severe disabilities, the transdisciplinary approach often is combined within a curricular and instructional model that yields especially successful outcomes. In this model, educational goals are derived from activities the student needs to perform to become a greater part of everyday life in the home and community as well as at school. Because most daily activities require the performance of integrated skills that cut across traditional developmental areas (e.g., gross-motor, fine-motor, language, and social skills), an instructional model that uses professionals flexibly (i.e., across traditional disciplinary borders) is highly compatible. Such a model significantly reduces problems learners traditionally have had in acquiring new skills or in synthesizing, maintaining, and generalizing skills already gained.

Apart from the consumer benefits from the curricular shift inherent in many applications of the transdisciplinary model, the fundamental way in which instructional plans are coordinated and delivered also has positive effects. Many learners with special needs, for example, engage in challenging behaviors. Instructional models that encourage independent and isolated approaches to the learners—often in settings apart from other children and professionals—result in fragmented and unsuccessful "behavior management" strategies. Conversely, teams that plan, implement, and evaluate approaches together tend to produce more effective outcomes for learners. Although no data are available to support this, it is plausible that teams working together are also more likely to view the intent of the students' behaviors more humanistically, i.e., as conveying specific unmet needs, and therefore to develop intervention strategies that are similarly more sensitive to the total needs of the child.

Finally, the student benefits by being worked with in typical settings across the day. In addition to the overall instructional gains from this approach described earlier, the learner experiences social benefits by not being removed from the ongoing flow of activities or, as is often the case, by being physically removed for isolated therapy.

For Families

Clearly, to the degree the child benefits—through instructional and social gains—the family members accrue secondary benefits. The transdisciplinary model also enables families to have an improved relationship with the school. Because services in the model are coordinated through one individual (typically the classroom teacher), parents do not have to "shop around" for information, seeking out each professional to discover what progress their child is making or to offer recommendations.

Perhaps the most important benefit for families, however, arises from the role that parents are afforded within the transdisciplinary model. A team operating within any model certainly can (and should) involve parents. As Carney and Atwood (1993) observe, however, teams best prepared to include parents in decision making are those that adhere to basic components of effective team functioning. The transdisciplinary model has long recognized the unique perspective and contributions of parents. This is especially true in early intervention programs (Hanson, 1985; Warren, Alpert, & Kaiser, 1986). "The role of the family is central to the transdisciplinary team. . . . All [transdisciplinary] programs consider the family not only as a full, decision-making member of the team but also as the consumer of early intervention services" (Garland et al., 1989, unpaginated). Readers seeking an especially helpful and practical perspective on the role of parents as team members are referred to Salisbury (1992).

For Professionals

Ideally, a transdisciplinary approach enriches each team member's professional skills and contributions. Because individuals on the team have a responsibility toward the overall development and implementation of the service plan, they become accountable both to the team and, of course, to the student. That accountability fosters personal growth and a sense of collegiality.

Moreover, skills in one's own discipline become more sharply focused around solving problems specific to individual learners. This also leads to greater creativity and an increased investment in practical outcomes for the child.

Finally, a transdisciplinary approach reduces the territoriality so common to many other team models. Success is measured not simply by an individual's contribution, but also by the degree to which the team works together to create and implement effective strategies.

APPLICATIONS OF THE MODEL

There are three major areas of application for the transdisciplinary model in educational settings: assessment, program planning, and delivery of services. Each of these will be explored briefly.

Assessment

In traditional models, professionals conduct their own independent assessments in their own disciplinary perspectives, using a combination of formal and informal instruments. Unfortunately, a disability in a particular area(e.g., movement) may restrict or alter performance in another area (e.g., communication), with no consideration of their interaction (Rainforth, Macdonald, York, & Dunn, 1992). Moreover, because each discipline typically develops a separate report, there is a need to pull the disparate reports together, coping with information that is either redundant or conflicting, if not irrelevant to the student's educational needs.

In contrast, assessment in a transdisciplinary approach is developed and implemented collaboratively. One model that has been used extensively to assess infants and toddlers is the *arena* model (Connor, Williamson, & Siepp, 1978; Wolery & Dyk, 1984). In the arena model, one team member interacts with the child and family while other members observe and record the child's responses. Family members are encouraged to participate as actively as they desire. After the assessment, team members and the family share their observations and reactions.

The arena model appears to be an improvement over traditional assessment processes. Nevertheless, it still typically relies on artificial settings and contrived tasks, which may fail to present a completely fair portrayal of the abilities of children with more severe disabilities (Rainforth, Macdonald, York, & Dunn, 1992).

As an alternative, Rainforth, Macdonald, York, and Dunn (1992) describe an assessment process based on a model of collaborative teams. The process is predicated on the importance of examining students' performance in natural environments and on typical tasks and routines. Discrepancies are then identified between the student's performance and the performance on those same activities by individuals without disabilities. From a transdisciplinary perspective, the critical feature of the collaborative model is that the assessment is planned, implemented, and summarized (via a comprehensive report) as a team. It is important to note that there is an important role within the approach for "diagnostic/discipline-referenced" assessment, that is, assessment by individual disciplines (York, Rainforth, & Dunn, 1990). However, it is a supplement to, not a replacement for, collaborative assessment on functional activities.

Program Planning

The assessment typically generates many more needs than an educational team can work on in a given year. Thus, the team must establish priorities for the learner's Individualized Education Program (IEP). While many questions must be addressed (e.g., Does the skill maintain health? Does it have multiple applications?), there are three particularly worth highlighting:

1. Will the activity make a real difference in the quality of the student's life?
2. Will performance increase the student's likelihood of interacting with peers?
3. Is the skill/activity a priority of the student and/or family?

The last question touches on a common concern of professionals, viz., parents' insistence on certain goals being included on their child's IEP, despite the professionals' "knowing what is best." Rainforth, York, and Macdonald (1992) present a helpful perspective:

Jeremy's mother wanted the team to focus on toilet training. For 2 years, team member disagreed about this priority and failed to put it on the IEP because some members considered it unrealistic. Finally, in the third year, toilet training was made a priority. After a couple of months, Jeremy's mother reported that she saw no progress, and thought they should move on to other needs. Some readers may conclude that the professionals 'beat' this unrealistic parent, but another view is that the team might have achieved a unified effort 3 years earlier if they had started by honoring the mother's priority. (p. 164)

Once priorities are established, goals must be written. The way in which they are developed and organized is critical to the implementation of the transdisciplinary model (Orelove & Sobsey, 1991). To be successful, the team must avoid the trap of having individual team members write goals for their own disciplines, with the resulting IEP becoming an exercise in collation, rather than collaboration. Rainforth, York, and Macdonald (1992) offer a variety of detailed examples of collaboratively developed IEPs.

Delivery of Services

Designing activity-based IEP goals and objectives with embedded motor, communication, and social skills sets the stage for collaborative teaching. It also is desirable to document the need for related services and the therapists' responsibilities. Two methods of doing this are: (1) to include a statement about required services within the IEP, and (2) to specify required services following each instructional objective (Rainforth, York, & Macdonald, 1992).

As suggested earlier, the transdisciplinary model presumes that most of the therapy will be integrated within instructional activities. Teams also may recommend direct therapy for students as a supplement to integrated therapy. For instance, a student who is highly distractible or who may require privacy for a particular procedure (e.g., suctioning) may benefit temporarily from time away from peers. Although many therapists believe that special equipment or specialized techniques justify isolated therapy for many children, usually alternatives can be devised and incorporated into the student's routine activities.

CHALLENGES TO IMPLEMENTING THE MODEL

The transdisciplinary model has numerous benefits. It must be recognized, however, that converting to the model presents a variety of challenges, fueled both by ideology and practicality. This section describes some of the common challenges to fully implementing the model and some solutions and perspectives to avoid the pitfalls and to resolve differences. The challenges are organized into three areas: (1) those that arise from differences in *philosophical or professional* perspectives, (2) those that relate to *personal or interpersonal* conflicts or issues, and (3) those that are basically *logistical* problems.

Philosophical and Professional Challenges

Differences in Philosophy and Orientation

Each individual brings to the team her or his own experiences and view of the world. Although diverse backgrounds enrich transdisciplinary teams, they also create potential barriers to working together effectively. Therapists, for example, typically work from a medical perspective, in which the underlying cause of a behavior must be determined prior to remediating the problem. Other team members who were taught to adopt a strict behavioral model may instead abandon a search for causes in favor of changing environmental events to effect behavioral change. Such a philosophical difference may be difficult to resolve, especially if the team members are used to learning to work in isolation and have not been provided with opportunities to solve problems cooperatively. Moreover, differences in professional jargon (e.g., "upper extremity" versus "arm," "bruxism" versus "teeth grinding") may further obscure communication between professionals, and especially between professionals and parents.

Such differences can be overcome, particularly when team members recognize that they are present. It is fine to use jargon, especially when it clarifies, rather than obfuscates, but it is preferable to use easily understood terms in speaking with family members and in writing any reports that they may read (i.e., virtually everything). Perhaps the key to remedying professional differences is to openly discuss and agree on the goal that everyone holds in common, i.e., the creation of better services and supports to the consumer.

Diminishment of Professional Status

Role release within the transdisciplinary model threatens the status that many professionals perceive for themselves. Bassoff (1976) pointedly observes: "The assumption that different disciplines on teams gather together as equals, while an overt statement of a desired state, cloaks the reality that some team members are more equal than others" (p. 224). Yet, as York, Rainforth, and Giangreco (1990) state: "Appreciation for the contributions of a therapist does not rise from selective sharing of information and skills and a territorial posture" (p. 78). The alternative, then, is for program administrators to encourage collaboration by continually pointing out to the team the common good they do through working together and openly sharing skills and information.

A special status problem occurs when a team perceives one member as being inferior (Landerholm, 1990). This happens, for example, when inexperienced teachers are hired to work in early intervention programs at salaries significantly lower than clinicians on the team. Landerholm (1990) suggests several practical solutions, including hiring experienced teachers at higher salaries and increasing staff training.

Role Conflict or Ambiguity

A related challenge arises from the fluidity of roles within the transdisciplinary approach. Some individuals have difficulty assuming greater flexibility, preferring instead to stay within the well-defined boundaries in which they were taught to perform. In other cases, roles are overly ambiguous, even within the more permeable team structure. Staff could be brought together to discuss their concerns and to help design solutions that they all can support, including clarifying one another's roles within the model (Landerholm, 1990).

Professional Ethics and Liability

Another challenge is the fear of some that reliance on indirect services may foster negligent behavior by not ensuring sufficient supervision by appropriately licensed or certified professionals (Geiger, Bradley, Rock, & Croce, 1986). A valid case in point are the restrictions imposed by a given state's Nurse Practice Act. Most of the acts specify the dependent and independent activities in which the licensed nurse can legally engage. For example, a nurse may be restricted from training a teacher or paraprofessional to perform tracheal suctioning in the absence of supervision by the nurse (Sobsey & Cox, 1991).

Clearly some highly specialized or potentially risky procedures should be performed by specifically designated, trained professionals (or parents). The reality, however, is that therapists and nurses are not available at schools all the time. The answer seems to lie in careful planning, staff training, and monitoring of policies and procedures to ensure the safety and well-being of the child and the personnel.

Misunderstanding of Approach

The final professional challenge to implementing a transdisciplinary model is overcoming its misapplication due to a failure to understand it fully. The model does not promote interchangeable team members or a reduction in therapy services. Administrators, however, may cite these "features" in an attempt to save money or to justify their inability to locate professional staff. As a result, teams find themselves doing a poorer job, trusting one another less, and feeling resentful. One likely reason for the transdisciplinary model not having been adopted more freely is its misapplication in the name of more flexible services.

Personal and Interpersonal Challenges

Inability to Work as a Team

This problem, of course, is not restricted to transdisciplinary teams. Because this model depends so heavily on team planning and consensus, however, difficulties in resolving conflicts, communicating openly, and so forth will render the team virtually useless. Much has been written about the "care and feeding" of teams, including the previous chapters. For more information, readers are referred to Bailey (1984), Johnson and Johnson (1987), Landerholm (1990), and Orelove and Sobsey (1991). Suffice it to say, successful teams are created and nourished. Transdisciplinary teams, like others, require thoughtful leadership and involvement of all members, in addition to administrative support and nurturing.

Threat of Training Others and of Being Trained

With role release being a prominent feature of the transdisciplinary model, it follows that successful teams depend on individuals both freely sharing with and accepting information from others. These actions, however, can be rather threatening because they place the individual's skills under close scrutiny, increasing one's personal risk, and demanding that team members trust others. Administrators would do well to watch for signs that staff members feel intimidated or uneasy. They could then encourage them to discuss the feelings, perhaps by sharing their own concerns. It also is important to remember that transdisciplinary teams, like others, develop over time and in somewhat predictable stages. Properly encouraged, trust, sharing, and acceptance will increase as team members work with and get to know one another better.

Resistance to Change

This is a common barrier, particularly when an outsider imposes a shift in direction. Resistance to change must be anticipated and confronted; left unchecked, it can destroy a team. Once again, successful teams understand and agree on a common mission that accounts for, but transcends, individual needs. As Giangreco et al. (1989) note: "Change is also the process by which team members continue to be challenged, to develop new skills, to feel a sense of accomplishment" (p. 61).

Logistical Challenges

It is the author's belief that the personal, interpersonal, and philosophical concerns raised earlier are central to the adoption of the transdisciplinary model. If teams can overcome those challenges, then they will find ways to deal with logistical problems as well.

Nevertheless, it would be unfair to dismiss real-world problems such as finding time to meet, developing processes that are efficient, and locating qualified personnel. Describing detailed procedures for implementing a transdisciplinary approach is beyond the scope of this chapter. Readers are strongly urged to consult Rainforth, York, and Macdonald (1992), who describe practical and tested solutions for scheduling personnel, conducting team meetings, and other important matters to implement programs. It should be evident by now that the transdisciplinary approach demands regular meetings that revolve around the specific needs of learners and team-generated solutions to those needs. It follows that the model requires understanding, organization, and commitment for success.

PREPARATION OF PERSONNEL

This chapter has focused on the application of the transdisciplinary model, particularly in school programs. Despite the numerous advantages of the model, however, most team members come to their professional positions with little or no understanding of the model or appreciation for its benefits. In fact, it would be fair to state that most university programs that prepare professionals in human services reinforce discipline-specific work at the expense of collaboration. Moreover, university faculty members themselves fail to model collaborative behavior, instead preparing and delivering lectures from the perspective of their discipline. This chapter's final section offers some recommendations for individuals responsible for preparing professionals to work collaboratively on transdisciplinary teams.

Appreciate Importance of Modeling Teamwork

We cannot expect students to do something that we preach but fail to practice. Actually using a collaborative approach to teaching university classes is probably more effective than spending a semester talking about the advantages of the approach. True collaboration includes more than the occasional guest lecture as helpful as they are; it means faculty from various disciplines designing and delivering courses and curricula.

Teach Skills on Collaborative Teamwork

Good teams are made, not born. The best teams not only share common values and a sense of purpose and commitment, but have the tools to work effectively within the team. Preservice programs afford an excellent opportunity to give students practice in skills such as resolving conflicts, sharing decisions, and solving problems in groups. These types of process skills can be applied in virtually any group assignment. The focus should be on collaborative outcomes, rather than on individual performance. These skills become even sharper and more useful when practiced with students from other disciplines.

Teach about Change Process

Teams do not work in a vacuum. It is helpful for transdisciplinary teams in educational settings to understand the reality and importance of the change process, particularly related to integration issues

(Giangreco, 1989). Understanding that change is inevitable should reduce professionals' anxiety and encourage their participation in the change process. Moreover, as team members increasingly assume consultative roles within the educational system, they will face more opportunities to serve as initiators or conduits for change (Giangreco, 1989). Finally, it is helpful for team members to appreciate the positive impact that their change efforts have on the students' education.

Select Field Placements that Support Collaboration

The impact of students' field experiences cannot be overestimated. Individuals tend to continue practicing in the manner they were first taught. Putting trainees in schools (and other placements) where collaborative teams flourish is perhaps the single most effective strategy available to a program. Naturally, the experience becomes even more useful when strong linkages are made to university supervisors who support collaborative teamwork.

Work with Consumers and Family Members

We should not forget that individuals with disabilities and their families are the reason why transdisciplinary teams exist in the first place. These individuals should be consulted in developing class readings and assignments and asked to participate in classes as guest lecturers, panel members, and so on.

Involve University Affiliated Programs

As of 1993, every state (except Wyoming) has at least one university affiliated program (UAP). These programs, supported by the Administration on Developmental Disabilities (U.S. Department of Health and Human Services), were created to provide *interdisciplinary* training to help professionals work more effectively with individuals with developmental disabilities. As such, UAPs offer a unique opportunity to rally support and to secure funding for the development of programs that involve university faculty and community service providers from a variety of disciplines. As one example, Virginia's UAP—the Virginia Institute for Developmental Disabilities—developed and continues to offer a course on interdisciplinary teamwork that is co-taught by faculty from different disciplines and enrolls students from seven different academic disciplines.

SUMMARY [1]

The transdisciplinary model requires commitment and hard work. In those ways, it is no different from any other approach to working with individuals in the human services field. The model, however, also incorporates a formal mechanism for sharing skills and information across traditional boundaries. In that respect, it asks a great deal from every single person on the team. In doing so, the model creates the opportunity for a richness of experience that comes from daring to trust another person and to risk displaying one's fear and uncertainty.

Finally, the transdisciplinary model says that the consumer of services is the ultimate judge of the team's success or failure. As we rightly continue to give more power and control to the consumer, the transdisciplinary team becomes more the servant than the master. As professionals we owe it to the consumer, as well as to the family, to demonstrate that we can pool our experiences and knowledge and rise above our biases to serve them as effectively as possible.

REFERENCES

American Occupational Therapy Association. (1989). *Guidelines for occupational therapy services in the public schools* (2d ed.). Rockville, MD: Author.

American Physical Therapy Association. (1990). *Physical therapy practice in educational environments.* Alexandria, VA: Author.

American Speech-Language-Hearing Association, Committee on Language Learning Disorders. (1991). A model for collaborative service delivery for students with language-learning disorders in the public schools. *American Speech-Language-Hearing Association*, 3(33) (Suppl.).

---

[1] Acknowledgment: I wish to thank Deana Buck and Elaine Ferrell for their help in preparing this chapter.

Bailey, D. B. (1984). A triaxial model of the interdisciplinary team and group process. *Exceptional Children*, 5(1), 17-25.

Bassoff, B. Z. (1976). Interdisciplinary education for health professionals: Issues and directions. *Social Work in Health Care*, 2(2), 219-228.

Bird, A. K. (1990). Enhancing communication within a transdiscplinary model. In C. J. Semmler & J. G. Hunter (Eds.), *Early occupational therapy intervention: Neonates to three years* (pp. 288-304). Gaithersburg, MD: Aspen.

Bricker, D. (1976). Educational synthesizer. In M. A. Thomas (Ed.), *Hey, don't forget about me!* (pp. 84-97). Reston, VA: Council for Exceptional Children.

Carney, I. H., & Atwood, B. (1993). *Beyond good intentions: Full inclusion of parents on decision-making teams.* Unpublished manuscript. Richmond, VA: Virginia Commonwealth University.

Connor, F. P., Williamson, G. G., & Siepp, J. M. (Eds.). (1978). *Program guide for infants and toddlers with neuromotor and other developmental disabilities.* New York: Teachers College Press.

Dunn, W. (1988). Models of occupational therapy service provision in the school system. *The American Journal of Occupational Therapy*, 42(11), 718-723.

Dunn, W. (1991). Integrated related services. In L. H. Meyer, C. A. Peck, & L. Brown (Eds.), *Critical issues in the lives of people with severe disabilities* (pp. 353-377). Baltimore: Paul H. Brookes.

Garland, C., McGonigel, M., Frank, A., & Buck, D. (1989). *The transdisciplinary model of service delivery.* Lightfoot, VA: Child Development Resources.

Geiger, W. L., Bradley, R. H., Rock, S. L., & Croce, R. (1986). Commentary. *Physical and Occupational Therapy in Pediatrics*, 6(2), 16-21.

Giangreco, M. F. (1989). Facilitating integration of students with severe disabilities. *Teacher Education and Special Education*, 12(4), 139-147.

Giangreco, M. F., Cloninger, C. J., & Iverson, V. S. (1993). *Choosing options and accommodations for children.* Baltimore: Paul H. Brookes.

Giangreco, M. F., York, J., & Rainforth, B. (1989). Providing related services to learners with severe handicaps in educational settings: Pursuing the least restrictive option. *Pediatric Physical Therapy*, 1(2), 55-63.

Hanson, M. J. (1985). An analysis of the effects of early intervention services for infants and toddlers with moderate and severe handicaps. *Topics in Early Childhood Special Education*, 5(2), 36-51.

Johnson, D. W., & Johnson, R. T. (1987). *Joining together: Group theory and skills* (2d ed.). Englewood Cliffs, NJ: Prentice-Hall.

Landerholm, E. (1990, Winter). The transdisciplinary team approach. *Teaching Exceptional Children*, 66-70.

Lyon, S., & Lyon, G. (1980). Team functioning and staff development: A role release approach to providing integrated educational services for severely handicapped students. *Journal of the Association for the Severely Handicapped*, 5(3), 250-263.

Orelove, F. P., & Sobsey, D. (1991). *Educating children with multiple disabilities: A transdisciplinary approach* (2d ed.). Baltimore: Paul H. Brookes.

Ottenbacher, K. (1982). Occupational therapy and special education: Some issues and concerns related to P.L. 94-142. *American Journal of Occupational Therapy*, 36, 81-84.

Ottenbacher, K. (1983). Transdisciplinary service delivery in school environments: Some limitations. *Physical and Occupational Therapy in Pediatrics*, 3(4), 9-16.

Rainforth, B., Macdonald, C., York, J., & Dunn, W. (1992). Collaborative assessment. In B. Rainforth, J. York, & C. Macdonald (Eds.), *Collaborative teams for students with severe disabilities: Integrating therapy and educational services* (pp. 105-155). Baltimore: Paul H. Brookes.

Rainforth, B., York, J., & Macdonald, C. (Eds.). (1992). *Collaborative teams for students with severe disabilities: Integrating therapy and educational services*. Baltimore: Paul H. Brookes.

Salisbury, C. (1992). Parents as team members: Inclusive teams, collaborative outcomes. In B. Rainforth, J. York, & C. Macdonald (Eds.), *Collaborative teams for students with severe disabilities: Integrating therapy and educational services* (pp. 43-66). Baltimore: Paul H. Brookes.

Sobsey, D., & Cox, A. W. (1991). Integrating health care and educational programs. In F. P. Orelove & D. Sobsey, *Educating children with multiple disabilities: A transdisciplinary approach* (pp. 155-185). Baltimore: Paul H. Brookes.

Stainback, W., & Stainback, S. (Eds.). (1990). *Support networks for inclusive schooling: Interdependent integrated education*. Baltimore: Paul H. Brookes.

Stainback, S., & Stainback, W. (Eds.). (1992). *Curriculum considerations in inclusive classrooms: Facilitating learning for all students*. Baltimore: Paul H. Brookes.

Symanski, E. M., Hanley-Maxwell, C., & Asselin, S. (1990). Rehabilitation counseling, special education, and vocational special needs education: Three transition disciplines. *Career Development for Exceptional Individuals*, 13(1), 29-38.

United Cerebral Palsy, Nationally Organized Collaborative Project to Provide Comprehensive Services for Atypical Infants and Their Families. (1976). *Staff development handbook: A resource for the transdisciplinary process*. New York: United Cerebral Palsy Association.

Villa, R. A., Thousand, J. S., Stainback, W., & Stainback, S. (Eds.). (1992). *Restructuring for caring and effective education*. Baltimore: Paul H. Brookes.

Warren, S. F., Alpert, C. L., & Kaiser, A. P. (1986). An optimal learning environment for infants and toddlers with severe handicaps. *Focus on Exceptional Children*, 18(8), 1-11.

Whitehouse, F. A. (1951). Teamwork—A democracy of processions. *Exceptional Children*, 18(2), 45-52.

Wolery, M., & Dyk, L. (1984). Arena assessment: Description and preliminary social validity data. *Journal of the Association for Persons with Severe Handicaps*, 9(3), 231-235.

Woodruff, G., & McGonigel, M. J. (1988). Early intervention team approaches: The transdisciplinary model. In J. B. Jordan, J. J. Gallagher, P. L. Hutinger, & M. B. Karnes (Eds.), *Early childhood special education: Birth to three* (pp. 164-181). Reston, VA: Council for Exceptional Children.

York, J., Rainforth, B., & Dunn, W. (1990). Training needs of physical and occupational therapists who provide services to children and youth with severe disabilities. In S. Kaiser & C. McWhorter (Eds.), *Preparing personnel to work with persons with severe disabilities* (pp. 153-180). Baltimore: Paul H. Brookes.

York, J., Rainforth, B., & Giangreco, M. F. (1990). Transdisciplinary teamwork and integrated therapy: Clarifying the misconceptions. *Pediatric Physical Therapy*, 2(2), 73-79.

4

Interagency
Collaboration: An
Interdisciplinary
Application

Vicki C. Pappas

As our understanding of how best to plan and provide services for people with complex and multiple needs has grown, so has our acknowledgment of the need for and benefits of being interdisciplinary. Ideals such as "coordinated," "comprehensive," and "appropriate" service delivery permeate professional literature and behavior in a variety of human service arenas and have undergirded advances in the use of interdisciplinary models to fulfill those ideals. Professionals from medical, educational, and social service backgrounds now routinely work together in interdisciplinary teams to assess children and adults, plan appropriate interventions for them, and evaluate their progress. Being interdisciplinary also has come to include teaming with parents, users of services, and even with other family members and friends from the community, in contemporary configurations called *circles of support* (Amado, Conklin, & Wells, 1990; Mount, Beeman, & Ducharme, 1988).

Our conceptualizations of being interdisciplinary have traditionally focused on the client or case level. Most definitions of interdisciplinary teams assume case-oriented interactions by a group of professionals, usually from one agency or program. School-based teams planning Individualized Education Programs (IEPs) for students with disabilities in public schools typically have included professionals employed only by the local education agency (e.g., teacher, psychologist, social worker, and speech pathologist) along with the mandated participation of parents. Hospital-based diagnostic teams generally have included a variety of medical and allied health professionals, social workers, and psychologists who have an affiliation with the hospital. Similar agency-based interdisciplinary configurations comprise teams in nursing homes that plan individual programs of active treatment under Medicaid regulations.

Since the mid-1980s, however, and the advent of changing service philosophies and practices, being interdisciplinary has come to take on a broader meaning. Because people with multiple needs cannot always best be served by one provider agency, case-oriented teaming is more frequently characterized by the interactions of professionals representing not only multiple disciplines, but also varied organizational affiliations. Today, teams frequently include participation of professionals from different agencies and organizations. This shift implies a need for even greater communication, cooperation, and collaboration to maximize effectiveness in serving consumers and families. For instance, as medically fragile children are legitimized to enter public school programs under expanded conceptions of "least restrictive environment" established by P.L. 94–142 (the Education of All Handicapped Children Act) and the movement toward "inclusive" schooling (Brown, Long, Udvari-Solner, Davis, Van Deventer, Ahlgren, Johnson, Gruenewald, & Jorgensen, 1989; Stainbeck & Stainbeck, 1990), school-based teams have begun to take on an interagency flavor. Educators interact with medical and allied health personnel from hospitals or public health nursing programs to provide appropriate health supports for these children while they are in school.

Similarly, early intervention advocates have raised consciousness about the need for educators and medical personnel to plan services so that more "comprehensive, coordinated community-based care" (Schorr, 1988) can occur before children reach the school age years. Passage of P.L. 99–457 in 1986 (Part H, Individuals with Disabilities Education Act) provided additional stimulus for interagency collaboration in the infant–toddler arena as professionals from multiple disciplines, and hence agencies, were mandated to collaborate with families to develop Individualized Family Service Plans (IFSPs) (Nash, 1990). Current conceptions of early intervention have come to mean the interaction of individuals from a variety of agencies to support young children and their families. Preschool screening and child find programs now include representative professionals from the schools, hospitals, public health nursing, and other social service agencies in the community.

Furthermore, as other programs (and concomitant funding streams) have oriented toward more community-based programming, guided by principles of community integration and family-based care, the need for professionals from multiple agencies to engage in program planning for people of all ages has become apparent. Community-based teams for adults with disabilities often include representatives from vocational rehabilitation, the residential or day program, mental health, and/or community recreation agencies. Providing adequate programs of family support has called for the cooperative involvement of community health, social services, and mental health providers. Aging services necessitate involvement from aging, medical, and social service agencies.

Finally, as community- and state-level programs struggle to meet burgeoning needs with significant budget constraints, interagency collaboration has become a preferred model for program- and system-level interaction (Audette, 1990; Johnson, McLaughlin, & Christensen, 1982). Nonduplication of services, resource sharing, and cost effectiveness have become desired operating procedures of service systems—ones that support the drive toward increased interagency collaboration.

Current trends such as these enable us to justify broader definitions of interdisciplinary teams. Our conceptions of being interdisciplinary can and should be expanded to assume participation of professionals from more than one agency and to consider the implications of interagency participation on teams at levels beyond the individual case level. While the basic characteristics and requirements of interdisciplinary teaming are similar for interagency groups, interagency participation also introduces variations in the standard model, primarily related to issues of turf, control, and funding. It is the purpose of this chapter to illustrate how interagency interaction at all levels is a logical extension of interdisciplinary teaming at the individual case level.

THE RATIONALE FOR INTERAGENCY COLLABORATION

Interagency collaboration is a concept that found its roots in the complex need to provide more efficient, coordinated human services amid a climate of economic constraints and accountability that has been present since the 1970s. Audette (1980) describes the "patchwork quilt" of human services—a system consisting of different eligibility criteria, intake systems, means of coordination, paperwork systems, and confidentiality requirements. Not only are there organizational and economic inefficiencies, but clients and families need to be very skillful to successfully negotiate services that are responsive to their needs, especially before and after the school age years when multiple agencies come into play.

A helpful definition of interagency collaboration was developed by the Regional Resource Center Task Force of the U.S. Office of Special Education (Johnson et al., 1982). They define the process of interagency collaboration as one that:

- Encourages and facilitates an open and honest exchange of ideas, plans, approaches, and resources across disciplines, programs, and agencies;
- Enables all participants to jointly define their separate interests by mutually identifying changes that may be needed to best achieve common purposes;
- Utilizes formal procedures to help clarify issues, define problems, and make decisions relative to them (p. 396).

Interagency collaboration received early impetus from policy directives issued by the then Department of Health and Human Services to establish service integration projects (Humm-Delgado, 1980) and in legislation designed for individuals with disabilities, with its provision of related services requirements (Johnson et al., 1982). In the disabilities field, both interdisciplinary teaming and interagency collaboration received particular attention not only to address how to provide comprehensive services to people with lifelong needs across an array of functional areas, but also to respond to cost considerations For similar reasons, interagency collaboration became an increasingly important part of early intervention programs, particularly Head Start in the 1980s (Nordyke, 1982) and the Education for All Handicapped Children Act Amendments of 1986 (Morgan, Guetzloe, & Swan, 1991).

TABLE 4.1   *Forces for Collaboration*

Individual level	Systems level
Multiple, diverse needs of individual	Multiple, diverse needs of system
Fragmented view of the individual	Fragmented agency services
Lack of responsiveness to individual needs	Lack of responsiveness to consumer needs
Lack of parental voice	Lack of consumer voice
Uncoordinated services	Uncoordinated services
Inadequate services	Gaps/duplicated services
Multiple professionals	Multiple/overlapping planning bodies
Differing treatment modalities	Different program models
Multiple billing procedures	Multiple funding streams
Professional jargon	Agency jargon
Professional territoriality	Agency territoriality

More recently, supports for and examples of interagency collaboration can be found in a variety of human service programs at local, state, and federal levels: child abuse, addictions prevention, long-term mental illness, juvenile delinquency, rural family services, therapeutic foster care, and perinatal substance abuse, to name a few. Likewise, instances of interagency collaboration frequently are found in other areas of government such as environmental policy, forestry, information resource management, international security, and public management.

Many have delineated an array of reasons why individual professionals and agencies need to work together (Audette, 1990; Elder & Magrab, 1980; Johnson et al., 1982; Kakalik, Brewer, Dougharty, Fleischauer, Genesky, & Waller, 1974; Lacour, 1982; Martinson, 1982; Zeller, 1980). Table 4.1 illustrates the parallels between individual and systems (interagency) levels of collaboration.

Whether at the individual or the system level, this array of conditions creates the demand for more collaborative ways of operating, particularly if there is pressure from clients, parents, advocates, or funding sources. The reasons agencies seek to engage in cooperative and collaborative interactions parallel the motivations professionals have for committing to interdisciplinary teamwork. In an era of consumer responsiveness and customer satisfaction, however, a focus on client needs ought to be basic to any col-

	Unidisciplinary ➤ *(Autonomous decision making)*	Multidisciplinary ➤ *(Parallel decision making)*	Interdisciplinary *(Integrated decision making)*
Professional	Professional competence and confidence	Cross-professional sharing	Cross-utilization of skills
Team	Role identification and orientation	Differentiated roles	Team cohesiveness
Program	Program identity	Joint activities without integration	Program identity subordinate to group goals
Agency	Agency identity	Joint activities without integration	Agency identity subordinate to group goals
	Cooperation ➤	*Coordination* ➤	*Collaboration*

FIGURE **4.1** A model for becoming interdisciplinary

laborative interaction: At the individual level, appropriately configured and coordinated services to meet consumer and family needs; and at the inter-agency level, a coordinated system must be responsive, accessible, and understandable to its consumers. For agencies or individual professionals to successfully work together toward these goals, they will have to address similar issues in communication, cooperation, and collaboration.

A CONCEPTUALIZATION OF BECOMING INTERDISCIPLINARY: A DYNAMIC MODEL OF MULTILEVEL INTERACTION

The development of integrated, collaborative functioning, whether interdisciplinary or interagency, is a dynamic, cyclical, and multileveled process. Functioning in this way is not always easily implemented, nor is it easy to achieve. Despite a plethora of terms and definitions, a useful way to understand collaboration is to consider it from a broad-based and inclusive conception. Figure 4.1 offers such a conceptual model, and positions interagency collaboration as a logical extension of interdisciplinary teamwork. The model assumes becoming interdisciplinary is a developmental process, and illustrates how *becoming* interdisciplinary has implications for individual-, team-, program-, and agency-level interactions.

The development of interaction styles occurs along a continuum, where stages of unidisciplinary, multidisciplinary, and interdisciplinary behaviors mature over time. Development of interdisciplinary behavior also occurs vertically, through various levels of an organization, beginning with individuals. There should be no assumption, however, that one stage or level in the model is a prerequisite for the next. Although becoming interdisciplinary grows and changes with time and circumstances, the process is dynamic and cyclical, rather than linear. Particular circumstances, such as funding cutbacks or particularly troublesome cases, can hasten development by creating an occasion for collaboration or hinder it by setting up barriers. Rates of professional development and attitudinal readiness for collaboration may vary, depending on personal styles, personalities, philosophies, or particular training experiences. Likewise, external events or individual personality characteristics can trigger or hinder movement along the continuum. The next sections will explore this conceptualization of becoming interdisciplinary in more depth and provide examples of interactions across each of the various stages and levels shown in Figure 4.1.

Unidisciplinary Behaviors

Unidisciplinary and the related term *intradisciplinary* refer to the independent attention of a single professional to a problem, with little input or consultation from professionals of other disciplines. Information may be shared with or communicated among professionals from other disciplines, but essentially one discipline is represented in the approach to problem solving; decision making is autonomous. A primary care physician performing an independent examination or a teacher acting alone to make a placement recommendation for a student are examples of unidisciplinary behavior.

At the *individual professional level,* gaining competence and confidence in one's own profession is the primary order of business. Most traditional professional preparation programs are geared to instill a unidisciplinary perspective in their students, with a focus on sound preparation and proficiency in the philosophy, tenets, and best practices of the particular discipline prior to licensing or certification. As new professionals move into practice, it is not uncommon for them to have a strong sense of the contributions their discipline can make to the field and to be concerned with further refining and building on the skills of their home discipline. Individual professional competence rests on a unidisciplinary focus.

A parallel situation can be found at the *team level*. In the area of team development, there is a literature that depicts the changing maturity of teams as they move through phases of problem solving (Shaw, 1981). In the initial stages, which parallel unidisciplinary interaction, teams are characterized by an emphasis on orientation—an exploratory phase where members come to understand the problems and the information possessed by other members that are relevant to the group decision. Early meeting phases often are characterized by ambiguity, positioning, questioning the agenda, uncertainty over goals, and tentative actions by members. Member behaviors are uncoordinated, and team members may not listen to each other.

Similarly, during the period of initial organization, *program- and agency-level* behaviors frequently are characterized by a concern for delineating individual missions and goals, realms of participation, and priority activities. Establishing "turf" and identity become primary concerns, and early efforts are characterized by these more self-centered activities. At this level, programs and agencies may cooperate with one another by offering general support or endorsements for each other's activities, but continue to engage in autonomous decision making and pursue their own internally determined objectives (Peterson, 1991).

Multidisciplinary Interactions

The term *multidisciplinary* is used to describe interactions where professionals from several disciplines or programs focus on a problem. However, they work in parallel, consulting and coordinating their work but still carrying out disciplinary or programmatic functions and decision making independently. Communication and sharing with others occur frequently, but integrated interaction does not. Examples of multidisciplinary interaction include special education-related services staff sharing their assessments of children at weekly staffings or agency program directors sharing progress on current activities at monthly staff meetings.

At the *individual level*, openness to multidisciplinary participation with other disciplines becomes more viable as the individual professional gains competence and confidence in his or her discipline. Especially when complex problems arise, demanding more expertise than any one individual can provide, recognition grows in the professional that other disciplines also may have important contributions to make in addressing the particular situation. Confident and competent in one's home discipline, the individual becomes more comfortable turning to other disciplines for advice and sharing and feels freer to look for other ways of describing and solving problems. Increased understanding and appreciation of the contributions of other disciplines lead the way to more open and cooperative relationships. While still operating individually, there is increased communication and exchange of ideas, more awareness of similarities and differences among professions, and discovery of alternative ways of problem solving. Also, there can be increased willingness for joint cooperation, working side by side in activities such as conducting assessments at a common site.

At the *team level*, operating at the multidisciplinary stage brings a certain dysfunction. As the team moves past orientation concerns, it enters what is termed the evaluation or conflict stage (Shaw, 1981). Differences surface as members judge the information relative to the problem and the proposed solutions. Group members seem to differentiate themselves more—opinions become more definite and attitudes more polarized. Often, this stage can be filled with dissension as the team struggles to identify their areas of contributions and limitations and find ways of working together.

For *programs and agencies*, moving into this multidisciplinary stage is often prompted when common audiences, programs, or needs are identified, and there is willingness to engage in a multiagency process. This level of interaction can be classified as one of coordination, where agencies work together on some common task while still remaining relatively autonomous from each other (Peterson, 1991). Morris and Lescohier (in Humm-Delgado, 1980) define such coordination as "various efforts to alter or smooth the relationship of continuing, independent elements such as organizations, staffs, and resources" (pp. 163–178). At this stage, programs and agencies enhance their avenues of communication, share information, and engage in joint activities where each can maintain their individual autonomy, such as co-locating programs or serving on each others' advisory boards. Conflicts and resistance can occur as agencies struggle to coordinate their efforts with others within the constraints of their individual missions, funding sources, or personnel resources.

Interdisciplinary Interactions

Interdisciplinary defines the process by which team members from a variety of disciplines focus on a problem in an integrated, cohesive, and comprehensive fashion. In an interdisciplinary interaction, each member of the team has the opportunity to influence all team decisions. Most important, individual roles and professional behaviors are subsumed for purposes of meeting the identified need or solving the problem. At this level, there is also increased involvement from nonprofessionals, including parents, clients, and other community members. Examples of interdisciplinary collaboration can be found when a team conducts a joint assessment—all observing the child at the same time, assessing from their own area of expertise as well as contributing observations about other disciplinary domains to other team members—and writes a unified assessment report.

Transdisciplinary, an extended conception of being interdisciplinary (Lyon & Lyon, 1980; Sears, 1981), describes an increased emphasis on role release and cross-skill training and utilization among the professionals involved. Transdisciplinary interaction might occur when one team member, the classroom teacher, agrees to take on responsibility for implementing a positioning program that is usually conducted by a physical therapist.

Magrab and Schmidt (1980) summarize what must be present to achieve the goals of truly collaborative and interdisciplinary processes: "interdisciplinary as a concept reflects an attitude—one of respect, trust, and interdependence" (pp. 395–399). These conditions of trust, respect, and mutual dependence are necessary at all levels of interaction. Often, this trust is exemplified even in the absence of formal agreements—when groups of professionals agree to function as a team to serve a particular person.

At the *individual level*, more value is added to interdisciplinary and cross-professional collaboration as the individual professional grows and matures along the continuum of becoming interdisciplinary. To an interdisciplinary professional, the solution of the problem becomes more important than the individual professional role. There is more openness to procedures such as shared assessment roles, joint decision making, integrated report writing, and utilization of skills and techniques from other professions. Willingness to give up traditional roles and responsibilities (within the bounds of professional standards) and to enter the give-and-take world of collaboration characterizes the individual who is well on the way to becoming interdisciplinary.

Likewise, at the *team level*, members achieve integration and cohesiveness as the team develops and matures (Shaw, 1981). Evident is more task orientation and increased reliance on the group to solve problems. Members begin to listen to each other and differences are respected and accepted. Consensus-seeking behaviors begin to appear. Group norms and roles are established, interpersonal relationships are strong; the group works well together, and problems are attacked rationally.

For *programs and agencies*, Morris and Lescohier define *integration* as "that action which brings previously separated and independent functions and organizations (or personnel, resources, or clientele) into a new unitary structure" (Humm-Delgado, 1980, p. 165). Peterson (1991) depicts collaboration as intense involvement over a long term that involves joint commitment and joint activity which is guided by a plan developed and approved by all. Some agency autonomy may be relinquished in the interest of accomplishing identified objectives, and adaptations to the agencies' normal operating policies and practices may have to occur. For instance, agencies may agree to use a common intake form in their assessments of children identified as being "at risk" during a community child-find program.

At any level, interdisciplinary collaboration takes time to blossom to its fullest advantages. Just as individual professionals grow toward responsiveness to collaboration, teams also experience a parallel growth process before true cohesiveness and collaboration appear. For programs and agencies, a similar developmental process can be assumed, first consolidating their unique areas of expertise and operation, and then becoming more receptive to coordinating and collaborating with others.

With these parallels drawn, and a model for considering the similarities and differences among the components presented, the remainder of this chapter focuses on one dimension of the model. Interagency collaboration is examined in more depth, and its applications at case, program, and policy levels are portrayed.

INTERAGENCY COLLABORATION AT WORK

Mittenhal and colleagues (in Humm-Delgado, 1980) characterize interagency collaboration as "a goal-directed process whose objective is the establishment of an operating, integrated human service system that addresses a range of an individual's needs and contributes to his or her status of personal independence and economic self-sufficiency" (p. 165).

At the outset, interagency teams, like interdisciplinary teams, begin the process of recognizing and appreciating individual differences and developing trust. The acquaintance process begins and continues, not simply with a focus on the individual participants, however, but also with the agencies they represent. While individual personalities, style, and readiness to collaborate certainly affect the interactions, the major issues being put on the table revolve around the agencies' individual interests, resources, and ideas about the potential outcomes around which the group will interact. Further, information about policies and procedures, eligibility requirements, target populations, geographic boundaries, legislative initiatives, confidentiality policies, and funding streams need to be shared and related to the other agencies' positions in these same areas.

The interagency team also must address the issue of developing and using a common language. Just as individual professionals are asked to explain their disciplinary jargon, so do the agency representatives need to present their agency-related terminology and concepts in terms acceptable and understandable to all. Legislative titles, rule and regulation numbers, departmental names, acronyms, or "buzz" words of a particular agency often are unfamiliar even to people from the same disciplines working in different agencies! Searching for common ground over definitions may entail selection of alternative wordings or even creation of team-specific phraseology.

Although it may be clear to client-focused teams what their objectives or reasons for convening are, interagency teams may need to spend more time identifying and agreeing on their purpose and objectives, particularly when dealing with administrative issues. A major goal among agencies is to agree to their common purposes and identify mutual benefits of engaging in the collaboration. As the process unfolds, agency participants will have to determine the appropriate balance between their agencies' separate interests and the degree of autonomy or self-interest that has to be subsumed to solve the problem. Agency administrative support will be critical to successful collaboration.

In interagency collaboration, it is frequently useful to develop written agreements. Just as individual plans demarcate the deliberations and the agreements of client-focused interdisciplinary teams, so do interagency agreements reflect the agreed-on common purposes and the negotiations over agency authority, resource constraints and contributions, and function. Again, securing administrative support for the procedures and "players" authorized to develop the agreements cannot be overlooked. One agency may designate authority to the service provider representative on the team to finalize the agreement; another may require the agency head to approve the final proposals.

Audette (1980) categorizes agreements into classes that have become standard for the field. First and most important are adoption of multi-agency standards that delineate who does what to whom, when, where, how often, and under whose supervision. A second class of agreements specifies the cooperative allocation of agency resources. The third class of agreements includes decisions related to uniform procedures, forms, and activities.

Audette's methods of cooperatively allocating resources give insight into the types of decisions interagency teams must negotiate to ensure that the agreements do not simply show "paper cooperation." He outlines six methods (1980, pp. 31–32):

1. *First dollar agreements*, where commitment is gained over which agency pays first for particular services. For instance, if an individual is eligible for vocational rehabilitation reimbursement, the vocational rehabilitation agency agrees to pay for services. The education agency agrees to pay when an individual is not eligible for vocational rehabilitation services.
2. *Complementary dollar agreements*, where each agency agrees to pay for certain services. For instance, when a Medicaid-eligible senior citizen needs speech therapy and reconstructive surgery, the aging program will pay for the speech therapy, and Medicaid will pay for the surgery.
3. *Complementary personnel/dollar agreements*, where one agency commits personnel and another commits to paying for other services. For instance, one agency employs the coordinator for an information and referral program, and the other agency pays for travel and equipment rental.
4. *Shared personnel agreements*, where both agencies commit personnel to carry out an activity. For instance, during a preschool screening program, each agency agrees to commit a staff member to conduct the screenings.
5. *Shared facility agreements*, where one agency agrees to use its facility for a collaborative activity. For instance, an agency contributes an office for use by a prevention program.
6. *Shared equipment and materials agreements*, where one agency agrees that its equipment and/or materials can be used for a collaborative activity. For instance, an agency will contribute use of its 800-phone line for an information and referral hotline.

Audette's examples of procedural and activity agreements lend insight into other areas for interagency collaboration. Some types of procedural agreements link directly to the needs of children and families: using uniform terminology and common intake forms, establishing single points of referral, coordinating participating agencies' entitlements, and agreeing to smooth transition procedures. Other kinds of procedural and activity agreements ensure that the collaborative arrangement is supported and maintained: use of uniform calendars for planning and budgeting, coordinated and comprehensive planning, co-training of staff, arrangements for payment for services to follow the client regardless of which agency provides the service, integrated databases and resource collections, and cooperative evaluations.

Despite the major proposition in this chapter that interdisciplinary teaming and interagency collaboration are similar, parallel processes, there are characteristics unique to interagency collaboration that affect team functioning. Perhaps most critical is the organizational affiliation of the participants. Unlike teams where all participants are employees of one agency, members of interagency teams have organizational loyalties elsewhere. They may respond to different jurisdictions, organizations, and stakeholders. They may have differing control over fiscal resources, differing levels of responsibility, and differing organizational policies regarding confidentiality, fundraising, and the like. Thus, an added element in negotiation and decision-making processes must be the recognition, discussion, and/or appreciation of the implications of these differences.

To further complicate the picture, agencies are essentially the key "actors" on the team. Thus the agency seat on the team will be maintained, but the individual representatives may change. Humm-Delgado (1980) suggests that the interagency team ought to be considered a "changing group of people, just as an agency has changing personnel." As individuals come and go, procedures need to be implemented to ensure minimal disruption of the team's progress. Further, team members may need to tolerate some disruptions or regressions in the developmental progress of the team; team cohesiveness may temporarily revert to the joining or conflict stages with the introduction of new team members.

Additionally, individual agencies may place different values on their representative's participation. In a single-agency team, the expectation to participate is usually uniform across the professional staff. That may not be the case in interagency teams, especially if participation is voluntary or if collaboration is superimposed on other responsibilities. Again, Humm-Delgado (1980) recognizes the need to legitimize participation as a regular and time-consuming administrative function of the participating staff member—perhaps by including it as part of a job description, decreasing responsibilities in some other areas, or giving public recognition to the team member's efforts.

Finally, because of varying administrative, policy, and fiscal features of the participating agencies, it may not be as easy to reach consensus as in a single-agency team. Further, because more than one agency has to agree to changes, "creative solutions" may not be as easily or quickly implementable across several agencies. Obtaining organizational consent to changes in policies and procedures may be easier when all professionals belong to one agency; creative problem solving may be more feasible when the locus of control is narrower. Varying budget cycles, target populations, eligibility requirements, state and federal authority, and legislative mandates, along with differential degrees of authority over them, may constrain interagency teams to limit their areas of collaboration as well as their expectations.

Despite these recognized constraints, interagency teams, especially those whose focus is administrative or policy oriented, are in a position to create systems change in a community, regionally, or at a statewide level. Instead of problem solving on a case-by-case basis, as client-focused interdisciplinary teams operate, the scope of the interagency team's influence is potentially much greater. Yet it is a double-edged sword, for these types of interactions and changes take longer, and individual professionals may view the process as taking too much time away from their day-to-day responsibilities.

EXAMPLES OF INTERAGENCY COLLABORATION

It is important to keep in mind that interagency teams are being conceptualized as applications of interdisciplinary teaming but with different focal points. Gans and Horton (1975) identify several categories of linkages that have become standard descriptions of interagency collaboration. Two focus on *direct services to individuals*: core services linkages, such as outreach, intake, diagnosis, referral, and follow-up services;

and case coordination linkages, such as case conferencing, case coordinating, and case teaming. Four additional categories describe collaboration related to *programmatic concerns*: (1) fiscal linkages, such as joint budgeting, funding, and purchase of services; (2) personnel practices linkages, such as consolidated personnel administration, joint use of staff, staff transfers, and colocation; (3) planning and programming linkages, such as joint planning, development of operating policies, programming, information-sharing, and evaluations; (4) and administrative support linkages, such as recordkeeping, grants management, and central support services.

Using the Gans and Horton categories as a base, a differentiated construct of interagency collaboration can be developed. Some interagency groups target a particular *case* (e.g., the child, family, or adult), and their purpose is to plan and/or provide direct services. A second type of interagency collaboration occurs with a *programmatic focus*, and these groups work to develop programs, particularly at the local level, to serve children, families, and adults. Still a third type of interagency linkage, not included in the Gans and Horton model, targets systems change and collaboration over *policy issues*. The following sections describe examples of each of the three classes of interagency groups.

Case-Centered Interagency Collaboration

Elder and Magrab (1980) provide a definition of interagency collaboration where the focal point is at the case level: "coordination efforts made by professionals and administrators across different agencies or organizations to ensure that the client is provided appropriate, nonduplicative services" (p. 7). Two examples of case-centered interagency collaboration follow, one related to youth and the other concerned with infants and toddlers.

Interagency Transition Teams in High Schools

Increased attention is being given to students with disabilities who are transitioning from school programs to adult services in the community. Early interagency planning is seen as critical for the students to obtain jobs after graduation, identify a place of residence, and identify resources and services that will enhance their community participation. Thus, transition planning is not simply the transfer of administrative responsibility for the individual's school program to the adult service system but a collaborative process of developing an ongoing support network that ensures a high quality of community life for the student after high school (McDonnell & Hardman, 1985).

Many states require schools to convene a transition team for each student with severe disabilities early in the secondary school years. The student's team is an interagency one, consisting of school personnel, parents, the student, a couselor from the vocational rehabilitation agency, and other relevant adult service providers from the community. The goal of many transition plans is for the student to leave high school with a job, a network of friends, and skills for actively participating in community life. With these goals as a backdrop, the team members work together to identify desired options, plan for availability of services, and determine who will do what to ensure the student's access to services and community activities. The formal interagency agreement—an individual transition plan—indicates vocational, residential, and leisure alternatives for the student; the training, experience, and supports needed for the student to achieve the desired alternatives; a program of establishing and monitoring eligibility requirements; a plan for future support, such as guardianship and establishment of trusts; and case management services (Trivelli, 1988).

Interagency Early Intervention Teams
Public Law 99–457—the infant–toddler provisions of the Amendments to the Individuals with Disabilities Education Act of 1986—requires that professionals collaborate with families to develop and implement an Individualized Family Service Plan (IFSP). The law mandates that the process be family centered, where family choice and responsiveness to family priorities are primary tenets of the interaction. In this model, families are not merely secondary to professionals providing services, they are in control of the interaction (McGonigel, Kaufmann, & Johnson, 1991).

The interagency agreement—IFSP—is developed through a less formal process. Families proceed at their own pace, beginning and moving back and forth between certain points of the process according to their needs and preferences. The ensuing plan delineates agreements about assessments to identify the child's and the family's strengths and needs, the desired outcomes to meet those needs, implementation activities, resource allocation, and evaluation of the plan. While often only one or a few professionals meets with the family, the system they design to meet child and family needs involves building collaboration among several agencies. Principles underlying the process assume that no one agency can provide the range of services needed to be responsive to the family and child—for instance, services such as medical interventions, preschool programming, parent training, speech therapy, physical or occupational therapy, counseling, respite care, case coordination, and/or advocacy.

Program-Centered Interagency Collaboration

The Elder and Magrab (1980) definition can be modified to take into account other foci of collaboration. These types of collaboration can be described as "coordination efforts made by professionals and administrators across different agencies or organizations to ensure that a [service system] provides appropriate, nonduplicative services" (p. 7). In program-centered collaboration, agencies gather together to plan collaborative programs that benefit a number of clients. Two examples of program-centered interagency collaboration follow, one triggered by community needs, and the other by federal legislation.

Family Services Center

Because it was concerned about low percentages of high school graduates and high rates of unemployment, teenage pregnancy, and families receiving public assistance, one community used an interagency approach to develop an innovative response. They envisioned a single center, where public and private services would be available under a single roof. What resulted was Kids Place—a family services center in southern Indiana selected as one of five most promising early intervention programs in the United States by the National Center for Clinical Infant Programs (King, 1991). The interagency team that planned and implemented this program consisted of a variety of child and family service providers as well as representatives from the business community.

The results of this interagency collaboration were a successful fundraising campaign, construction of a new facility, co-location of several agencies in the building, and linkages established with other relevant agencies. By grouping services together, this interagency agreement enhanced communication between families and providers and reduced parents' transportation problems. Working parents benefit from the centralized day care and a variety of other health care services so time-off from work to keep appointments is reduced. The "one-stop shopping" concept of Kids Place includes the collaborative involvement of the county health department, local physicians, the WIC program (the federally funded supplemental food program), an early intervention program, a day care and preschool enrichment program, special education, Head Start, and child protective services.

Interagency Coordinating Councils

Under Public Law 99–457, local interagency councils are mandated to develop and provide a comprehensive interagency system of direct and indirect services to meet the needs of children in their geographic area who are under age 5 and who have disabilities or are at risk. Because of the comprehensive needs of young children at risk, professional involvement that crosses jurisdictions and legislated program responsibilities is necessary (Peterson, 1991). Thus, agency representatives who are responsible for public awareness, child find, referral, evaluation, case management, family support, parent education, and a variety of medical, educational, and social services can be participants on the team. Parent organizations and the private sector (e,g., physicians, United Way, child-related businesses) also are often represented on the teams.

The council conducts a needs assessment and a review of existing community resources. The interagency agreement is to include ways to coordinate, expand, modify, or refine services in such a way that duplication of effort is reduced, gaps are filled, and agencies are able to target and expand their resources in the most advantageous ways (Morgan et al., 1991). Results of collaboration for some interagency councils include establishing a collaborative early childhood screening program, identifying a coordinator and a location for centralized information and referral, developing public awareness materials for parents, and conducting interdisciplinary assessments and evaluations. The councils are expected to be ongoing, serving both a direct service and a policy function as they mature.

Policy-Centered Interagency Collaboration

At the systems level, interagency groups are often convened for the purpose of advising, influencing, planning, and/or recommending policy changes that affect larger systems, most commonly at state or national levels. Two examples of policy-centered interagency collaboration follow, one funded through legislative appropriations and the other through a federal grant program.

Developmental Disabilities Councils

Under disabilities legislation passed in 1975, each state is to designate a developmental disabilities council. Membership on each state's council is to include representatives of relevant state agencies and representative local service providers. At least 50 percent of the council must be people with disabilities, including some parent representatives. Some councils also include legislators and members of the business community. The council is to meet on a regular basis to advocate for people with disabilities and influence state policy.

One of the council's primary tasks is to develop a coordinated state plan, including identification of service system gaps, designation of objectives, and action steps that state agencies agree to undertake, either singly or in concert with others. The council also reviews and comments on the plans of other state agencies whose programs affect people with disabilities either directly or indirectly such as the plans of the health department, Medicaid division, public transportation, vocational rehabilitation, and special education. Through councils, real attempts at systems coordination can take place.

Beyond planning, the council often stimulates other collaborative ventures. These can include co-sponsorship of statewide conferences, joint support of legislation, co-funding of interagency systems change grants, co-hiring of coordinating or consulting personnel, and joint development of statewide databases.

Disability and Business Technical
Assistance Centers

In 1991, the National Institute on Disability and Rehabilitation Research awarded 10 regional grants to provide technical assistance to businesses in the implementation of the Americans with Disabilities Act. The Act prohibits employers, organizations, and businesses from excluding people from jobs, services, leisure activities, and benefits based on any disability. Businesses must provide "reasonable accommodations" to protect the rights of individuals with disabilities in hiring, promotion, and accessibility. The centers' overall objective is to develop ways to work constructively with businesses to effectively implement the provisions of the law.

The 10 centers bring together agencies that have not traditionally worked together. Their collaboration reflects all disability interests involved in championing the passage of the law, the wide range of business and governmental interests affected by the Act's passage, and the university community. While each regional center varies, one regional center has established state interagency steering committees, consisting of representatives from the state Chamber of Commerce, the state Developmental Disabilities Council, several disability advocacy groups and independent living centers, the state university, and people with disabilities. Each state steering committee develops a plan for providing technical assistance, conferences, and informational materials to businesses and government agencies. More important, the state teams forge relationships between business and the disability community, and also among various subgroups within the disability community itself—e.g., those with physical/sensory disabilities and those with more severe cognitive and functional limitations.

THE FUTURE: WHAT LIES AHEAD?

Throughout this chapter, parallels have been drawn between interdisciplinary and interagency teams. An integrating model has been presented to illustrate the continuum along which individual professionals, teams, programs, and agencies grow toward collaboration. A variety of examples were presented to portray interagency interactions that are case centered, program centered, and policy centered.

Interagency collaboration is not necessarily a new way of interacting, and its frontiers continue to be pushed outward. Several of the examples included in this chapter allude to a broadening conception of "agency." No longer is it adequate to conceive of interagency collaboration as the interactions among professional service providers and administrators of several agencies or programs. In today's climate of outreach and inclusiveness, attention is being given to building more inclusive teams, ones that move into the private sector and particularly into the business world.

Perhaps a better definition would be to consider *interagency* as meaning collections of individuals representing varying organizational or personal affiliations working together. This broader conception allows for the inclusion of other than typical human service providers on collaborative interagency teams. Business and churches could easily be considered "agencies," and teams might be enlightened by the perspectives they bring to deliberations.

Individuals, family members, and friends are others who are now being considered as members of interdisciplinary teams. Theirs is a personal affiliation, and they too add new dimensions to team deliberations. Many legislatively mandated teams already require this type of representation. A contemporary model of an "interagency" team under this new definition is worth noting. Called *circles of support*, this model represents a reversal of common practices, for professional and paid representatives are considered peripheral members of the team. A discussion of this type of team is included here to illustrate how common conceptions of collaborative planning are being extended.

A circle of support is a group of people who agree to meet on a regular basis to help a person with a disability accomplish a personal set of goals (Mount et al., 1988). A circle exists totally in the interest of the focus person. Most typically it includes friends, family members, co-workers, and community members, each from different organizations, but most often, *not* from a service agency. Professionals sometimes do play a part in circles, but only because they have some personal commitment to the person and can provide an essential resource to the circle.

The circle meets frequently, depending on the needs and wishes of the focus person, and works on strategies for achieving the person's plan for the future. The group lays out strategies to overcome barriers to achievement of the person's goals, makes commitments to action, evaluates progress, and recommits to new strategies until the person achieves his or her goals. A circle may help someone find a job, join a community group, move out of a nursing home, get transportation, make new friends, or even get married. Who facilitates the meetings is decided individually and is based on the skills that are a part of the group; sometimes, the facilitator is the focus person. With other circles, it may be an advocate or an outside process person.

In this model, the circle can become the lynch pin for interagency collaboration. Once the focus person's plan is known, the circle becomes instrumental in establishing the collaboration among service providers, community members, and friends that may be necessary to achieve a certain goal. Not all goals, however, need paid, agency-based interventions or paid professionals to be accomplished. The role of the human service representative(s) is to support directions defined by the group, to share knowledge about available resources, to assist in negotiating service systems, and to provide direct service to the focus person. The human service professional also supports delivery of needed services by negotiating a collaborative agreement among participating agencies to shift or redesign services to meet the focus person's wishes. Although not a typical team, a circle of support could stimulate an interagency agreement on behalf of a person. Its work is informal; its modus operandi is committed, creative problem solving; and its accountability is to the person—the center of the circle. As one of its functions, the circle pushes for the creation of a coordinated and responsive interagency system for an individual.

Technology is also pushing the frontiers of interagency collaboration forward. Again, from business, new systems are becoming available to support the group process and task-orientation aspects of teaming. Called electronic meeting systems (or similarly, group decision support systems or collaborative work technology), these computer and software configurations enable groups to overcome some of the barriers to effective group interaction and productive meetings. While not eliminating face-to-face discussion, they become effective supports to interagency collaboration (Pappas, Schroeder, Noel, & Herschel, 1991).

A growing innovation in corporate America, electronic meeting systems are relatively rare in human services, primarily because of their expense, but also because human services usually lag behind in the use of computers for planning and policy development purposes. Electronic meeting systems allow brainstorming to be more efficient, because all members can "talk" simultaneously by entering their ideas into a computer. Further, because these systems enable even the quietest person to enter ideas into the discussion electronically, more equitable participation by all group members is possible. Additionally, ideas entered into the computer are anonymous. Still another advantage of electronic meeting systems is that they add a structure to the meeting, helping to keep the group focused and on task. Finally, the systems maintain an ongoing record of the group's electronic commentary, and minutes of the meeting can be produced and reproduced for all participants at any time (Collaborative Work Lab, n.d.).

Electronic meeting systems can support interagency groups in a variety of activities. Mission statements can be developed, possible solutions can be brainstormed, goals and objectives can be negotiated, and ideas can be evaluated. Also, such systems enable groups to come to agreement over program criteria, develop policy recommendations, identify pros and cons to a situation, or come to consensus. Their potential for enhancing human service collaboration is great.

These two examples merely surface possibilities for the future of interagency collaboration. New ways of defining team membership and the addition of technology to the group process pose interesting challenges to our traditional ways of conceiving and operationalizing interdisciplinary interactions. Creative opportunities extend our vista to work together to create even more responsive, integrated ways of serving people and developing programs and policies.

REFERENCES

Amado, A. N., Conklin, F., & Wells, J. (1990). *Friends: A manual for connecting persons with developmental disabilities and community members*. St. Paul, MN: Human Services Research and Development Center.

Audette, R. H. (1980). Interagency collaboration: The bottom line. In J. L. Elder & P. R. Magrab (Eds.), *Coordinating services to handicapped children: A handbook for interagency collaboration* (pp. 25-34). Baltimore: Paul H. Brookes.

Brown, L., Long, E., Udvari-Solner, A., Davis, L., VanDeventer, P., Ahlgren, C., Johnson, F., Gruenewald, L., & Jorgensen, J. (1989). The home school: Why students with severe intellectual disabilities must attend the schools of their brothers, sisters, friends, and neighbors. *The Journal of the Association of Severe Disabilities, 14*(1), 1-7.

Collaborative Work Lab. Introduction to an electronic meeting. (n.d.). Bloomington, IN: Institute for the Study of Developmental Disabilities.

Elder, J. L., & Magrab, P. R. (Eds.). (1980). *Coordinating services to handicapped children: A handbook for interagency collaboration*. Baltimore: Paul H. Brookes.

Gans, G. T., & Horton, G. T. (1975). *Integration of human services: The state and municipal levels*. New York: Praeger.

Humm-Delgado, D. (1980). Planning issues in local interagency collaboration. In J. L. Elder & P. R. Magrab (Eds.), *Coordinating services to handicapped children: A handbook for interagency collaboration* (pp. 163-178). Baltimore: Paul H. Brookes.

Johnson, H. W., McLaughlin, J. A., & Christensen, M. (1982). Interagency collaboration: Driving and restraining forces. *Exceptional Children, 48*, 395-399.

Kakalik, J., Brewer, G., Dougharty, L., Fleischauer, P., Genesky, S., & Wallen, L. (1974). *Improving services to handicapped children*. Santa Monica, CA: The RAND Corporation.

King, C. (1991). Kids Place: A successful family center in rural Indiana. *Family Resource Coalition Report*, no. 1. (Available from Family Resource Coalition, 200 South Michigan Avenue, Suite 1520, Chicago, IL 60604.)

Lacour, J. A. (1982). Interagency agreement: A rational response to an irrational system. *Exceptional Children, 49*, 265-267.

Lyon, S., & Lyon, G. (1980). Team functioning and staff development: A role release approach to providing integrated educational services for severely handicapped students. *The Journal of the Association for the Severely Handicapped, 5*, 250-263.

Magrab, P. R., & Schmidt, L. M. (1980). Interdisciplinary collaboration: A prelude to coordinated service delivery. In J. L. Elder & P. R. Magrab (Eds.), *Coordinating services to handicapped children: A handbook for interagency collaboration* (pp. 13-23). Baltimore: Paul H. Brookes.

Martinson, M. C. (1982). Interagency services: A new era for an old idea. *Exceptional Children, 48*, 389-394.

McDonnell, J., & Hardman, M. (1985). Planning the transition of severely handicapped youth from school to adult services: A framework for high school programs. *Education and Training of the Mentally Retarded, 20*, 275-286.

McGonigel, M. J., Kaufmann, R. K., & Johnson, B. H. (1991). A family-centered process for the individualized family service plan. *Journal of Early Intervention, 15*(1), 46-56.

Morgan, J. L., Guetzloe, E. C., & Swan, W. W. (1991). Leadership for local interagency coordinating councils. *Journal of Early Intervention, 15*(3), 255-267.

Morris, R., & Lescohier, I. H. (1978). Service integration: Real versus illusory solutions to welfare dilemmas. In R. C. Sarri & V. Hasenfeld (Eds.), *The management of human services* (pp. 21-50). New York: Columbia University Press.

Mount, B., Beeman, P., & Ducharme, G. (1988). *What are we learning about circles of support? A collection of tools, ideas, and reflections on building and facilitating circles of support.* Manchester, CT: Communitas, Inc.

Nash, J. K. (1990). Public Law 99-457: Facilitating family participation on the multidisciplinary team. *Journal of Early Intervention, 14*(4), 314-326.

Nordyke, N. S. (1982). Improving services for young, handicapped children through local interagency collaboration. *Topics in Early Childhood Special Education, 2*(1), 63-72.

Pappas, V., Schroeder, H. J., Noel, T., & Herschel, R. (1991). EMS in a human service environment: Promising opportunities. *Proceedings of the Twenty-second Annual Meeting of the Midwest Decision Sciences Institute* (pp. 42-44). Muncie IN: Ball State University.

Peterson, N. L. (1991). Interagency collaboration under Part H: The key to comprehensive, multidisciplinary, coordinated infant/toddler intervention. *Journal of Early Intervention*, 15(1), 89-105.

Schorr, L. B. (1988). *Within our reach: Breaking the cycle of disadvantage.* New York: Anchor Books, Doubleday.

Sears, C. J. (1981). The transdisciplinary approach: A process for compliance with Public Law 94-142. *The Journal of the Association for the Severely Handicapped*, 6, 22-29.

Shaw, M. (1981). *Group dynamics: The psychology of small group behavior.* New York: McGraw-Hill.

Stainbeck, S., & Stainbeck, W. (1990). Inclusive schooling. In W. Stainbeck & S. Stainbeck (Eds.), *Support networks for inclusive schooling* (pp. 3-23). Baltimore, MD: Paul H. Brookes.

Trivelli, L. U. (1988). Transition plans, teams, and agreements. *HEATH*, 7 (September/October), 4-5.

Zeller, R. W. (1980). Direction service: Collaboration one case at a time. In J. L. Elder & P. R. Magrab (Eds.), *Coordinating services to handicapped children: A handbook for interagency collaboration* (pp. 65-98). Baltimore: Paul H. Brookes.

TEAMS IN ACTION

5

World of Practice: Early Intervention Programs

Corinne Welt Garland

THE NEED FOR TEAMWORK

Professionally she is a magician and a clown. She is also the mother of a child with a disability. Addressing a group of early intervention professionals in New Hampshire, in her hand she holds a tiny foam rubber mother and father on their way to the maternity unit of the hospital. Closing her fingers around the couple, she tells of their hopes and dreams for their family. When she closes and opens her hand, they have magically increased in number—now a mother, father, and tiny foam rubber baby. She reveals a second foam couple in her other hand. When she closes and opens her hand again, a dozen or more tiny foam figures tumble out. The audience oohs appreciatively. "This baby has been born with severe health and developmental complications," she explains. "They thought they would come home with a baby, but this family also got a neonatologist, physical and occupational therapists, a pediatric neurologist, a speech pathologist, an early intervention specialist, a public health nurse, and a social worker."

The family of a very young child with a disability immediately faces a number of difficult tasks. First, they must reconcile, emotionally and cognitively, to the difference between the child they had planned for and anticipated and the birth of a child with a diagnosed disability. Frequently, medical care decisions must be made, requiring the family to sort out complicated information and alternatives, and to consider information in light of their family's concerns, resources, priorities, and values.

Decisions that would tax any new parent are even more difficult when each of the many specialists involved with an infant's diagnosis and treatment has acted alone to arrive at a diagnosis and make a recommendation for treatment. The family is left to weigh and judge the relative merits of the varied professional perspectives. For families and for early intervention professionals, the need for and benefit of a team approach to information sharing, decision making, and treatment has become increasingly clear; the team approach is widely viewed as best and standard practice. The foundations for teamwork are found not only in the experiences of families and professionals, but in legislation and research.

Legislative Authority for Teamwork

The complex nature of disabilities and the overlapping and interactive effects of a disability on a young child's development (Antoniadis & Videlock, 1991) frequently require the services of a wide variety of professionals, sometimes even exceeding the dozen or so specialists intruding unexpectedly on the little foam family. When P.L. 99–457—the Education of the Handicapped Amendment—was passed in 1986, there was, within the field of early intervention, "near unanimity" that a team approach was necessary and that families were essential members of the team (McGonigel & Garland, 1988, p. 10). The regulations for P.L. 99–457 and its successor, the Individuals with Disabilities Education Act (IDEA), passed in October 1990, give additional recognition to the need of the young child and her or his family for a wide array of services from multiple disciplines. IDEA defines early intervention services as including, but not being limited to, audiology, service coordination, family training, health services, medical services for diagnostic and evaluation purposes, nursing services, nutrition services, occupational therapy, physical therapy, psychological services, social work, special instruction, speech–language pathology, and transportation (Part H of IDEA, Rules and Regulations, 34 CFR, Part 303.12, July 30, 1993).

IDEA goes beyond defining early intervention services in a broad and multidisciplinary way. This legislation makes public policy of teamwork, encouraging the collaborative efforts of independent programs and agencies in a state by making funding contingent on each state having a governor-appointed interagency coordinating council. The law requires that early intervention systems developed by states be "comprehensive, coordinated, multidisciplinary, and interagency" (Part 303.1), building on the many services already in place through an interagency commitment to collaboration, rather than creating a new, independent program. Although there are gaps that will need to be filled in statewide early intervention systems (Clifford, 1991), a variety of state and federal initiatives form the basis on which state planners can build and fund collaborative systems.

In a 1988 survey, Gallagher et al. (1988) found that states were using, on the average, over 11 different federal, state, and local programs to fund early intervention services. Funders of early intervention were, for the most part, health-related sources, including Medicaid, and public education. The Maternal and Child Health (MCH) Services Block Grant has, since 1981, enabled states to provide rehabilitation services for blind and disabled young children. Amendments to the MCH Block Grant program include the goal of providing and promoting family-centered, coordinated care for children with special health care needs (Sciarillo, 1989). State education agencies are required by P.L. 94–142, the P.L. 99–457 amendments, and now by IDEA to locate, identify, and evaluate all children with disabilities from birth. Recognizing the array of agencies involved in serving disabled young children, states have chosen the lead agency for early intervention services from among state departments of education, public health, human resources or public welfare, mental health and mental retardation, and others.

A team approach to early intervention and to early education for children with disabilities is clearly needed if states are to build on existing programs and funding sources to provide services that are coordinated and comprehensive. IDEA requires states to develop policies that require and foster interagency and interdisciplinary collaboration at the local level. Such policies, along with interagency agreements developed at the state level, enable and encourage local health care, child development, education, social service, and other community-based settings to participate in the multidisciplinary team assessment and development of an Individualized Family Service Plan (IFSP) to which each eligible child and family is entitled (Section 671). "The development of a state system of interagency coordinated services is one of the most important and challenging policy issues that the states are wrestling with" (Harbin & Van Horn, 1990, p. 1).

Unfortunately, it is easier to see the need for a team approach to early intervention services than it is to restructure services to meet this need. "Because fragmented services are too often accepted as the norm, a revolutionary change will be required to achieve the goal of integrating services for handicapped children" (MacQueen, 1984, p. 128).

MODELS FOR EARLY INTERVENTION TEAMS

Programs for children with disabilities have a long history of experimenting with models for providing the complex web of services needed by the young child with a disability and by his or her family. Traditionally, responsibility for meeting the needs of a child with a disability rested primarily with a single individual or discipline. The determination of that responsibility largely has been a function of the organizational context for services. In community health care and hospital settings, the physician has, historically, been responsible not only for the medical management of the child but also for choosing other services that the child and family might need. In public schools, children were traditionally "served by a single discipline, most frequently a classroom teacher, while other specialty services were recommended based on a child's primary presenting problem" (Garland & Linder, 1988, p. 8). The team approach grew from an increasing appreciation of two facts: the young child with a disability is an interactive and integrated whole, not a collection of separate parts (Golin & Duncanis, 1981); and, more often than not, the nature and complexity of developmental disabilities in young children required the services of more than one discipline (Holm & McCartin, 1978).

Multidisciplinary Teams

The multidisciplinary team model was the first attempt to bring together professionals from a variety of disciplines (Child Development Resources, 1991). The multidisciplinary team, in which members work "independently, providing services directly, with little coordination" (Briggs, 1991, p. 1), is largely a team "by association" (McCollum & Hughes, 1988, p. 131).

On the multidisciplinary team, families have access to specialists from a variety of disciplines. The professionals on the team, however, assess or diagnose separately, each developing his or her own treatment plan without any systematic coordination or information exchange (Bennett, 1982; Fewell, 1983). Each team member is concerned primarily with his or her own clinical issues, functioning more like an independent specialist than like an interactive team member. Each specialist on the team meets individually with families to provide diagnostic conclusions and treatment recommendations. An example of the multidisciplinary team with which many health care professionals are familiar is the hospital-based specialty clinic where children are scheduled for several consecutive appointments by specialists on the same team. Peterson (1987) compares the multidisciplinary model of team interaction to parallel play in young children, "side by side, but separate" (p. 484).

The multidisciplinary model does have advantages in a context in which neither administrative practices nor billing procedures support the time that clinical specialists need for the purpose of sharing information and developing a treatment plan based on their collective experience with the child and family. In those settings, time for collaborative planning is neither built into the schedule of practitioners on the team, nor does it constitute a billable service. For children whose diagnostic evaluation and treatment planning require lengthy, complex, and highly technical procedures, the multidisciplinary approach may be the most practical and economical. However, Woodruff and McGonigel (1988) suggest that teams that work only as "a collection of multiple disciplines each pursuing his or her own task" fail to live up to the potential of a team approach (p. 164). In fact, the lack of coordination and communication among multidisciplinary team members often places the responsibility for coordination of evaluations, integration of information, and resolution of differences on the family (Orlando, 1981). "The process is one of piecing information together rather than coordinating information to form a unified, coherent picture" (McCollum & Hughes, 1988, p. 132). The patchwork of a multidisciplinary team can result in services that are fragmented and duplicative, if not conflicting.

Hannah

Ms. Key brought her two-and-a-half-year-old daughter to a regional child evaluation clinic. Hannah had been developing typically until 22 months when language ceased to improve. At that time, she began to show unusual repetitive behaviors and seemed to be emotionally distanced from her mother. She was referred by the classroom teacher in an early intervention program for children with disabilities where she had been accepted because of severe expressive language delays. Hannah saw several specialists in succession and each prepared a separate report. Ms. Key took time off from her job on three separate occasions for Hannah to be seen by a psychiatrist, an audiologist/speech pathologist, and a pediatric neurologist. She met with each, in turn, to hear the findings.

The psychiatrist explains that Hannah's father left the family during a critical period in her language development, resulting in a disruption in both expressive language development and the development of normal attachment. She is concerned about autistic-like behaviors Hannah has shown and recommends play therapy. The audiologist/speech pathologist reports that Hannah is severely delayed in expressive language. Although she has normal hearing, she has some auditory processing problems, particularly in auditory recall. These, he believes, can be addressed through special education and speech therapy. The pediatric neurologist is concerned that Hannah's periods of unresponsiveness are due to petit mal seizures and recommends medication and further testing.

Ms. Key is confused and even more worried about her child than she was prior to the evaluations. The classroom teacher, who works in an entirely different system that has little or no contact with the clinic, was not asked to provide input and will receive no specific recommendations for education intervention.

Interdisciplinary Teams

Partly in response to the problems experienced by multidisciplinary teams and by the families they served, early intervention programs have experimented with other models of interaction. The interdisciplinary model builds on the strengths of the multidisciplinary team by continuing to draw on the expertise of several disciplines. The interdisciplinary team, however, has a formal structure for interaction and communication that both encourages members to share information and enhances team decision making (Fewell, 1983; Peterson, 1987). Interdisciplinary teams, like multidisciplinary teams, conduct separate assessments by discipline. However, interdisciplinary teams come together to discuss individual results and to plan, in collaboration, for intervention. Frequently, the family is involved in program planning, if not in assessment. Many of the children's specialty services or child evaluation clinics now use an interdisciplinary model.

Jeron

In a large urban teaching hospital, an interdisciplinary team comes together to plan services for a young child with a severe feeding disorder. Gastroenterologist, nurse, social worker, psychiatrist, nutritionist, speech and occupational therapists, and others conduct separate clinical evaluations and meet to share information, to reach a common conclusion, and to develop a treatment plan. At this hospital, each team member is responsible not to the team but to her or his own department head, and it is clear during their rushed meetings together that time for collaborative planning is stolen from other responsibilities and is without fiscal support.

Like most interdisciplinary teams, the feeding disorder team has included the family in the team meeting. On this team, Mr. and Mrs. Howard are perceived by other team members as an important source of information about their son Jeron who has cerebral palsy. The team asks many questions about Jeron's eating at home, his problems with sucking and swallowing, his food preferences. However, as is true with some interdisciplinary teams, the parents are not viewed as decision makers. In fact, the team seems surprised, and taken somewhat aback, when the Howards ask if they will receive a copy of the report that the nurse will prepare to summarize the meeting.

The individual team members, in their separate evaluations of Jeron, address only their own disciplinary areas of expertise and are responsible for implementing his treatment plans separately. Jeron's family, like Hannah's mother, will have to make time to see each team member individually for the program to be carried out.

The interdisciplinary team has the advantage of bringing together a variety of professionals who are committed to working together and who recognize that working together will lead to more effective decisions than working alone would. However, communication and interaction problems are prevalent. Professional turf issues complicate team interaction (Fewell, 1983; Linder, 1983). Some members, particularly physicians, seem to carry more weight in decision making than other team members. Parents, although typically present, may not be seen as having valuable information to share (Brinkeroff & Vincent, 1986; Gilliam & Coleman, 1981; Nash, 1990). Although team members frequently have widely differing views about etiology and preferred treatment, they may lack a protocol for resolution of conflict. They may lack understanding of the professional training, expertise, or responsibilities of their colleagues on the team. The physician sometimes may fail to recognize the skill of the speech–language pathologist or the occupational therapist in assessing a child's skills or planning for treatment. On the interdisciplinary team, "the physical therapist takes the legs, the speech therapist takes the mouth, the cardiologist takes the heart" (Shelton, Jeppson, & Johnson, 1987, p. 32). As a result, there are gaps in reports and plans, and some problems fall between team members' responsibilities and are missed. Sometimes "emotional development . . . has taken a back seat to more easily detectable . . . condition(s)" (Nover, 1985, p. 3).

Although the interdisciplinary feeding disorder team has eliminated the need for the Howard family to meet separately with each member for the development of the treatment plan, after the meeting the family will continue to be involved with a large number of professionals and to work out problems of scheduling and coordination. "The speech therapist says 'Do half an hour of therapy after dinner.' The physical therapist says 'Do 30 minutes of therapy in your spare time.' What spare time? . . . I had to choose between being my child's . . . therapist and being his mother. And I chose being his mother" (Shelton et al., 1987, p. 33).

Transdisciplinary Teams

In the mid-1970s, the United Cerebral Palsy (UCP) Collaborative Infant Project began to experiment with a model of team interaction in which professionals from a variety of disciplines, together with families, could come together to plan an integrated service plan in a way that would be cost-effective—the transdisciplinary (TD) team (Haynes, 1976; United Cerebral Palsy, 1976). Designed specifically for early intervention, the transdisciplinary team not only collaborates in planning but also conducts collaborative assessment and routinely shares information, knowledge, and skills so that one person, together with the family, is primarily responsible for the implementation of the early intervention plan (Woodruff & McGonigel, 1988).

Crossing disciplinary boundaries, transdisciplinary team members teach and learn basic terminology and simple intervention procedures of disciplines represented on the team (Wolery & Dyk, 1984), carrying out team plans with authorization from, and in consultation with, their specialist colleagues. An occupational therapist working on oral motor and eating skills with a child who has a high degree of tactile defensiveness will, after consultation with the speech and language pathologist, encourage the child to point to or name the cup when he is ready to drink. The therapist also will consult with the parents and child care providers to learn what liquids the child prefers and what surfaces and textures seem least objectionable, at the same time showing parents ways to decrease the tactile sensitivity and to make feeding easier. The pediatrician and nutritionist will gain a realistic grasp of the problems in feeding this child from parents and therapist before they make dietary recommendations that reflect concern for the child's caloric intake and suggest high-calorie liquids. A physical therapist on the team will show parents and the occupational therapist how to position the child to allow him to breathe and swallow more easily.

Some professionals have expressed their concern that transdisciplinary practice inappropriately obliterates the distinction between professional responsibilities and a team approach (Holm & McCartin, 1978). The developers of the transdisciplinary model, sensitive to such concerns, give clear directions about occasions when transdisciplinary role release is inappropriate. Role release should not occur when one team member has learned a new technique of intervention but has not yet practiced or mastered the technique sufficiently to teach it to another team member. Neither is role release appropriate when a team member, who is teaching a new intervention technique, does not see evidence that the new skill has been fully mastered by the colleague. Finally, there are some interventions that are, by their very nature or by laws or policies regulating professional practice, too highly specialized to be taught to other team members.

The delivery of highly specialized services by a professional from the appropriate specific discipline is known, within the transdisciplinary framework, as role support—a critical and necessary feature of the transdisciplinary model. The provision for role support is, unfortunately, often overlooked by critics of the transdisciplinary approach who fear that interventions will be carried out by inadequately prepared personnel (Holm & McCartin, 1978).

An essential feature of the TD team is the role of the family on the team. Because "TD team members are interdependent, all must commit themselves to assist and support one another, including . . . supporting the family and . . . including them as equal team members who have a say in all decisions" (Woodruff & McGonigel, 1988, p. 179). In fact, many transdisciplinary teams acknowledge the family's "ultimate decision-making power" (McGonigel & Garland, 1988, p. 13). This feature of transdisciplinary interaction has been embodied within the requirements of

IDEA and, therefore, will become common practice by all early intervention teams regardless of the team model they use.

When teams acknowledge the decision-making power of families, they do not relinquish professional responsibilities. For families to be full decision makers, they must have full and open access to all information and access to the best judgment of the other specialists on the team. Early intervention team members do not abandon their roles as experts, but rather assume new roles as expert consultants who share the information they have with families, the options available, and the potential consequences of each option. Team members respect families' right to choose, even their right to choose to let the team or a single team member make a decision for them. IDEA regulations promote respect for families' rights to choose in all matters, including the level and extent to which they wish to be involved as decision makers on the team.

Carla

Carla's team is meeting in the small conference room of the public health department to develop an Individualized Family Service Plan (IFSP). The infant development specialist, who works with Carla at home and in a play group for toddlers, is present as are a physical therapist employed by the hospital and the public health nurse. The nurse has spoken with Carla's developmental pediatrician and has reviewed her extensive orthopedic and other medical records. Carla's parents also have asked their family therapist to attend. She is helping them find ways to interpret Carla's cerebral palsy and multiple health and developmental problems for their large extended family. Like Carla's parents, all the other team members have prepared for the meeting and will share their observations of Carla's developmental strengths and problems based on the assessment in which they all participated.

Together the team will determine Carla's strengths and needs and will set priorities for intervention. The family will let the team know, to the extent that they are willing to share information, about their own concerns and priorities for intervention services as well as about their family's resources. Carla's family will decide what, among their financial, social, emotional, and intellectual resources will be relevant to the plan that is developed for Carla, and what they need to tell the team.

One member from among the team will be selected to bear primary responsibility for integrating the team's plan and for carrying out that plan in collaboration with the family with full team support and assistance. In this case, the infant development specialist, and family members who see Carla daily, will be given ideas about how to position and handle Carla to facilitate her movement and development of motor control. The family lets the team know that Carla's mother is already skilled in these techniques. Carla's mother agrees to spend some time working with Lee, the infant development specialist, until Lee is also comfortable handling Carla. The physical therapist also will work directly with Carla and Lee until Lee has mastered new skills she can use when Carla comes to play group.

The transdisciplinary team model has many advantages over other early intervention team models for children and families, for participating professionals, and for program administrators. Particularly suitable for services for infants and toddlers, the transdisciplinary team service plan avoids unnecessary duplication and fragmentation by addressing the child's strengths and needs across developmental domains. Transdisciplinary treatment goals are functional and holistic. By integrating goals and programming for skills that cross developmental domains, the team can increase the opportunities for learning in the context of a child's daily routine. The transdisciplinary model offers professionals and family members on the team an opportunity to teach and learn from one another (Wolery & Dyk, 1984), making professional development a routine and continuing process. At its best, the transdisciplinary approach can limit the intrusiveness in and disruption of family lives that occur when teams require families to work separately with each discipline. For administrators, the transdisciplinary approach offers a cost-effective way to provide the comprehensive team assessment, planning, and services that young children with complex needs require, avoiding wasteful and duplicative efforts.

The TD model is not without its problems. This model requires a high degree of commitment on the part of team members. Like the interdisciplinary team, the team must be made up of members who are willing to give up disciplinary turf. Transdisciplinary team members must be people who will enjoy the teaching and learning that allow them to release some roles and skills while acquiring new ones. Successful transdisciplinary teams need strong leaders (Bennett, 1982; Orlando, 1981) who can establish the climate of mutual trust and support that is necessary for teamwork to occur. TD team members must be willing to work in a highly interactive context, acknowledging, respecting, and supporting the role of each person on the team and, most important, that of the family. Because participation on the TD team requires such a high level of team interaction, it is most successful when team members' professional preparation has including training in teamwork. Those involved in the development of programs of preservice, inservice, and continuing education have only recently begun to bring an interdisciplinary focus to those programs (Bailey, Farel, O'Donnell, Simeonsson, & Miller, 1986; Burke, McLaughlin, & Valdiviseso, 1988).

Many teams experience problems resulting from a lack of administrative support. The TD team requires administrative commitment to team building and maintenance activities (Woodruff & McGonigel, 1988), and teams must be allowed the time and space in which teamwork can occur. When team members report to different supervisors in the same agency, or when they come to the team representing several different agencies, all must be authorized by their supervisors to participate in and to support the decisions of their teams. Occasionally, the needs of individual agencies must be deferred to in favor of the priorities of the team and the needs of the child and family. If professionals are to participate on TD teams, they must know that making decisions in favor of children and families will be supported by their supervisors and administrators. Any limits on team members' ability to make commitments of time and services must be unambiguous so as not to compromise their team participation or the resulting team plans.

Team Models: Common Issues for Early Intervention

Each of the three models discussed—multidisciplinary, interdisciplinary, and transdisciplinary—is characterized by both strengths and limitations. None of these models is immune from problems of personnel shortages, although transdisciplinary advocates suggest that the TD model makes the best use of limited time. Shortages of early childhood specialists, particularly of pediatrically trained physical, occupational, and speech therapists, are widely reported (Burke et al., 1988; Yoder, Coleman, & Gallagher, 1990). Without the participation of all disciplines needed by a child and family, the team assessment is inaccurate, planning is incomplete, and service delivery is inadequate.

Teams using any one of the three models discussed are particularly challenged to incorporate medical input into team assessment and planning and to integrate a child's health care and developmental services. Physicians may be accustomed to having a higher degree of status than other members of a team (Bennett, 1982), creating problems for teams committed to consensus decision making and to the absence of traditional hierarchical structure on the team.

Although health and allied health care providers are key players on early intervention teams, the problems caused by lack of adequate training for team interaction are exacerbated by the problems of securing financial support for the physician's participation in team assessment and planning. Infant interventionists working in health care settings do not always have the knowledge and skills needed to be comfortable on a hospital-based team, limiting the extent to which they can be effective in early intervention that is delivered in a hospital setting or planned in the context of discharge from the hospital. Early childhood special educators may be unfamiliar with the vocabulary of the hospital setting, with limits on insurance coverage that affect treatment choices, with the origination of the health care system, and with the medical implications of a child's disability for planning intervention (Bailey et al., 1986). Similarly, pediatricians, family physicians, and other pediatric specialists interested in having an active role on a community-based early intervention team may have received little information or training concerning IDEA and the early intervention service system.

In considering which team model might be most successfully adapted for use in a particular work setting, it may be helpful to consider the three models discussed not as separate systems but rather as points on a continuum of team interaction. Teams seeking models for their work together are served best when, in addition to evaluating the strengths and limitations of each model, they explore the institutional values and resources of the settings in which the teams will operate. A system for team interaction should provide a match between the team's view of best practice and the organizational context in which the team must work. Similarly, teams will work best when they abandon traditional views of health and allied health care and child development as separate systems and view them as an integrated system for supporting the growth and development of young children.

CRITICAL ISSUES FOR EFFECTIVE EARLY INTERVENTION TEAMS

Selecting a model of team interaction is only one hurdle facing groups of professionals who have chosen to work together as a team toward shared goals. Rebecca Fewell's observation that "teams are not born but made" (1983) has become early intervention's own shorthand description of the need to develop strategies for effective teamwork in the face of multiple challenges. Even when early intervention professionals share the common goals of ensuring needed support for the family and good developmental outcomes for the child, they are frequently limited in their team interaction by different philosophical bases, operational policies, procedures for communication, definitions of the family role and, in fact, of their own roles on the team. "The values that members bring to the team influence members' roles, team goals, and team norms" (Nash, 1990, p. 320).

When professionals from multiple disciplines come together to plan and deliver coordinated services to infants and toddlers with special needs and their families, they must establish teamwork procedures (1) for leadership and decision making that will be equitable and functional, (2) for communication that will be accessible and intelligible, and (3) for standards that hold both the group and its individuals members accountable, across the disciplinary and bureaucratic boundaries that typically separate them (Dyer, 1987).

Leadership and Decision Making

"Effective early intervention teams must be more than collections of individuals, each pursuing his or her own interests and tasks" (Child Development Resources, 1991, p. 5). It is not sufficient for team members to share commitment to a common goal. A team requires a leader who not only can articulate clearly the goal of the team but also who can keep the team moving toward that goal or vision. In the case of the early intervention team, for which the goal, of course, is to provide comprehensive, collaborative services to children with disabilities and to their families, the team leader cannot be the only one who accepts responsibility for accomplishing the goal. To the extent that each team member must share responsibility for working diligently toward the goals of the team, each member also accepts a measure of responsibility for team leadership.

Each member of the team inevitably perceives his or her role on and responsibility to the team through the lens of his or her own training, experience, and value system, and each may expect to have greater or lesser input to the decision-making process. Teams need to decide in advance how they will go about the process of decision making (Briggs, 1991; Brill, 1976; Parker, 1990; Russo & Shoemaker, 1989). Team members must be clear about the parameters for determining which decisions can be made by the group and which must be made by parents, other individuals on the team, or by agency administrators.

Some decisions require the action of a single individual, perhaps because time does not allow for consultation or group process or because policy or law places responsibility with that person. Surgeons make some decisions that social workers do not; in protective service cases, the reverse is true. Other decisions are made by an individual in consultation with others—checking the perceptions and opinions of one or more other members of the group. Administrators or team leaders may have the sole responsibility for some fiscal or personnel decisions.

When decisions can be made by the team as a whole, the team must have established procedures for their decision-making task. If a group is large, voting is quick and easy, readily accepted as the familiar and democratic process. Voting, however, produces winners and losers and does not ensure the full commitment of the team to the decision.

Many teams choose to use consensus decision making—a process that allows each team member to have his or her voice heard until the team reaches a conclusion that all can support. Teams that make decisions by consensus place the collective wisdom of the group above individual expertise, agreeing in advance that the best decision is the one on which the team agrees. Teams using consensus review and evaluate their decisions and action plans on a regular basis to ensure that the decision has had positive results and that it continues to have the full support for the team.

Although consensus decision making is associated, by many, with optimal team functioning (Brill, 1976), consensus is acknowledged to be difficult and time consuming. Some team members find consensus decision making to be incompatible with their professional values and norms and find it difficult, in particular, to share the decision-making process with families (Turnball & Winton, 1984). It is not unusual to find that some team members have been trained to assume that professionals, not family members, are in control of the decision-making process (Bates-Smith & Tsukuda, 1984). Conversely, early intervention professionals who have been trained in the provisions of IDEA may see families not only as having the option to be full and participating team members but as having the right to choose and include those professionals whose expertise they value on their child's team (McGonigel & Garland, 1988).

Dominic

The team is meeting to plan for Dominic who is three years old. As a result of his mother's long-term substance abuse problem, Dominic is in the custody of his maternal grandparents, the Corellis, both in their seventies. Dominic was enrolled in an early intervention program because of concerns about delays in his language and cognitive skills and because of behaviors that his grandparents found extremely difficult to manage. Having made great gains, he was not eligible for public school special education services.

When he left the early intervention program on his third birthday, the transition plan on his IFSP was for Dominic to attend a Head Start program in the morning although the Head Start program in his community accepts few three year olds. Because his grandparents still work, it was planned that Dominic would attend a child care center in the afternoon when the Head Start program is not in session. After the first six weeks, the Head Start staff, who were involved in the transition planning, are having great difficulty managing Dominic whose behavior they describe as hyperactive. The teacher at the child care center, a much less structured environment, finds Dominic a challenge although neither hyperactive nor unmanageable.

Dominic's physician at the public health department, who is unable to attend the meeting, is considering prescribing medication based on the reports of the Head Start center's staff. Mrs. Corelli has told the physician that after she meets with the rest of the team she will decide whether she wants Dominic on medication. Because of the problems she has had with her daughter, she is unhappy with the idea of giving Dominic "drugs."

Mrs. Corelli has asked Gladys, the teacher from the early intervention program, to attend the meeting. Gladys expresses her concern that, with medication, Dominic will not be alert enough to respond to the many learning opportunities at Head Start and will lose the gains he has made. Teachers from day care and Head Start each present their assessment of Dominic and their recommendations. It is clear that each perceives Dominic's behavior very differently. The Head Start mental health consultant presents the report from the psychologist who evaluated Dominic, but who makes no clear-cut recommendation about medication.

After a thorough discussion of Dominic's skills and behavior problems, the team weighs its options, and the benefits and potential consequences of each possible choice. Clearly, team members have divergent views, but air them in a free and open atmosphere of mutual respect and trust. After Mrs. Corelli listens to the other team members, she decides to keep Dominic in all day child care, without medication, for the fall semester. She understands that there are some negative consequences of her choice. Her child care costs will double, whereas Head Start charges no fee. She also will lose some of the services that Head Start provides such as home visits.

Although the staff had hoped that Dominic would remain at Head Start but be put on medication, they understand the concerns of their team colleagues and recognize that Dominic is young and immature compared to the many four year olds who are enrolled. They agree to work with the child care center staff so they can help Dominic acquire the social skills he will need to succeed in Head Start when he reenters. The health services coordinator from Head Start will review the information that the pediatrician will need to have after the meeting with Mrs. Corelli and will, with Mrs. Corelli's permission, send the pediatrician a copy of the psychologist's report. The coordinator will follow up with the pediatrician to be sure he has no other concerns that the team did not address.

Dominic's team has reached consensus. After airing many points of view, the team, in reaching full consensus, agrees to support the decision of the family who, after all, bears the final responsibility for the outcome.

Conflict Resolution and Communication

"Conflict is inherent in team process" (Nash, 1990, p. 322). Members of the team differed widely in their assessment of Dominic's strengths and needs and in their ideas about services needed. Dominic's team, however, had a process that was successful for dealing with conflicting points of view and for reaching consensus. Each person on the team had an opportunity to present his or her views and to hear the ideas of others. The team accepted ownership of all the options offered, not attributing specific strategies to specific team members. Each option was weighed in terms of the outcomes that were desired for the child and the family. Each member was chosen because of the Corellis respect for their expertise. Likewise, the team's decision reflected their respect for Mrs. Corelli as a full member of the team and for her ultimate responsibility for Dominic. Once the decision was made, each team member, having felt respected and listened to during the decision-making process, was committed to ensuring the success of the team's plan.

Leroy's team worked differently.

Leroy

Leroy, who has fetal alcohol syndrome, has been participating in a community-based early intervention program since the public health nurse made a referral several months ago. The nurse participated in the assessment and in the development of Leroy's IFSP along with staff from a local early intervention program—a speech pathologist, an occupational therapist, and an early childhood special educator who is also Leroy's service coordinator.

When the service coordinator became concerned about continued parental substance abuse and its impact on Leroy, she made a child protective service referral. The protective service worker has called a meeting of workers from all agencies involved, by now including the early intervention program, public health, mental health, court services, and child protective services. The service coordinator works in an early intervention program governed by IDEA and public policy that calls for families to have the option to be full participating team members in any decisions that affect them. She wants and believes she is obliged to invite Leroy's mother to attend the meeting. The child protective service worker and the public health nurse are unable to agree with the service coordinator about whether the mother should be informed of the meeting and invited to attend. Plans for support for Leroy and his mother are on hold until the team can work out procedures for holding this meeting.

Leroy's team reached an impasse on the issue of whether it was appropriate for the team to meet without providing Leroy's mother an opportunity to participate as a team member. The team lacked procedures necessary for resolving this serious procedural and philosophical disagreement. In fact, they lacked the climate in which such serious dissent could be raised without damaging the working relationships that would allow them to continue on this case and others in the future. The failure to build a relationship and emotional climate that could withstand conflict, as well as the failure to establish procedures the team could use to resolve conflict, was also a failure to acknowledge that in any working group there are occasions when individuals or subgroups will disagree (Dyer, 1977). Without clear procedures for dealing with conflict and for making decisions, endless discussion without resolution can destroy the emotional climate of trust necessary for teamwork. Perhaps in greater trouble is the team that is unable to air conflict at all.

Airing of and resolution of conflict can occur only in a climate of trust and open communication. Team members can participate in decision making and shared leadership only to the extent that they have access to all the information needed to make good decisions and to move the team toward mutually agreed on and commonly held team goals. Many early intervention teams have developed highly refined protocols for child assessment and IFSP planning that ensure that all team members will have equal access to information. Successful communication, however, is "a learned process influenced by the participants (e.g., their socialization, culture, values, goals) and by the environment" (Nash, 1990, p. 321).

Thorp and McCollum (1988) mention communication as one of two broad categories of skills needed by team members. "Team members from multiple disciplines [should] have a common vocabulary that enables them to share their disciplinary expertise, to plan interventions, jointly, to incorporate parents in planning, and to incorporate shared disciplinary knowledge into their own interventions" (p. 154). Communication among team members, especially communication with families, frequently falls short of that goal. One parent described her experience with health care and early intervention professionals as being like a "Martian speaking to an Earthman" (Thomas, 1986). "Parents and professionals must find ways to understand each other's language" (Shelton et al., 1987, p. 15). Technical vocabulary and professional jargon have so invaded the lives and work of team members that they may be unaware of the ways in which their language results in unclear communication and misperceptions and sometimes even closes the door for future interactions. "Each time I call my social worker," one father said with disbelief, "they tell me she's working in the field." Pointing to the rainstorm outside his window he asked, "What kind of field could she work in on a day like this?"

Vocabulary may not be the only barrier to clear communication. Although honest, open communication with a family is widely held to be a critical factor in the early intervention team process (Kramer, McGonigel, & Kaufmann, 1991), some team members, administrators, and team leaders deliberately withhold information. Knowing that knowledge is power, they seek to control and limit that power by sharing information selectively. Ironically, such power differentials limit not only the ability of groups to function as teams but also the ability of the administrator or team leader to ensure that team goals are achieved.

Accountability and Evaluation

One of the most difficult issues facing early intervention teams is the evaluation of the extent to which their goals have been met. Most professionals have been trained to expect that their accomplishments rise and fall on their efforts. Participation in a team process means sharing not only decision making but responsibility for results. Team members are, however, generally accountable in a literal sense to their immediate supervisors rather than to the team. On transagency teams, each team member may report to a wholly different administrative system. Even within a single, but highly departmentalized agency, team members from different disciplines may be supervised by department heads who may have little or no understanding of the team's work or of the skills needed to carry out that work effectively.

Administrators involved in the hiring of early intervention professionals who will work as part of a team will wish to address in the recruiting, interviewing, and hiring process not only the clinical skills needed for early intervention but the communication and decision-making skills necessary for teamwork. *The Skills Inventory for Teams* (Child Development Resources, 1992) offers a number of factors to consider in assessing one's own or a job applicant's capacity for teamwork. These include:

- Consistency between the individual's goals and philosophy and the team's philosophy and goals;
- Understanding of one's own and other members' roles on the team;
- Openness and clarity of communication;
- Willingness to use the resources of other team members' knowledge and skills and to offer one's own;
- Decision-making and problem-solving skills;
- Willingness to accept responsibility for the work of the team;
- Ability to manage and use conflict productively;
- The ability to seek and use performance feedback from team colleagues and from one's supervisor.

Assessment of job performance and of the need for training and clinical supervision for early intervention team members should be based on these teamwork skills as well as on clinical skills.

If appraisal of teamwork skills is important for individual team members, it is critical for teams to evaluate their work as a group. Evaluation of the process of teamwork is no less important than evaluation of the outcomes. Unfortunately, for most early intervention teams, evaluation is a self-imposed process. Parker (1990) encourages early intervention teams to ask, "How are we doing?" This question can be asked and answered informally at the end of team meetings. Some teams regularly debrief after infant assessments, meeting together for a few minutes to ask: "Did we learn what we wanted to?" "Did everyone feel comfortable during the process?" "Did we each have a chance to ask questions and be heard?" "If there was conflict, did we handle it well?"

Families should have an opportunity to evaluate their experiences on the early intervention team and be able to provide feedback on whether they felt valued as members of the team and felt free to share ideas, ask questions, contribute to the decision-making process. Some teams will choose to appraise their work together in a more formal way, using written team assessment rating instruments to examine areas of team interaction such as the clarity of their goals, responsibility sharing, decision making, communication, conflict resolution, group cohesion, and others. Team members who feel truly informed and part of the decision-making process will feel a strong commitment to team accomplishments of shared goals. Teams will set their own timelines for action and will build strategies for reviewing accomplishments into their work plans.

Project PRIDE

Project PRIDE is an early intervention program in rural New England. Its staff of forty includes special educators, nurses, and therapists who work as a team with family members and with representatives of other community agencies. They have a long waiting list for their program and are feeling overwhelmed and overworked. They meet as a team two times a month, with a good deal of time given to discussing program problems, but never seem to get anywhere. Out of frustration with the process, they use a formal team evaluation instrument and are not surprised with the results.

Communication at PRIDE is open and honest. Members have a strong sense of loyalty and affiliation with the team. Discussions of problems are lengthy and forthright. However, there is no process for decision making. Team members aren't sure who can make what kinds of decisions, or even how they know when a decision has been reached. Many things that have been decided never get acted on. Problems eventually resurface, the same topic comes back again at staff meetings, and no one remembers what was decided the last time the issue was discussed. Many staff members are part time, and their young staff has had many family leaves. People returning to work after a leave have no way of learning about decisions affecting the team or its procedures that have been made during their absence.

The PRIDE staff develops a written work plan for improving their decision-making and communication procedures. They will clarify the kinds of decisions they are empowered to make as a team with the executive director. A recorder is appointed for all team meetings, and decisions will be highlighted, along with responsibilities for implementation and timelines for accomplishment. A central place is decided on for posting team minutes. People absent or on leave are responsible for reading the minutes of meetings missed. The team plan specifies trying these strategies for twelve weeks and reevaluating at that time to ask again, "How are we doing?"

Team building is not an event but a process. Without periodic reevaluation and reexamination, Project PRIDE and other early intervention teams are unable to maintain themselves as effective and efficient work groups. High staff turnover in early intervention (Palsha, Bailey, Vandiviere, & Munn, 1990) contributes to the need for planned team building and maintenance efforts to ensure that new team members are successfully incorporated into the team.

Personal and Professional Development

Few professionals entering health care, education, or human services have had the opportunity to learn skills needed to build, maintain, participate on, or lead successful teams. The process of learning to work as a "well-functioning, effective team does not occur overnight" (Briggs, 1991, p. 8). Rigorous evaluation of team interaction requires a high degree of openness to the possibility of change "as individuals learn to move beyond traditional roles and expectations" (Briggs, 1991, p. 8). Increasingly, programs of professional preparation are beginning to address the new roles required for teamwork and to offer interdisciplinary training as part of the preservice experience.

Although the ability to provide the coordinated, collaborative, comprehensive early intervention services to which infants and toddlers with disabilities will soon be entitled is sorely limited by inadequate preparation for teamwork, the current economic climate makes wasteful, duplicative effort unthinkable. The complexity of the needs of the children and families served in early intervention will encourage each clinician to assume new roles within teams. For the early intervention professional, the rewards of teamwork are the incentives for the development of the requisite teamwork skills. Clinicians involved in teaching and learning across disciplines as part of an early intervention team will find satisfaction in their own professional development as they expand their roles.

Early interventionists seeking to develop their skills in working as part of a team can begin with relatively small but significant efforts. Reading journals beyond one's discipline and attending conferences outside one's area of primary interest are good ways to start. Asking to observe a colleague from another discipline at work with a child, asking follow-up questions about the intervention technique, and asking for help in acquiring those new skills all enhance team interaction. Asking for observation and feedback from colleagues in other disciplines on one's work expands the extent of team interaction. Receiving and making use of feedback to evaluate and modify one's own behaviors occurs easily in a climate of openness and mutual respect. A team environment in which members can freely express their ideas fosters not only the professional development of individual team members, but also the development of innovative, state-of-the-art treatment and program approaches (Antoniadis & Videlock, 1991).

Future Challenges for Early Intervention Teams

As early intervention services become an entitlement in all 50 states, existing community-based teams will be challenged to refine their teamwork practices and procedures in light of the new legislation, while in other communities new teams will develop. Professionals and agencies will work in collaboration. A service coordinator will be appointed for each individual infant and toddler and his or her family to serve as the link between the family and the formal service system to ensure that children and families receive the services they are entitled to in a coordinated, collaborative way. All will be called on to develop a new inclusiveness of families and of private practitioners previously excluded from the teams of publicly funded agencies. For private practitioners, there will be new challenges to find adequate financial support for their participation on the community-based teams that serve their patients and clients. People who worked alone will need to become part of teams if they are not to be irrelevant.

Teams that existed within single agencies will need to expand their parameters to incorporate the broad range of community providers and consumers who are stakeholders in early intervention. As increased numbers of children with severe health impairments return to our communities needing the support of early intervention services, early intervention systems will need to respond with new methods for respite care, home care, specialized medical and adaptive equipment, support services, transportation, and a new commitment to serving those children in natural, inclusive environments.

For teams to meet the challenges of a legislative mandate of full services for all eligible infants and toddlers, consumers and providers alike will need to carefully monitor the implementation of newly developed state policies and procedures to ensure they are adequately reflected in local early intervention team practice. They will need to ensure that the policies of agencies that participate in the early intervention process not only permit but also foster participation on community-based teams and support their employees who are members of interagency teams. Higher education institutions and other sources of preservice and inservice training will need to follow the examples of excellence set by the network of University Affiliated Programs and by federally-funded inservice training models, such as Trans/Team Outreach, Project Dakota, and Project Copernicus, in developing training that prepares professionals to participate as members of community-based teams.

SUMMARY

No one discipline or agency is able to meet the needs of infants and toddlers with disabilities and of their families. Legislation, best practice, and the interrelatedness of development in infancy all combine to require a team approach to early intervention. Multidisciplinary, interdisciplinary, and transdisciplinary team models all have evolved in response to the need for collaboration across agency and disciplinary boundaries. The strengths and problems of each team model must be weighed in light of the service delivery setting and its resources, as well as in light of the needs of families.

Regardless of the model used as a structure for team interaction, the IFSP stands as a guarantee that families will not be left to resolve duplicative and even conflicting service plans. Service coordinators who serve as the link or bridge between the family and the formal service system are available to facilitate team assessment, planning, and coordination of services and to advocate for services that are needed but unavailable. However, state and local public policy will need to be developed to support and encourage teamwork among professionals and agencies to decrease wasteful and duplicative efforts. Administrators of agencies that participate as part of community-based early intervention systems will need to acknowledge and authorize the teamwork required of their personnel. Professionals entering early intervention will need to reconceptualize their roles, moving away from a role definition of individual clinician to one of team member. Personnel preparation and supervision will need to address not only clinical intervention skills, but skills needed for teamwork. Most importantly, professionals, regardless of their discipline or agency affiliation, will need to redefine the role of families on the team, giving new status and respect to families not only as consumers but also as primary decision makers for themselves and for their children.

"They thought they would come home with a baby," the mother and clown continues, "but this family also got a neonatologist, physical and occupational therapists, a pediatric neurologist, a speech pathologist, an early intervention specialist, a public health nurse, a social worker . . . all of whom will work together with them as members of their family's team."

REFERENCES

Antoniadis, A., & Videlock, J. L. (1991). In search of teamwork: A transactional approach to team functioning. *Infant Toddler Intervention: The Transdisciplinary Journal*, 1(2), 157-167.

Bailey, D. B., Farel, A. M., O'Donnell, K. J., Simeonsson, R. J., & Miller, C. A. (1986). Preparing infant interventionists: Interdepartmental training in special education and maternal and child health. *Journal of the Division for Early Childhood*, 11, 66-77.

Bates-Smith, K., & Tsukuda, R. (1984). Problems facing multidisciplinary teams in a large psychiatric facility. *Clinical Gerontologist*, 2(3), 64-66.

Bennett, F. C. (1982). The pediatrician and the interdisciplinary process. *Exceptional Children*, 48, 306-314.

Briggs, M. H. (1991). Team development: Decision-making for early intervention. *Infant-Toddler Intervention: The Transdisciplinary Journal*, 1(1), 1-9.

Brill, N. (1976). *Teamwork*. Philadelphia, PA: Lippincott.

Brinkeroff, J., & Vincent, L. (1986). Increasing parental decision-making at the individual educational program meeting. *Journal of the Division for Early Childhood*, 11, 46-58.

Burke, P. J., McLaughlin, M. J., & Valdiviseso, C. H. (1988). Preparing professionals to educate handicapped infants and young children: Some policy considerations. *Topics in Early Childhood Special Education*, 8(1), 73-80.

Child Development Resources (1992). *The team approach to assessment, IFSP, and case management.* Unpublished. Lightfoot, VA.

Clifford, R. M. (1991). *State financing of services under P.L. 99-457, Part H.* Carolina Policy Studies Program, Frank Porter Graham Child Development Center, Chapel Hill, NC: University of North Carolina.

Dyer, W. G. (1987). *Team building: Issues and alternatives.* Reading, MA: Addison-Wesley.

Federal Register, Vol. 58, No. 145, July 30, 1993.

Fewell, R. R. (1983). The team approach to infant education. In S. C. Garwood & R. R. Fewell (Eds.), *Educating handicapped infants: Issues in development and intervention* (pp. 299-322). Rockville, MD: Aspen.

Gallagher, J. J., Harbin, G., Thomas, D., Wenger, M., & Clifford, R. (1988). *A survey of current status on implementation of infants and toddlers legislation* (P.L. 99-457 Part H). Carolina Policy Studies Program, Frank Porter Graham Child Development Center, Chapel Hill, NC: University of North Carolina.

Garland, C. W., & Linder, T. (1988). Administrative challenges in early intervention. In J. B. Jordan, J. J. Gallagher, P. Hutinger, & M. B. Karnes (Eds.), *Early childhood special education 0-3* (pp. 5-28). Reston, VA: Council for Exceptional Children.

Gilliam, J., & Coleman, M. (1981). Who influences IEP committee decisions? *Exceptional Children*, 47, 642-644.

Golin, A. K., & Duncanis, A. J. (1981). *The interdisciplinary team.* Rockville, MD: Aspen.

Harbin, G. L., & Van Horn, J. (1990). *Elements for inclusion in interagency agreements.* Carolina Policy Studies Program, Frank Porter Graham Child Development Center, Chapel Hill, NC: University of North Carolina.

Haynes, U. (1976). The National Collaborative Infant Project. In T. D. Tjossem (Ed.), *Intervention strategies for high risk infants and young children* (pp. 509-534). Baltimore, MD: University Park Press.

Holm, V. A., & McCartin, R. E. (1978). Interdisciplinary child development team: Team issues and training in interdisciplinariness. In K. E. Allen, V. A. Holm, & R. E. Schiefelbusch (Eds.), *Early intervention: A team approach* (pp. 97-122). Baltimore, MD: University Park Press.

Kramer, S., McGonigel, M. J., & Kaufmann, R. K. (1991). Developing the IFSP: Outcomes, strategies, activities, and services. In M. J. McGonigel, R. K. Kaufmann, & B. J. Johnson (eds.), *Recommended practices for the individualized family service plan* (2d Ed., pp. 57-66). Bethesda, MD: Association for the Care of Children's Health.

Linder, T. (1983). *Early childhood special education: Program development and administration*. Baltimore, MD: Paul H. Brookes.

MacQueen, J. C. (1984). The integration of public services for handicapped children: Myth or reality. In E. Eklund (Ed.), *Developmental handicaps: Prevention and treatment II* (pp. 115-129). Silver Spring, MD: American Association of University Affiliated Programs.

McCollum, J. A., & Hughes, M. (1988). Staffing patterns and team models in infancy programs. In J. B. Jordan, J. J. Gallagher, P. Hutinger, & M. B. Karnes (Eds.), *Early childhood special education 0-3* (pp. 129-146). Reston, VA: Council for Exceptional Children.

McGonigel, M. J., & Garland, C. W. (1988). The IFSP and the early intervention team: Team and family issues and recommended practices. *Infants and Young Children*, 1(1), 10-21.

Nash, J. K. (1990). Public Law 99-457: Facilitating family participation on the multidisciplinary team. *Journal of Early Intervention*, 14(4), 318-326.

Nover, A. (1985, January). *State of the art in working with families*. Paper presented at a meeting of the Ad Hoc Family Advisory Committee to Habilitative Service Branch, Department of Health and Human Services, Washington, DC.

Orlando, C. (1981). Multidisciplinary team approaches in the assessment of handicapped preschool children. *Topics in Early Childhood Special Education*, 1(2), 23-30.

Palsha, S. A., Bailey, D. B., Vandiviere, P., & Munn, D. (1990). *Employee turnover in home-based infant intervention*. Frank Porter Graham Child Development Center, Chapel Hill, NC: University of North Carolina.

Parker, G. M. (1990). *Team players and team-work*. San Francisco, CA: Jossey-Bass.

Peterson, N. (1987). *Early intervention for handicapped and at risk children: An introduction to early childhood special education*. Denver, CO: Love.

Russo, J. E., & Schoemaker, P. J. H. (1989). *Decision traps*. New York: Fireside.

Sciarillo, W. G. (1989). P.L. 99-457, Part H, Challenges and Opportunities for State Title V Programs, PIC-III Technical Report, Series 89-04. Baltimore, MD: Department of Maternal and Child Health, School of Hygiene and Public Health, The Johns Hopkins University.

Shelton, T. L., Jeppson, E. S., & Johnson, B. H. (1987). *Family-centered care for children with special health care needs*. Washington, DC: Association for the Care of Children's Health.

Thorp, E. K., & McCollum, J. A. (1988). Defining the infancy specialization in early childhood special education. In J. B. Jordan, J. J. Gallagher, P. Hutinger,

& M. B. Karnes (Eds.), *Early childhood special education 0-3* (pp. 147-162). Reston, VA: Council for Exceptional Children.

Thomas, R. B. (1986). The family's experience with a child's complex health concerns. Unpublished manuscript. Seattle, WA: Children's Hospital Medical Center.

Turnbull, A., & Winton, P. (1984). Parent involvement in policy and practice: Current research and implications for families of young, severely handicapped children. In J. Blocker (Ed.), *Severely handicapped young children and their families: Research in review* (pp. 377-395). Orlando, FL: Academic Press.

United Cerebral Palsy National Collaborative Infant Project. (1976). *Staff development handbook: A resource for the transdisciplinary process.* New York: United Cerebral Palsy Associations of America.

Woodruff, G., & McGonigel, M. J. (1988). Early intervention team approaches: The transdisciplinary model. In J. B. Jordan, J. J. Gallagher, P. Hutinger, & M. B. Karnes (Eds.), *Early childhood special education 0-3* (pp. 163-182). Reston, VA: Council for Exceptional Children.

Wolery, M., & Dyk, L. (1984). Arena assessment: Description and preliminary social validity data. *Journal of the Association for Persons with Severe Handicaps, 9*(3), 231-234.

Yoder, D. E., Coleman, P. P., & Gallagher, J. (1990). *Allied health personnel: Meeting the demands of Part H, Public Law 99-457.* Carolina Policy Studies Program, Frank Porter Graham Child Development Center, Chapel Hill, NC: University of North Carolina.

RESOURCES

Trans/Team Outreach, Child Development Resources, P. O. Box 299, Lightfoot, VA 23090, (804) 565-0303.

Project Dakota, 680 O'Neill Drive, Eagan, MN 55121, (612) 454-2732.

Project Copernicus, The Kennedy Institute, 2911 E. Biddle Street, Baltimore, MD 21213, (301) 550-9700.

6

□ □ □
□ □ □
□ □ □

Teamwork and the Involvement of Parents in Special Education Programming

Stuart M. Losen and Joyce G. Losen

The primary function of the special education team in any public school setting is to develop an appropriate Individualized Educational Program (IEP) to meet the identified needs of each handicapped or exceptional child brought to its attention. The team also is obligated to make every effort possible to involve the child's parents or guardians in all decision making regarding the development of the IEP. But our experience and recent research by Friend and Cook (1992) have underscored a variety of problems experienced by multidisciplinary special education teams in their efforts to comply with state and federal special education regulations.

This chapter, therefore, is intended to describe some of the successes achieved by school personnel in their attempts to work together as a team, the difficulties commonly experienced when school staff, who represent different professional orientations, disagree in their view of a particular child's educational needs, and some of the frustrations that have to be overcome when attempting to encourage meaningful parent involvement in the team's decisions.

Before discussing some of the problems experienced by special education teams, however, it is imperative that we emphasize the view, based on our experience, that the special education team approach to developing programs for special education-identified students more often than not *works*, and it usually works very effectively, particularly when parents are meaningfully involved. We have found that the team approach encourages mutual problem solving by providing a system of checks and balances regarding the diagnosis or identification of the problem, and by comparing ideas, including those expressed by the child's parents, regarding what is most likely to work to help them and their child toward better understanding, accepting, and easing the child's learning difficulties. When parents are respected for their knowledge of their child and encouraged to take an active part in the plan ultimately agreed to by the team, the results can be extremely gratifying for all involved as was the case with one of our parents.

Mrs. Conrad, the single parent of a third-grade little girl, expressed it best when, at the conclusion of our annual review of Nancy's first year in our special education resource program for children with Attention Deficit Disorders and Learning Disabilities, she sought to thank each member of the team individually. She was effusive at first in her round of compliments, but she then stopped short when she saw that we were beginning to react somewhat self-consciously, and instead, said to us, "You know I fully expected you all would give me a hard time at the beginning of the year when I told you that I suspected Nancy had a learning problem, especially when I told you that I thought she might have ADD. I had once heard teachers in her previous school complaining that ADD was the new fad that parents were making big fusses over—blaming all of their kids' problems on it. But you've been great, you took me seriously, you seemed to be up on all the new stuff about ADD, and you made me feel comfortable about my concerns—like I wasn't some idiot, or an alien from outer space. I want you to know I appreciated that, and all you've done to help Nancy this year—she doesn't feel stupid or out of it anymore. At the end of last year, she told me she thought there was something wrong with her—it was painful—it really hurt! But this year has made a big difference—like we have a handle on her problems, and we know now how to help her. I want to thank you for helping ease our pain."

The teamwork in this case had been an obvious success. In fact, our efforts to work with Mrs. Conrad had evolved helpfully *despite* some of the team members' privately expressed attitudes that ADD concerns were being used by parents as a smokescreen, often to avoid coming to grips with family or emotional issues affecting their child's school performance. We had researched the recent literature on ADD, were aware of the Fall 1991 clarification of federal regulations governing the identification of students with ADD as "Other Health Impaired," and, having found that Nancy's distractibility *was* having "an adverse effect" on her better than average learning ability, we proceeded to involve Mrs. Conrad in an appropriate plan to meet Nancy's needs, which, thankfully, proved extremely successful. We knew of other school districts where children with ADD had to meet the more stringent learning disability criteria to be eligible for service, but our system's pupil–personnel administrator and our psychiatric consultant had designed interim procedures to take account of the 1991 federal advisory from the Office of Special Education and Rehabilitation Services (OSERS) to develop appropriate programs for children like Nancy.

Of even greater importance, however, was our attitude of willingness to take parents at their word, to respect what they knew or sensed about their children, and to investigate their concerns as fully as we could before passing further judgment. In our experience, that attitude of respect for parents being capable of becoming problem-solving partners is vital to the success of the special education team process and crucial to involving them in long-term effective programming for their "special" children. Later in this chapter, we will further discuss how the effective involvement of parents, even resistive, angry, and/or extremely defensive or litigious ones, can be pursued constructively.

PLANNING AND PREPARING FOR TEAM SUCCESS

Other authors have stressed the concern that staff member territoriality, ambiguous role definition among team members, accountability confusion, lack of trust, and inconsistent or loosely construed decision-making procedures were found to be among the various factors resulting in significant team inefficiency. We have found that to avoid such problems and encourage parent participation, it is imperative that the special education team leader or coordinator play an active role in the preparation of staff who may be expected to contribute to IEP planning for, or the annual review of, progress with any given child. The following discussion, therefore, focuses on specific actions we feel can improve team functioning.

Clarifying Staff Roles and Expectations

All staff members should have a clear idea, before the meeting, of the role they are expected to play. They should know in advance what data they may be asked to present or explain, what specific descriptions of the child's present performance or suggestions for the child's future program they may have, or whether they will be asked only to answer questions. They also should be prepared for the kinds of questions that are likely to arise.

Staff members also need to have a clear understanding of the specific objectives of the particular meeting. Classroom teachers, who may not have attended team meetings previously, should be briefed about the nature of the meetings, informed of the team's objectives, and told who will be in attendance. Staff members should also know the order in which they will be called on to speak if serial presentations generally characterize such meetings.

In addition, the staff needs to know that any advance planning is not meant to predetermine outcomes or to control their input; but that it is intended to prepare staff members so they do not find themselves working at cross purposes or cause confusion for the parents. When an IEP is developed, staff members should also understand what their responsibility may be for implementing the services, attaining certain objectives, monitoring the child's progress, writing future reports, and so on.

Without such advance preparation and clear understandings among the staff, communication problems are likely to develop. These problems may be exacerbated if the team leaders are uncertain of their roles and/or if the parents are harboring resentment and antagonism or are fearful about the meeting. Furthermore, unless staff members are aware of the procedural requirements and the "due process" safeguards that must be formally offered and explained to parents, they may find the meetings overly formal and intimidating. Obviously, this is most likely to occur in the case of teachers who may have attended few if any meetings. Procedural matters often seem routine to regular team members, but they should never be omitted or treated too lightly as such oversights can become an important source for serious legal complications later if parents disagree with team decisions and choose to invoke their legal due process rights. We know, in fact, of many hearings where a neglected procedure, for whatever reason, has reinforced an adversarial stance by the parents and ultimately proven costly to all concerned.

Occasionally, serious communication problems can develop when the meeting is run by a dominating leader who fails to ensure that everyone has had a chance to make a real contribution. No matter how clear or well prepared the other members are, regarding their potential contributions, the tone and pace will most often be set by the leader. It is the leader's expectations, more than anything else, that will ultimately determine whether everyone will leave the meeting satisfied with his or her role. For a more complete discussion of how certain leadership factors affect group communication and problem-solving efficiency, the reader is directed to Chapters III and IV of our book entitled *The Special Education Team* (Losen & Losen, 1985).

One other factor related to team members' expectations is often neglected. With increasing frequency, regular classroom or subject-area teachers are being involved in team conferences, but most are prepared poorly, if at all, for the role they will be expected to play. Consequently, the teacher's attitude may vary from feeling completely left out—through a defensive reaction to the parents' or other staff members' questions about their work with the student—to annoyance that a special education student has been "dumped" in their classroom. Therefore, unless these mainstream teachers are better prepared for their part in the team process and feel comfortable about the extent of their contribution and/or responsibility for the program or for the child, their active involvement in the team meeting may, at best, prove meaningless and, at worst, disruptive.

To accomplish the job of better preparing mainstream teachers for such roles, the federal law requires each state to develop inservice training programs to acquaint all teachers with special education issues and procedures. P.L. 101–476 funding is made available to both the states and the local school districts for such activities. But the ordinary facts of school life, i.e., time pressures on teachers, budget demands in other school program areas, lack of inservice trainers, and so on, often block the development of effective, continuous inservice training to the extent needed.

It usually remains for the special education leadership, therefore, to do the job of preparing mainstream teachers for their team involvement. Team leaders can encourage teachers to learn about available special education and support services. The principal, for example, can and should inform all regular staff of their potential responsibility for team involvement and assistance in planning for special children. Whoever coordinates the team can inform specific teachers what will be expected of them with regard to a particular child prior to a meeting. But, unless the general expectation that they will be involved and *need* to be involved, has been established through leadership of the principal or a team coordinator, the mainstream teacher is not likely to be the informed colleague that the special education planning process requires. Instead, unprepared teachers are likely to feel that they were forced into a needless, unjustified waste of their time, which they may also perceive as an unproductive process designed to help only a few children. Consequently, their forced participation can, and sometimes does, undermine the whole team's efforts.

Clarifying and Enhancing Parents' Expectations

Much of the success or failure of efforts to involve parents and elicit their cooperative participation depends on what their expectations are prior to team meetings and how those expectations are either changed or reinforced.

Parents whose children are experiencing difficulty in school are likely to be apprehensive. Their reactions may range from fear about their child's future to feelings of guilt over what they might have done or neglected regarding their youngster's problem whether it is a physical handicap, an emotional disorder, an attentional difficulty, or a learning disability. Some of their reactions may be irrational. However "guiltless" they may be in reality, parents whose youngster suffers from cerebral palsy, for example, may harbor some secret feeling of responsibility over possible genetic causes, birth trauma, or other causative factors for which they blame themselves. Similarly, they may feel defensive if their child seems to suffer from difficulties that are less well defined such as attention deficit disorders. This is true particularly if there appears to be social or emotional overtones for which the parents may either blame themselves or for which they may feel others hold them accountable.

Even in the absence of such personal apprehensiveness, the idea of coming to school for a conference with the principal and/or other specialists may be difficult for some parents to handle. Associations about returning to school may go way back to their school days. Regardless of the source of the apprehension, and the groundlessness of their fears, it is important to understand that these feelings may exist and be prepared to deal with them.

Some parents, rather than being apprehensive and defensive, may feel extremely angry or resentful toward the school system or toward particular school staff members if they believe that their child has been "singled out," "mishandled," "labeled," or that their child has not been given enough attention and that his or her difficulties have been overlooked, ignored, or even caused by the school. Even the formality of the notices regarding scheduled meetings and parental consent procedures for proposed evaluations may create additional negative parent reactions.

It is, therefore, recommended that initial contacts with parents always precede team meetings when staff resources and time permit. Such preliminary meetings provide the most suitable occasion to first inform parents about their children's school difficulties—a task that should *never* be attempted at a team meeting. If conducted effectively, the initial contacts can go a long way toward allaying at least some of parents' apprehension. A more complete discussion of ways in which parents' initial apprehensiveness, anxieties, fears, hostility, and other concerns can be channeled into constructive cooperation as described in *Parent Conferences in the Schools* by Losen and Diament (1978).

When finally ushered into the presence of "the team," parents must be treated with courtesy and introduced to all staff members present. Each member's role regarding their contact with the child should be briefly explained, and the parents need to be encouraged to ask questions that might be of concern to them about the nature, size, or purpose of the meeting. It should be acknowledged that large team meetings, especially, tend to inhibit parents who are new to the process and do not realize that their active input is desired. Parents should not be intimidated or rushed into agreements about evaluations or an IEP. They need to be given ample time to consider the staff's suggestions if they seem hesitant or confused. It is better to wait or even to have another meeting, if necessary—than to risk having to deal with uncertain, angry, or resentful parents all year.

As a general rule, parents may be expected to assume that the best program possible will be provided for their child. They also will likely assume that the staff will recognize and recommend what would be ideal for the child. Given these expectations, parents often react negatively to the suggestion of a program or services that might seem to fall short of the ideal. To help avoid such a situation, therefore, parents should be given a written description of the school district's special education program alternatives, detailing the law's requirement that a program at least be realistic, appropriate, and adequate to meet a child's needs. This description needs to include a full explanation of why, within the financial resources of a public school system and under the limits of the law, it may not be possible to provide what might be considered "ideal" for a child.

The school staff also should be straightforward with the parents in explaining their due process rights, and the fact that they have a right to invite advocates to future meetings, to obtain an independent evaluation at school expense, to employ the counsel of an attorney, to challenge recommendations, and so on. It should also be made clear to the parents that they do not have to agree to the staff's classification of their child's needs or to any proposed special education placement. They need to understand that they have the right to request additional or different services, or a different placement, and that their request will be seriously considered. In other words, the more parents feel assured that they have a real voice in the decision-making process and are not powerless to affect decisions about their child, the more they are likely to be persuaded of the good intentions of the planning team and to be willing to cooperate with the staff. The extra time taken to afford parents such early assurances has often proven to be time well spent.

After the initial team meeting, if it is suspected that a child has a serious problem, the parents should be provided the opportunity to discuss and deal with their feelings about it in a separate meeting with the staff member who has the most direct knowledge of their child. The next team meeting, when evaluations are reviewed and the IEP is developed, is not the time to break "bad news" about a child's identified difficulties.

Similarly, at annual review team meetings, if there has been little or no progress during the course of the school year and the parents have not been regularly informed about the child's lack of anticipated success, that kind of bad news also is never welcome and a parent's exclamation, "Why wasn't I told about this before!" can be expected. The point is that new disclosures should always be acknowledged *when* they occur. The risk of distressing parents with negative or surprising information at initial program development or annual review meetings can and should be avoided. This is particularly true at the annual review when planning for the future is hard enough. Introducing new information about which the parents should have been informed may make planning for the future impossible.

Some Comments about Parents' Prior Notice and Other Rights

The law requires that parents receive appropriate notice of team meetings to identify a child's special needs and to plan to modify a special education program suitable to the child's needs. The law further stipulates that such notice must be communicated to parents in a language they can understand, within a prescribed period of time prior to the meeting, and that the notice contain information apprising parents of their due process rights. In addition, the notice must state that regulations, consistent with the intent of P.L. 101–476, have been developed to urge active parent participation in team meetings, to allow for surrogate-parent representation when appropriate, and to encourage parents to bring their own educational advisors or legal counselors to assist them with their team involvement.

These statutory rights obviously are intended to increase parental involvement in school decisions. However, their implementation has resulted in at least three unexpected negative side effects that tend to be antithetical to the best interests of the children the laws are intended to serve.

First, the paperwork and necessary attention that need to be devoted to procedures (e.g., written notices of meetings, records of having mailed notices and subsequent telephone calls, preparing arrangements for taking accurate minutes or recordings of meetings, the need to sign a variety of release forms, waiver of notice forms, and permission for testing forms), have created an aura of red tape around all formal team meetings that is extremely time-consuming and frustrating.

The idea of having to wait a certain number of days before school personnel and parents can officially meet is, in itself, a necessary but often time-wasting precaution. Waivers signed by the parents can alleviate some of this red tape, but then the proceedings may be slightly tinged with an aura of illegality because of the omnipresent feeling that everything needs to be done just right, that the "case" may have been jeopardized in some way, or that certain due process rights will have been violated. This whole matter of following legally prescribed procedures also tends to be alien to the school staff, teachers, and parents who have not been legally trained. Administrators, who may be more generally comfortable with procedural matters, are also frequently uneasy about special education regulations because such procedures are dictated by state or federal statutes rather than by local or district Board of Education policies with which they are more familiar. Most team members, therefore, including many parents, frequently perceive the bulk of regulatory procedures as unnecessary and time-consuming even if they do protect the parents' rights. Consequently, many view the parents' due process rights as a boon to lawyers more than as a genuine aid to parents. However justified these or opposing views may be, the fact remains that the imposition of regulatory procedures creates, at the very least, the subtle awareness that over and above the desirable circumstance that all parties might *want* to get together, the team *must* get together and *will be recorded* as such. This fact of current special education life is what also creates the second and perhaps most important negative side of the law's effect: The reinforcement of adversarial attitudes and the anticipation of conflict between parents and staff.

Although the law requires that some positive action be taken by a team to meet a child's identified needs, adversarial channels created by due process regulations often tend to be used too quickly by parents or school personnel. What may be lost as a result is the necessary airing of underlying issues and concerns that might ultimately aid in developing the most comprehensive and mutually desirable program of remediation for a child. In other words, parents and staff may bypass valuable though uncomfortable confrontations about real, causative issues by prematurely pursuing due process procedures, i.e., by turning matters over to lawyers.

Finally, it should be recognized that formal notices and formalized procedures in and of themselves, however protective, often arouse mistrust and suspicion plus unnecessary or premature defensiveness when no such feelings existed previously. Comments from parents, like the following, unfortunately are becoming increasingly commonplace:

> Do I really have to sign all these permissions? What is it that you're planning to do to my child anyway?

I received your letter and those official sounding notices. I will certainly be coming in with my husband next week, but I get the feeling that we ought to bring our lawyer too.

Obviously, laws and regulations have been enacted primarily as a means of correcting existing injustices. And, with regard to parents' rights, the clear intent of the law is to *involve* parents meaningfully in those school situations that have in the past either discouraged or circumvented parent participation in decisions affecting their children. There is little point in arguing now for an alternative, nonstatutory way to proceed, which might encourage and ensure greater parent involvement in decision making. P.L. 101–476 and its effects are with us for some time to come. Therefore, to enhance effective team functioning, we must acknowledge the fact that potential negative expectations may be aroused by the law and its concomitant regulatory procedures. Such reactions must then be confronted, discussed openly, and resolved as fully as possible if the team is to do its job. Otherwise procedural steps such as the prior notice, which is intended to start a helping process for a needful child, may, indeed, backfire and become the *final* notice that very little can or ever will be done.

COMMON PROBLEM AREAS FACED BY THE TEAM

Even with the most careful planning and preparation, the nature of the team process is such that there are always potential stumbling blocks that need to be acknowledged and faced. Among the most frequent are negative or defensive reactions by staff to the presence of parents' advisors, conflicting opinions among staff members, the problems stemming from overlapping roles, conflicts between staff members and leaders, and, finally, extreme parental reactions such as overpassivity, on the one hand, or an overly aggressive, assertive stance, on the other.

Staff Reactions to Parent Advisors or Legal Counsel at Team Meetings

P.L. 101–476 encourages parents to invite others to attend team meetings. These may include lawyers, outside professional specialists they have consulted, or others who they feel will support or help them to articulate their concerns. The positive intent of this aspect of the law is to provide parents better representation via informed advocacy, thereby increasing their power in the decision-making process. It is most suitable in school situations in which the parents' contribution has usually been ignored, minimized, and/or circumvented. Unfortunately, in those school situations where parents have characteristically been encouraged to participate actively in the team process, the net effect of the presence of the "experts" or the "legal eagles" brought in by the parents is, at the very least, distracting. At worst it is potentially disruptive, if not demoralizing for the school staff who believed they were trusted and respected, but who may view the parents' utilization of outside advocates as evidence that they ought to be questioned.

To make matters worse, school personnel generally are not trained in matters of law. While they probably are familiar with special education regulations and with school policy, they usually feel uncomfortable regarding formal, legal issues and procedures they may not fully understand. They often feel that their involvement in quasilegal processes should not even be part of their job. When lawyers are present, in particular, most staff members react with feelings that range from defensiveness and agitation to outright fear and open antagonism. At the very least, they appear to be easily intimidated by lawyers who are obviously more at home in confrontational situations and who seem to have no qualms about openly challenging a staff member's background, training, experience, and other qualifications. Most teachers are not used to being challenged or having their credentials regarded with skepticism when they make evaluative judgments about a child's performance in school—particularly if they have worked closely with the child for some time. Similarly, support services staff (i.e., school psychologists, social workers, and counselors) are threatened by the implication frequently present in a lawyer's questions that they are not really looking at things from the point of view of what they feel might be best for the child, but rather from the point of view of the school system's or the staff's needs and limitations. It becomes even more difficult when the parents, who have invited a lawyer to attend, turn matters entirely over to the lawyer and refrain from any participation in the meeting themselves. Communication under such circumstances can sound more like a series of courtroom-style exchanges than a discussion about a child's needs or problems. It is too easy for such a meeting to deteriorate rapidly into a flurry of charges and countercharges unless attention is redirected to the real purpose for everyone being there—to *identify* the child's present difficulties and the team's purpose in meeting them.

For their part, lawyers ordinarily do not feel bound by the team's usual procedures, especially if they have been asked to pursue a complaint on behalf of the child's parents or guardian. In fact, sometimes they will behave provocatively or state a position prematurely—e.g., "We've heard enough! Whom do we contact to arrange for a hearing?"— well before the parents would normally have even considered that possibility. On the other hand, if the lawyer and the parents have not predetermined their course of action, there is no reason to anticipate undue, unreasonableness simply because a lawyer is present. It may be quite possible that a lawyer, despite her or his potential to be intimidating, will be eager to assist the team to pursue full consideration of all relevant issues and concerns.

The point is that the very presence of an attorney is a significant variable to be taken into account regarding what, and with what ease, matters of importance will be openly discussed. It is often helpful, therefore, for the chairperson to acknowledge at the outset that the presence of the lawyer may have an initial inhibiting effect on communication, but that the team intends to overcome such inhibitions and do its job. Chairpersons' comments like the following may be useful to set the stage for cooperation rather than confrontation:

> We should acknowledge, before we begin, that Mr. Lagiano is here to represent the Clarks as their attorney. He may be helpful to all of us in our proceedings, but since most of us are unaccustomed to working with lawyers present, we will need to be sure that our discomfort does not lead us to be overly cautious in what we say or how we say it.
>
> Ms. Coltin is here as the Smith's lawyer and advisor, but let's not get too caught up in and distracted by legal or due process issues until we've worked through the main purpose of the meeting today, which is . . .

Recognizing the probable impact of a lawyer's presence on the rest of the team, openly acknowledging that fact, and proceeding from there to the main business of the team meeting are about all a leader can do to diminish the possible negative impact of the lawyer's presence on what everyone does and says. The lawyer's actual behavior from there on will determine whether his or her presence seriously impairs open communication. Although it must be reemphasized that a lawyer's presence may have a profound effect on team members' level of comfort, it is the chairperson's job to keep everyone's attention focused on best identifying and meeting the child's needs.

The presence of other specialists invited by the parents may have an impact similar to the presence of a lawyer at a team meeting. For one thing, psychologists, social workers, and other educational specialists are often perceived by the staff as having expertise similar to their own. However, the guest specialist, unlike the lawyer, often elicits a more urgent need to communicate more material, in greater depth, and with more substantiation. More effort tends to be directed toward the exchange of professional opinion. Jargon often flows more freely, and, consequently, communication may suffer not from inhibition, but from too much specificity. To maintain perspective, the chairperson may comment:

> What we seem to be getting into about the comparative validity of these two tests is certainly important, but we may be losing the main point of our discussion . . .
>
> We seem to be disagreeing over the interpretation of this particular subject, but can we get back to what this all means relative to Jenny's program?

The clear message to be conveyed when a guest specialist is present is that we share similar knowledge and skills, perhaps to varying degrees, but we know a lot about one another's ideas to begin with and, therefore, can communicate more openly and less defensively. As a result, the communication problems that occur with guest specialists may be addressed differently than those that occur with lawyers present.

Finally, to ease the strain being felt by everybody at the meeting, and to acknowledge immediately the potential adversary-reinforcing nature of the guest's presence, the team chairperson should always affirm the parents' right to have legal or specialist assistance at the meeting. But the leader should also note that the presence of the outsider, especially if unexpected, is likely to make the school staff feel somewhat guarded in what they wish to say, particularly if the session is to be tape recorded. In addition, the team leader should note that while guests are welcome, it is important for them to clarify their interest in the case or their relationship to the parents. In that way, any adversarial attitudes or preexisting antagonistic views may be made clear at the outset. Thereafter, it is probably a good idea to actually encourage the guest to participate in the proceedings whenever it seems appropriate to elicit the parents' reaction to something reported or presented.

On the other hand, attempts to limit the guest's participation should be kept to a minimum to avoid unnecessarily alienating the parents, who are undoubtedly depending on their guest's aid. Clearly, the leader can and should intervene when the guest pursues a line of discussion or inquiry that seems premature, or inappropriate to the task at hand. The point to be made in such situations is that the meeting was called to fulfill a particular objective and the guest's contribution should not be allowed to deviate too far or detract from the team's primary purpose—meeting the child's special needs.

School administrators, of course, should be particularly aware of the need to assist their special education staff, as well as their regular classroom teachers in preparing for guest expert and lawyer encounters. Inservice training should include simulated role-playing exercises that provide staff with the opportunity to explore their likely reactions to a variety of possible encounters, including taped sessions with parents and parent advisors in potential or actual adversarial relationships. The better prepared all staff members are, the more successful they will be in turning potential adversaries into working allies.

Having to Contend with Conflicting Points of View among Staff Members

An especially difficult problem occurs when, during the presentation of evaluation data for program planning purposes, one or more staff members disagree with the general consensus. When anticipated, therefore, the possible premeeting resolution of such differences between staff members, and related role-contribution conflicts, should be pursued as quickly as possible by the team's chairperson or coordinator. At the very least, when differences arise at the team meeting, is is imperative that:

1. Any persisting differences or dissenting opinions should be annotated to the team's decisions.
2. Such differing opinions must ultimately be resolved through further examination of a child's performance—possibly via further, independent evaluation.
3. Such differences should not diminish the team's effort to at least reach a tentative decision regarding a child's program—pending further evaluation.

But it needs to be emphasized again that prior to the team meeting, every effort should be made to resolve expected staff member differences. Nothing is more discouraging for parents than to see staff members sharply disagreeing among themselves about evaluations, squabbling over role responsibilities, or acting confused about who should follow-up the team's decisions. We have already described how some of those difficulties can be resolved through encouraging greater staff preparedness, by clarifying role functions in individual conferences with staff members, and by providing inservice training sessions for the whole staff to increase awareness of one another's strengths and weaknesses as well as of different job functions.

It also should be noted that we feel it is important, from our experience, for each team of specialists to learn to compliment one another's professional skills and to defer to the specific strong points of other specialists rather than insist on or bicker about job delimitations relative to titles when determining who should best implement the team's decisions. This idea is likely to be rejected by administrators in school districts where crossing over disciplinary lines is frowned on, because it will be argued that such practice blurs role distinctions. In practice, however, we have found that a well-knit team can and, whenever possible, should employ skill rather than credential distinctions to provide the best available service to individual children.

Problems Stemming from Overlapping Staff Roles

Despite all administrative efforts to clarify staff members' roles and functions and despite a table of organization that specifies responsibilities and lines of authority, it is in the nature of the work of special educators that their similar skills and work methods create an overlap in functions that sometimes becomes a source of conflict. Many speech and language–development clinicians, for example, are now trained to use some of the same assessment devices formerly considered the private domain of school psychologists. Social workers, counselors, and clinically trained school psychologists all may possess similar interviewing and counseling skills. Special education teachers are trained in the administration of diagnostic and achievement tests that used to be considered the private domain of reading specialists, educational consultants, and school psychologists. Therefore, no job description is likely to clarify perfectly where one specialist's job begins and the other one leaves off.

Some school districts make arbitrary assignments: Psychologists do testing but do not confer with parents—the latter constituting a role function delegated only to counselors or social workers. Such an arbitrary division of labor sometimes appears to work smoothly, but it tends to create resentment and morale problems when the people in the various roles are well-rounded in their training and object to artificial job limits because they feel perfectly capable of performing broader functions.

As already noted, while staff members' credentials should be viewed as establishing primary areas of responsibility within each team, we strongly advise that formal credentials should be considered *secondary* to personal *strengths* and *skills*. For example, a speech clinician who can use screening measures of cognitive ability effectively should be encouraged not only to do the IQ screening of children referred primarily for speech or communications disorders, but also to do screening of other groups of children (prekindergarten screening, for example) instead of reserving that task only for the psychologist. Similarly parents who need follow-up or ongoing counseling may be assigned to those psychologists, social workers, counselors, and even administrators who have had training in counseling. Among team members, job assignments may thus be distributed according to individual skills rather than on the basis of title, or according to the extent of caseload rather than on the basis of formal credentials. Then, when conflicts arise over who should perform a function, the issue may be decided on the basis of who has the time and the *necessary skills* rather than who has the correct title. Each staff member could then have designated caseloads, and for later reference, the minutes of team meetings should specify the delegation of assignments.

Finally, the implications for inservice staff training are clear. Staff members should be trained to work together as a group of individual professionals with individual, overlapping strengths that need to be capitalized on rather than ignored because one may lack certain credentials. The superordinate goal always must be to provide the best combination of services to meet the child's needs.

Coping with Staff Member Incompetence or Inadequate Performance

Perhaps the team's greatest internal headache is the need to contend with staff members who have shown a marked personality change, who have not kept up with current skills, or who have never possessed appropriate competence for their current role function. Teacher tenure laws create some of these difficulties. Changes in role assignments sometimes create problems. For example, a teacher may have completed enough additional schooling to become certified as a specialist late in his or her career because he or she has become bored with teaching or is seeking a salary increase that is tied to dual or additional certification. Possession of proper credentials may not, therefore, really ensure a high level of competence or motivation regarding a particular assignment, but according to certification laws, that person is unlikely to be displaced without evidence of gross incompetence.

Conversely, sometimes a person may have become certified in a specialty many years earlier but never really worked in the field. Reduction in a school's staff may suddenly push the person into the specialty area on the basis of "paper" credentials when the individual is really not able to function at a high level of expertise. Tragically, these staff reassignments can result in the displacement of a highly skilled and experienced specialist by a person who possesses a much lower level of skill and has less or no experience in the specialty, simply because she or he has greater seniority in the district. Finally, some staff members close to retirement may begin to "coast"—to ride out their last few years as a specialist without enough experience in the field.

All of these situations can create circumstances where effective service to children is jeopardized. For the sake of the children, these situations must be resolved on a case-by-case basis.

In some instances, it may be possible to delimit such a staff member's functioning to small groups of those kinds of children with whom the staff member can work effectively. Sometimes, reassignment to a more compatible team or to a special project are possibilities. Occasionally, concentrated inservice training or special course work may enable a staff member to make up certain skill deficiencies such as improving educational-diagnostic testing knowledge. Often, however, none of the options work, so something must be done about a difficult situation.

With the cooperation of the local teacher's association, some school districts have legally worked through a competency review procedure. Such procedures require filing documented complaints about the staff member and prescribed suggestions for improvement that include carefully specified means and timelines for review of progress.

In the interest of fairness to the teacher, meetings to review professional improvement must be elaborately documented. Unfortunately, direct straightforward confrontation and counseling may be discouraged when legalistic procedures are undertaken. Yet, this always should be an option available for special education administrators to use with their staff.

At the very least, the annual staff evaluations of performance and/or professional growth routinely required in many systems may be the best vehicle for direct confrontation. In addition, inservice training programs should be developed to establish the acceptability of regular self-evaluations by team members, to encourage group members to "share" reactions and give feedback to one another, to set the standards desired for professional development, and to help each other achieve mutually gratifying "quality" work.

Resolving Conflict Between Members and Leaders

Those possessing effective leadership characteristics often may not need to contend with intrateam revolt. The sensitivity, awareness, knowledge, and other skills of such leaders provide the best assurance that little more than occasional disagreements among team members will arise. But they *do* arise, and they are usually not a function of anyone's inadequacy or incompetence. They may occur because of differing philosophies, differing views on how to use certain staff, or differences in personal style.

With respect to style differences, one team may generally function in an orderly, businesslike fashion, except for what is perceived as the humorous, but distracting, antics of one or another team member. Another team may reflect the team leader's "casual" attitude about many matters, especially the formal procedures, except for one or more team members who want things taken "more seriously." Such stylistic differences are probably best met by simply acknowledging their existence. If anything, differing styles probably work as a check and balance to one another.

With respect to the more intense conflicts, and inherently more disruptive issues, direct confrontation may be necessary. For example, certain members of the team may regularly tend toward recommending placements outside the school district fairly quickly rather than following the slower, more gradual withdrawal process consistent with "least-restrictive environment" principles. They may argue, with some justification, that the student is likely to experience increasing frustration until his or her school environment is totally changed. This occurs most often when working with secondary level students with social–emotional handicaps, and/or when parents are easily willing to accede to a recommendation for "out-placement." This kind of situation may also be further complicated by the team leader's concern over budgetary constraints—a factor that, in itself, can exacerbate intrateam conflict over legitimate child-oriented versus budget-oriented approaches.

The best strategy for dealing with such sources of conflict is to openly address them. Whatever the conflict that may lead to intrateam squabbling, whether it is a potential disagreement (on the basis of budget problems or program issues) over the advisability of placing a student out of the district, or a difference in professional opinion based on background or training differences, the team format should enable open reference to those differences. The more issues that may potentially lead to conflict are allowed to surface, the more the team may be able to confront one another directly and constructively. The more those issues remain hidden, or are allowed to subtly influence the team's deliberations, the less likely the team will be able to serve the students' best interests. It is entirely up to the team leader to initiate and maintain a receptive attitude that will permit open confrontations of this kind. To reemphasize an important point, one of the most critical attributes required of team leaders is the ability to listen to what is *not* being said as well as to what is— to listen for the genuine concerns expressed by staff members who have a professional difference of opinion and then to be able to deflect those differences, sometimes even before they are stated.

The Problem-Solving Role of the Case Manager or Team Contact Person

Many day-to-day problem situations, including some of those already cited, may be handled best by delegating certain responsibilities to a case manager or team contact person. Such a person might serve as the team's spokesperson for a child, for ongoing coordination of the child's program, for follow-up contact with the child's parents, and for keeping the rest of the team aware of the child's progress on a more frequent basis than would otherwise have been possible.

In school districts where the case manager concept is employed, case assignments are often made during the initial team meeting for IEP development, and the case manager may actively be written into the IEP as the child's program coordinator. Then, in addition to the role functions noted above, the case manager may act as the liaison between the staff who work directly with the child, helping bring out questions and concerns expressed by different staff members about the child's program, and enabling the team's leaders to be aware of any developing, critical issues before they become serious problems. In some instances, the case manager may provide the team coordinator or chairperson with needed information or "warning" cues, so that one or the other of them can act quickly to avert a potential problem. Particularly when a regular classroom teacher has a complaint or question about a child's special education program, intervention of the case manager may bring appropriate action from the building principal before the issue has had time to fester.

At other times, the case manager may be able to handle the situation directly, depending on the leader's confidence in the case manager and the amount of latitude permitted. How nice it is to hear things like the following from a case manager to whom such follow-up responsibilities had been delegated:

> Mrs. Frankel, a classroom teacher, was annoyed that Hank would have to miss some additional homeroom time during the next two weeks because Mr. Carpenter, a special education resource teacher, had to reshudule the session Hank had missed when he did the sixth grade screening, "but I think I straightened it all out. Mrs. Frankel just needed to know that it wasn't likely to happen again until the spring—she seemed satisfied by what I said, but you know her, she was getting ready to raise the roof about kids missing time from homeroom before I reassured her."

For secondary-level students, the case manager idea is almost a must. The role is frequently assigned to a guidance counselor who has close ties with special education staff, to a special education supervisor, or to any of the special education staff whose schedules permit them to maintain contact with all of the subject teachers with whom a special education student comes into contact. Without such coordination by a staff member who knows everyone who may need information about a particular student or suggestions on handling or responding to the student, the youngster might easily run into a difficult situation that is aggravated by a teacher's lack of awareness of her or his special needs or problems. The case manager, therefore, can help prevent, if not entirely avoid, a comment like the following:

> If only I'd known about that kid's reading problem, I would have had him give his report orally. No wonder he got so upset when I insisted he read some of his material to the rest of the class.

Obviously, even the best of case managers cannot cover the whole range of possible student daily contacts to constantly ease the way or prevent all forms of frustration to which special education students may be subjected. But, at all school levels, the case manager's daily contact with most other staff who teach these students can be of tremendous value.

Dealing with Extreme Parental Attitudes or Reactions

Parental Passivity

Persistent, continuing parent passivity generally thwarts everyone's efforts to involve them more meaningfully in helping their children. It reinforces defensive behavior on everyone's part, and often portends future difficulty. George Gilmore (1974), the present authors, and others have cited the importance of encouraging parents to take an active participatory role. Passive, reticent parents usually defer too readily to the team's authority for a variety of reasons. While such deference may reflect a more complex and significant history of prior deferential behavior, it is the immediate task of the team to encourage change via whatever concrete ways the team can devise. This might begin with the expressed acknowledgment that the parents, thus far, have probably gained something by their passive role—that it has served a positive purpose for them in their past, but that it may not be the most helpful for their child now. This may be more difficult than it seems because the staff may too readily perceive and dismiss these parents as nonchallenging, nondemanding, or even noncaring. The team must, therefore, guard against its own tendency to do nothing about such parents' passivity and to too quickly take advantage of the opportunity to move on to more pressing issues, with other children, and with other parents.

Parental Domination

In sharp contrast to the need to draw the passive parent into an active team role, parents who are vocal, demanding, and hypercritical need to be encouraged to listen more to what others have to say. Such parents are already too active and tend to dominate team meetings to the extent that mutual problem solving becomes impossible. Again, the dynamics of the aggressive, dominant parent must be addressed immediately rather than, as is often the case, briefly tolerated and then ignored or avoided as much as possible. Unfortunately, such parents are not easily ignored or avoided—they keep letting you know that they must be dealt with somehow. But the frequent error, in such cases, is to remain on the defensive—a stance continually reinforced by the parents' aggressive actions—and to avoid or otherwise not come to grips with the potentially undermining character of the parents' behavior.

It is more difficult to respond immediately to parents' aggressive stance during a team meeting than to the passive parents' behavior. Because such behavior is often a function of their defensive reactions against feelings of helplessness and vulnerability, but certainly not an immediate reflection of such vulnerability, it needs to be left to the staff member who has already most closely worked with the parents or parent to meet with them separately and to discuss openly the disadvantages of their attitude and behavior. If this is attempted during the team meeting, it is likely that the aggressive parent will misconstrue the message and react with statements such as "Don't try to shut me up!" "Are you telling me that you know my child better than I do?" In other words, parents' aggressive behavior ought to be more carefully investigated in terms of the *purpose* it serves them before efforts can be successful to get such parents to listen or reflect on what the team really has to say.

A Final Comment about Team Meetings

The first time team members come together to share information about a child is like any other encounter between people meeting for the first time. Overriding objectives, therefore, need to be clearly stated before the meeting has ended and be agreed on by all in attendance. Surprisingly, objectives often are not clearly stated either in initial meetings or in later team meetings designed to assess progress. At initial meetings, everyone "knows" or at least "says" the team has gathered to help a child "do better in school," or "enjoy school more," or "realize more" of his or her potential. Such generalizations are always palatable and easy to make. But the most meaningful and tangible objectives often remain ambiguous in everyone's mind. Therefore, more than merely stating generalizations, at any team meeting, it is important to identify one or two specific goals for future or further reference, such as "providing additional strategies to help Tommy overcome his low self-esteem," or "helping Carol further compensate for her expressive writing difficulty," or "finding ways to reduce Eric's distractibility."

When such specificity has *not* been achieved during the team's first and subsequent meetings, it is not uncommon to hear parents raise questions later on that surprise everyone—particularly when it is clearly felt that their questions should have been answered a long time ago. In other words, when questions such as "I'm still puzzled. What *is* my child's problem anyway?" arise at a later, even a triennial meeting, it is evident that too much has been left unclear previously. Therefore, the single most important emphasis in the problem-solving approach to team meetings that we recommend is clearly stating, restating, and adhering to a few specific, mutually agreed on, work objectives. In the absence of consistent group interest in carefully delineated objectives, we have found that hidden agendas, unresolved personal concerns, within-group alliances, intrateam squabbling, and a variety of other nonchild, help-related issues can seriously undermine the important ultimate purpose of the team.

SUMMARY

This chapter has highlighted the role of the case manager in helping coordinate the team's and the parents' daily involvement with the child, and underscored the leader's role and responsibility for keeping staff members appropriately involved in evaluating and making decisions about the child's progress. The one special feature of the special education team process, which is somewhat unique when one compares this to other team problem-solving efforts in other settings, however, is that the special education team has a superordinate goal to pursue that holds intense personal meaning for all involved.

In closing, we wish to reiterate that the team approach to identifying and meeting children's special education needs does work more often than not, especially if parents are meaningfully involved, respected for their knowledge about their child, and encouraged to contribute actively to the programming process. All in attendance, particularly the child's parents, *usually* have an abiding investment in providing what will be in the child's *best interest*. When conflicts arise, when presentations or impressions are disputed, when financial or program considerations are at stake, when personal styles, attitudes, or competencies clash, the team leader may subtly or directly invoke the issues of what will *best* suit the child's needs. This is a potent point of reference for most, if not all, of the team's members, and helps keep everyone working constructively, and perhaps even more important, together.

REFERENCES

Friend, M., & Cook, L. (1992). *Interactions: Collaboration skills for professionals.* White Plains, NY: Longman.

Gilmore, G. (1974). School psychologist–parent contact: An alternative model. *Psychology in the Schools*, 2, 170-173.

Losen, S., & Diament, B. (1978). *Parent conferences in the schools.* Boston: Allyn and Bacon.

Losen, S., & Losen, J. G. (1985). *The special education team.* Boston: Allyn and Bacon.

7

□ □ □
□ □ □
□ □ □

Teamwork: An Organizational Priority in Residential Child Care

Martin L. Mitchell and Christine A. Ameen

Organizations that are interested in implementing teamwork will have to address three major issues that impact how well teams function. First, an organizational structure will need to be developed that results in teams of staff having the time and resources to function as a team. Second, the process for how teams interact and make decisions needs to be developed. Third, the quality of the staff who make up the teams, in terms of formal training and experience, will have an effect on how well teams function.

THE NEED FOR STRUCTURE AND PROCESS

The successful implementation of teamwork requires that its approach be an organizational priority. Teamwork is best implemented where both effective structure and process are present. The structure for teamwork requires, for example, that teams have time to meet, are given the resources necessary to support their decisions, and are granted administrative sanction for their work. The process for teamwork requires that each team member contributes to the quality of communication, decision making, conflict resolution, and relationship building (see Brendtro & Mitchell, 1983, and Lafferty, Weber, & Pond, 1978, for a more complete discussion of these two elements).

We recognize that it may not be feasible for all organizations to structure themselves to the fullest extent within the framework of the team concept. Nevertheless, the closer an organization can get to providing for the full structure and process that an ideal team requires, the more successful the implementation of teamwork will be. This concept is more clearly delineated in Figure 7.1. The use of the grid allows the reader to see how the combination of the variables of structure and process impacts the implementation of teamwork. The following definitions emerge:

Low Process Low Structure	=	No Team
High Process Low Structure	=	The Frustrated Team
Low Process High Structure	=	The Poorly Functioning Team
High Process High Structure	=	The Ideal Team

As indicated on the grid, the Ideal Team is characterized by high teamwork structure and high teamwork process. In this case, the organization has provided the structure necessary for teamwork, i.e., time for teams to meet, resource support, and administrative sanction for teams to do their work. Simultaneously, the organization has recognized the need for teams to develop the process skills of communication, decision making, problem solving, conflict management, and relationship building.

Often we find instances where the organizational structure does advocate for teamwork, but the process is missing. In this case, the organization provides time for teams to meet and the necessary resources (for example, coverage) for those meetings to be productive, but the staff are not capable of functioning as a team. Very simply, staff members fail to communicate, make decisions, solve problems, and manage conflict as a team. The relationship building that is such a key to quality teamwork does not exist. This situation is characteristic of a Poorly Functioning

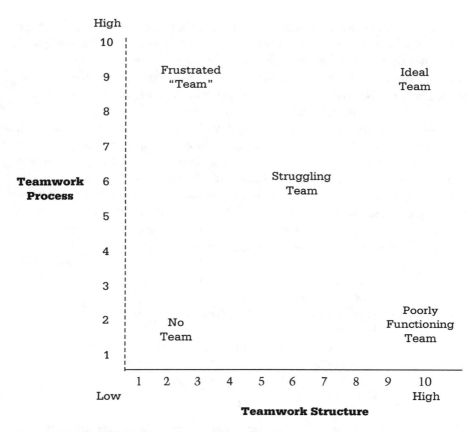

FIGURE 7.1 The Mitchell–Ameen teamwork grid.

Team. This scenario is very often the starting point for an organization that decides to commit itself to teamwork. In essence, the process by which teams function needs to "catch up" with the structure the organization has provided. In these cases, training, consultation, and time are what is needed to bring process into sync with structure.

    There are also occasions when the organization provides no structure, but the staff does possess the skills for working together as a team. When this occurs, we see the emergence of a Frustrated Team. They are motivated to work together, they possess the skills to do so, and they are committed to the organizational goals. But the "system" fails to recognize the benefits of the teamwork philosophy. In fact, by failing to provide time for people to work together, support resources for coverage, and administrative sanction for teams to make decisions, the organization actually undermines the motivation and commitment of the staff.

If the commitment to both structure and process is lacking, there is, in essence, No Team. Not only does the organization fail to encourage teamwork from a structural point of view, but the staff do not know how to work in a teamwork climate.

It has been our experience that a total lack of either element is very rare in residential treatment. Even agencies that do not consider themselves to be teamwork oriented may provide some structure, with something as minor as providing two therapists the time to consult on a specific case, or encouraging teachers to talk to clinicians about their students. There are also times when staff may be brought together on an ad hoc basis to discuss a treatment approach or to give feedback to administrators about specific issues. While some structure is provided by virtue of the fact that there is a meeting time, place, and topic, the staff may not possess the teamwork process skills to get the most out of the opportunity to work together.

In these examples, the concept of teamwork is implemented with such inconsistencies that staff get a fragmented view of how teamwork works and what its benefits are. It is difficult to be a nonteam player most of the time and a team player part of the time. When staff members are brought together under these circumstances, they struggle with the demands and expectations placed on them by their nonteam roles and become a Struggling Team.

Another example of the Struggling Team arises when the organization creates unsanctioned roadblocks to successful teamwork implementation. These may be organizational in nature, for example, an administrator impinging on the time set aside for team meetings by asking team members to be in a different meeting. On the other hand, they may be process roadblocks, imposing priorities on the team that are different from those they have developed themselves.

STAFF QUALITY AND THE IMPLEMENTATION OF TEAMWORK

The ability to be a fully functioning member of a team is dependent on more than organizational structure and teamwork process. The quality of the staff who work within the setting is also an integral part of the equation. Quality, in this context, consists of two elements. First, staff must possess the clinical skills to provide treatment. This is a

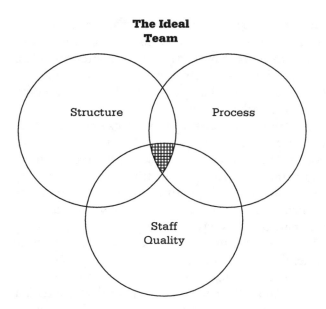

The Ideal Team

Structure

Process

Staff Quality

FIGURE 7.2   The interrelationships of teamwork structure, process, and staff quality.

prerequisite whether an organization uses teamwork or not. Second, staff must possess certain characteristics that allow for a match between their personal working style and the teamwork model. For example, staff whose preferred style is to work independently will fare much better with teamwork than staff who do not. Staff who are willing to assume responsibility will be better matched for the challenges of teamwork.

The process of teamwork provides much less direction to staff and is open-ended. In essence, the team sets the direction for making decisions and outcomes are, by the nature of teamwork and the treatment environment, less predictable. Staff who have a high tolerance for ambiguity will respond more effectively to these conditions than will staff who need clear direction set for them with outcomes clearly identifiable. Finally, being committed to the purpose of the team is a necessity.

The quality of the staff will make or break a team as surely as organizational structure and process. The interrelationship of all three variables is shown in Figure 7.2.

The Ideal Team is defined as the group that is structured for the support of teamwork, skilled in the teamwork process, and competent in their roles. All of the components necessary for teamwork to grow and develop exist to their fullest extent. The Frustrated Team is, perhaps, more frustrated because its members not only have the teamwork process skills, but they also have competence in their jobs. Yet, the organization fails to capitalize on these benefits by not structurally supporting teamwork. The Struggling Team continues to struggle. These staff members have experienced some of the process and structural elements of teamwork on a limited basis. Another component of the struggle is lack of competence on the job. The Poorly Functioning Team still functions poorly, in spite of the fact that team members have competence with regard to their jobs. They continue to suffer from the lack of skills in communication, decision making, problem solving, conflict management, and relationship building.

An organization that commits itself fully to the implementation of teamwork must go beyond setting the concept as a priority. Teamwork requires a commitment to providing the organizational structure and process in which teams operate. Equally important, teamwork requires a commitment to recruitment, retention, and development of quality staff.

ISSUES TO BE CONSIDERED

We believe in the effectiveness of teamwork as a management and treatment philosophy. There are a number of issues, however, that need careful attention when giving consideration to the philosophy of teamwork as a way of doing business.

Goal Specificity

As an organization begins to develop an attitude that is consistent with good teamwork practices, it is important for teams to be goal specific. For example, the goal in a residential treatment setting might be treatment teams that will work with a specific client population to effectively implement the program. It is possible then for teams to be assigned a specific population (see Figure 7.3). In this case, the specific goal of the team is to provide treatment services and care to a given client population.

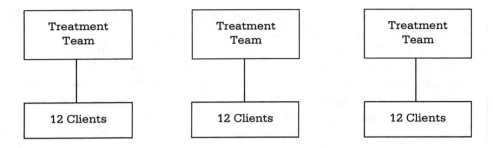

FIGURE 7.3 Goal specificity for treatment teams.

The very existence of a team requires goal definition. The team's purpose and reason for existing must be established. Teams that lack goal specificity and clarity of purpose will not be able to fully contribute to the success of an organization; they simply will have no sense of where they fit into the organization's comprehensive mission. A team that knows it exists for specific, clearly defined purposes that fit into the larger mission of the organization, however, will have a direct effect on the success of the organization as a whole.

Size Integrity

The size—actual number of persons on a team—can range from 2 people to as many as 10. Size will have an impact on two critical characteristics of the team: communication and creativity. Obviously, the smaller the team size, the greater the potential for increased communication. It is much easier to maintain communication with 6 people, for example, than with 10 people as illustrated in Figure 7.4.

If a team is too large, not only is it difficult to maintain communication, there is a tendency for subgroups to form, in which communication lines are dominated by how information flows between certain, select team members. This fragmented type of communication is very much in conflict with the goal of equal, high-volume communication that should occur within a fully functioning team.

While the need for quality communication would imply that team size needs to be restricted, there is a concern, should group size be too small, that the creativity of a team could be impeded. Fewer team mem-

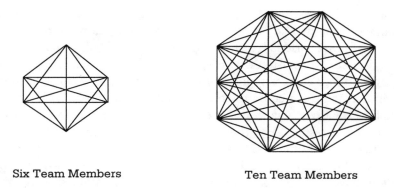

Six Team Members   Ten Team Members

FIGURE 7.4 Relationship of lines of communication to size integrity.

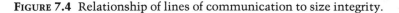

bers will result in fewer ideas generated for treatment planning, problem solving, and decision making.

Team size, then, is relative and must support the functions of effective communication and creativity. It has been our experience that the ideal range that achieves a balance of these two important characteristics is five to eight people per team.

Team Loyalty Versus Professional Loyalty

In most cases, when the process of teamwork is established in an organization, existing professional or departmental loyalties are often in competition with teamwork. Staff members are pulled in two different directions: loyalty to their discipline or department, and loyalty to the team. This creates a situation of serving two masters and a condition where staff must choose sides. While it is possible to have departments and still organize effective teams, more effort and time are required to make sure that both the department and the team are dealing with appropriate issues.

For example, in a residential setting where teachers are assigned to teams, it is necessary for teachers to still relate to some form of an educational department. There are issues and decisions that are more practically made by a group of teachers than a treatment team. For instance, when ordering materials or working on book selections or even attending a workshop on classroom instruction, the content of the meeting is quite relevant to teachers and not very relevant to other team members.

The same scenario is true for counselors/group leaders in a residential setting, where information that is specific to the task of being a counselor is being shared. Progress reports, how to run group meetings, or any discussion that is task specific to being a counselor might be addressed.

In both of these examples, members of a team become involved in topics that are so specific to their role that it is very appropriate to address them outside of the team. However, for those issues that are very much central to the team and to its goals, it is essential that loyalty to the team's process and decisions take precedence. To establish this loyalty, all that is necessary is to focus on the team goals. In actuality, loyalty should be to the clients being served or to the specific task to be accomplished. If staff members are always encouraged to keep that premise in mind, their energies are not wasted on the political strategies so often found in unhealthy work situations. It is possible for staff to be supportive of their professional group and their team without either suffering. The word professionalism certainly describes this type of characteristic in an employee who is capable of achieving this balance effectively.

Diversity of Power

Power and authority are invested in all team members; thus, there is diversity of power rather than unilateral power. Each team member, regardless of perceived status, has the same decision-making capabilities as any other team member. This practice is in sharp contrast to hierarchial structures quite frequently found in many human service systems.

In a hierarchial structure, someone always has the ultimate responsibility and/or power, depending on one's perspective, to make final decisions. If the decisions made by this person are frequently effective, then this individual becomes even more powerful and his or her position is established based on credible performance. However, if the person is an ineffective decision maker, power will be established based on position only. Co-workers and subordinates will learn that the way to survive in this circumstance is to work around the leadership.

Another weakness inherent in a strict hierarchial structure is that those who are subordinates to the designated leader frequently take on less leadership than they are capable of handling. Ideas that might have been just what was needed in a prescribed situation are frequently left undiscovered, or unsaid, and the overall performance of the organization is negatively affected.

There is another reason why diversity of power is important to good team process. An entire team of people can be held accountable for decision making and implementation rather than just one individual. No one is scapegoated, not the subordinates or the designated leader, as everyone is responsible for decisions made.

The question that often arises is: "Won't a leader emerge in any situation?" The answer is yes. Leaders do emerge, but the critical difference is the fact that an emergent leader has *earned* the power, where the prescribed leader has merely been *given* power based on title. In addition, anyone on a team has the opportunity to be a leader and, with the diverse number of issues with which teams must deal, leadership from a variety of people is certainly welcomed. Diversity of power allows for each member to exercise authority and leadership. Through consensus, the team can then implement decisions that have been made. Because everyone has been a part of the decision-making effort, team members are more likely to fully implement decisions.

Optimum Responsibility/Shared Management

It is said that the whole is greater than the sum of the parts. This is certainly true of fully functioning teams. Together, they accomplish more than the staff, as individuals, could achieve. The synergistic effect of teamwork makes it possible to delegate a tremendous amount of responsibility to teams, even those responsibilities traditionally thought to be management oriented. To fully experience this synergistic benefit, it is critical that teams be allowed to grow and have opportunities even to fail, for through these experiences team members learn what works and what their capabilities are. Allowing teams to develop to their fullest potential also enables individual team members to be fulfilled through their work responsibilities. Much of the literature on motivation stresses the fact that individuals need to feel they are a meaningful contributing part of an organization. Having the ability to help set the direction of a team can be a strong motivator for wanting to implement decisions effectively.

Employees who have optimum responsibility also have more opportunities to receive various forms of positive reinforcement. In the book *In*

Search of Excellence, Peters and Waterman (1982) speak about how "excellent companies are not only designed to produce lots of winners; they are constructed to celebrate the winning once it occurs." They describe these systems as being full of "hoopla." The old adage "nothing succeeds like success" seems to be the cornerstone of their premise, and they cite that "researchers studying motivation find that the prime factor is simply the self-perception among motivated subjects that they are in fact doing well."

The basic premise of "optimum responsibility" is that in order for employees to receive the "hoopla" an organization has to offer, they must first be given the opportunity to take on major roles of responsibility. Depending on a team member's level of maturity and willingness to work, the scope and breadth of the responsibility offered are limitless.

Operationalizing optimum responsibility requires managers to be willing to share the decision-making process. Often work groups in various settings are given the task of making decisions about identified organizational problems or interests. Once a decision has been made, however, it is not uncommon for management to reverse the decision or alter it in some form. Those on the staff work group, who devoted much time and energy to generating ideas and trying to determine a specific course of action, often are dismayed when even seemingly small changes are made to the plan of action. This occurs because they were not a part of all the decision making from beginning to end. The practice of teamwork and the achievement of optimum responsibility require that managers change their paradigms about how decisions are made and adopt a philosophy in which management of the work at hand is shared.

Interdisciplinary Balance

The most powerful teams are those who have available resources from a variety of backgrounds and disciplines. Teams that tend to have like thinkers in terms of individual skills and knowledge brought to the job run the risk of practicing group think. *Group think* is a phrase used in the literature to describe a situation where people working together feel, for a variety of reasons, that they must concede to the group's wishes to avoid conflict or bad feelings within the group. The result is that everyone begins to think the same way to avoid conflict. While building a team of staff with similar backgrounds does not always mean that this will occur, there is a greater risk that doing so will lead to group think.

Team members must have enough in common in their approaches to implement a plan of action, but also must have differing viewpoints to stimulate more creative thinking. At times, these differing opinions may result in conflict that in this circumstance should be viewed as healthy and helpful. While it is often typical to avoid conflict, highly functional teams that have interdisciplinary balance will actually stimulate conflict because they generate a wide variety of creative and challenging ideas. Some of the best solutions to problems often surface in this process. A synergistic effect occurs when the combined ideas of many and different people are merged.

Structured Meetings

Often situations can be found where employees are asked to accept certain responsibilities but never are given the meeting time to make sure implementation occurs. Planning has been cited by many as one of the most important functions within organizations and yet often it is the function conducted most inadequately. Organizations do not fail because of a lack of good ideas, but rather for two other reasons: The opportunity for ideas to surface from anyone in the organization is not realized, and, if the ideas are generated, members of the organizations often fail to implement the ideas.

A specific time for team members to meet and conduct planning is essential. At a minimum, team members should meet weekly. There may be certain issues that arise that require even more time.

Meetings must be designed in a way that promotes decision making, rather than giving everyone an opportunity to socialize or tell "war stories." A clearly defined agenda is essential to the process. Meetings need to be arranged at times that allow all members to attend. These events should have an important status within the organization—an organizational priority—and deserve the staff's full attention.

The meeting structure must also allow for each member to serve as secretary and chairperson. The importance of this is obvious. Any position of power, such as chairperson, should be rotated so that, by design, we avoid creating a situation where any one team member has more influence over the agenda and decision-making process than others.

Similarly, the role of secretary needs to be rotated among team members. It is essential that this task and role, as any other responsibility held by a team, be shared by all.

At the conclusion of meetings, each member should have an excellent grasp of what her or his responsibilities are for short-, medium-, and long-range decisions. A meeting is ineffective if team members leave and cannot account for the decisions made.

Situational Leadership/Participative Management

Teamwork has little chance of working when the administrative style of an organization is autocratic. If teams are going to be given the responsibility to make decisions for the organization, in return, it is critical that those decisions be supported administratively, when appropriate. Therefore, the management style of the organization must support the functions of teams.

Hersey and Blanchard (1977) offer the best description of this process. They describe their theory of situational leadership in the following way:

> According to Situational Leadership Theory, as the level of maturity of their followers continues to increase in terms of accomplishing a specific task, leaders should begin to reduce their task behavior and increase relationship behavior until the individual or group reaches a moderate level of maturity. As the individual or group begins to move into an above average level of maturity, it becomes appropriate for leaders to decrease not only task behavior but also relationship behavior. Now the individual or group is not only mature in terms of the performance of the task but is also psychologically mature. Since the individual or group can provide their own "strokes" and reinforcements, a great deal of socioemotional support from the leader is no longer necessary. The individual or group at this maturity level sees a reduction of close supervision and an increase in delegation by the leader as a positive indication of trust and confidence. Thus, this theory focuses on the appropriateness or effectiveness of leadership styles according to the task-relevant maturity of the followers.

One of the goals of teamwork is to delegate as much responsibility as possible to staff. Within this context, if teams are to develop maturity in terms of the kinds of tasks they manage, they must be given the latitude to exercise decision-making power. The leadership style used to facilitate the teamwork process must respond to the maturity level of the individual teams and encourage that maturity to reach the highest level possible.

Teams that are very mature in this regard have the potential to participate in decision making at all levels of management. Many issues, ranging from those related to the daily responsibilities held by the team to those issues typically managed by administrators, are open to discussion by a team, provided those issues impact the team in some way. In this respect, many decisions previously thought to be the sole province of administration fall within the parameters of the teamwork structure.

The Most Valuable Team Player

There is a longstanding tradition in the field of athletics to celebrate the achievements of an individual player with an award called the "Most Valuable Player." This award typically is given to an individual who has developed exemplary skill and is seen as a "stand-out" from the other members of the team. It is interesting to note that this celebration of individual success is often made at the expense of the success of the overall team. For example, a basketball team may have one outstanding player who rebounds, shoots, and handles the ball well. Often, all of the attention, resources, and development are spent on making this one player even more outstanding. The development of other individual team members gets much less attention and the collective capabilities of the team go unchallenged and underdeveloped. It is often the case that such teams enjoy the individual success of the MVP and never realize collective success as a team. However, other teams that avoid promoting a superstar and focus their attention and support on developing the optimum of all team members do celebrate collective success.

This same scenario applies to organizational teams. The explicit goal is optimum development of all team members. The working definition of this approach is "we are only as strong as our weakest link." The MVP, then, becomes the Most Valuable **Team** Player. This is the team member who is committed to the staff development of every team member—who is open to offering constructive criticism, providing professional support, and giving help in whatever way possible to promote the skills of each and every member of the team. This approach requires a willingness on the part of each team member to help others and an openness to seek help from others. As each team member adopts this perspective, the foundation for a highly successful, highly skilled team is built, on which the organization's mission and goals will be accomplished.

Consensus Decision Making

Effective decision making depends on two important concepts: The quality of the decision and the acceptance for the decision. Common sense would dictate that a high-quality decision that is not accepted by a team will not be well implemented. A poor-quality decision, on the other hand, which may be well accepted, will simply be a poor decision. There are some important implications of these observations for how teams make decisions.

When making decisions, teams must strive for consensus versus a majority vote agreement. There is a sharp contrast and distinction between the two decision-making methods.

Majority vote, averaging, coin flips, and bargaining are all conflict-reducing techniques. Using these methods immediately implies that differing opinions and conflict are negative and unhealthy. As indicated earlier, the very nature of a highly functioning, interdisciplinary team will result in differing opinions. Therefore, methods that squelch the generation of varied ideas are unhealthy to the team process. They will result in poorer quality alternatives being generated for consideration in the decision-making process.

Furthermore, when conflict-reducing methods for arriving at decisions are employed, the risk of part of the team being less than committed to full implementation of the decision is very high. For example, if six people serve on a team and three of the team members are advocates of one idea and the other three team members are advocating for another idea and coin flipping is used to make the decision, it is likely that the actual implementation of the "winning" ideas will be less than effective. However, if the team, after full discussion of all alternatives, can use consensus to agree to a decision, the process itself builds support for a decision that everyone can see through to full implementation.

Effective decision making requires the generation of quality ideas and a consensus process to achieve acceptance for the final decision. Lafferty et al. (1978, p. 19) suggest several guidelines for this process:

1. Work groups must always strive for the best answers. Think in terms of cause and effect while attempting to identify actual problems, not just symptoms and solutions.
2. Assume problems are solvable. Avoid win–lose situations. Discussions do not have to reach stalemates.
3. As work groups attempt to involve everyone in the discussion and decision-making process, disagreements can enhance the quality of the decisions made. Seek the best alternatives.
4. When making decisions concerning other human beings, it is important to consider your own reactions to the group choice as if it were to affect you personally. There is value in "Walking in the other person's shoes."
5. Avoid conflict-reducing techniques such as majority vote, averaging, coin flips, or bargaining.
6. Be alert to the human needs of the group and work in ways to reduce tension, formality, and resolve differences. Do not substitute camaraderie, harmony, and good fellowship for sound decisions.
7. Be time and cost effective.

The true measure of whether a team has reached full consensus or not can be seen in results, or the degree to which an idea was fully implemented. After teams have made decisions, the actions of the next day or through the next week are the critical indicators regarding the degree to which consensus was achieved.

Once team members make a commitment to each other to fully implement an idea, it will become quickly apparent if true consensus was reached. For example, if a team agreed that the students in their care needed to be involved in more service projects, then a series of decisions would be made. The team might discuss first what types of projects would be most appropriate, how each student will be involved, the days of the week the events will be conducted, and the lessons to be learned from such activities. Many decisions would be necessary from this exchange, and consensus for implementation would be critical even if there was disagreement among team members on some of the significant issues.

Over the next week, if all the plans went smoothly and it was apparent that all decisions had been implemented, a team would know that at its last team meeting, they had truly reached consensus. However, if some critical elements of the plan were not implemented, team members did not follow through on their specific responsibilities, their goal of getting students involved in more service projects was not achieved, or the actual process of the projects turned out to be disastrous, three conclusions are possible. Perhaps extenuating circumstances impeded implementation, e.g., some of the group members caught the flue and could not participate. On the other hand, perhaps the staff responsible for the actual implementation lacked the skills necessary to successfully follow through on the decisions made. Or, finally, perhaps the staff responsible simply did not implement because they made decisions counter to those previously made by the team. It is in this last case that the team would know that consensus had not been reached.

SUMMARY

Making teamwork an organizational priority requires that the leadership strive to create high functioning "ideal teams." While reaching the goal of creating ideal teams is challenging, the process of striving for these highest of ideals is what makes excellent organizations and the people that manage them at all levels highly successful.

Ideal teams are defined as work groups that are structured for the support of teamwork, with team members who are both skilled in the teamwork process and in their treatment roles. To foster the development of these ideal teams, organizations must address a number of critical issues—goal specificity, size integrity, team loyalty versus professional loyalty, diversity of power, optimum responsibility and shared management, interdisciplinary balance, structured meetings, situational leadership and participative management, the most valuable *team* player, and consensus decision making.

REFERENCES

Brendtro, L. K., & Mitchell, M. L. (1983). The organizational ethos: From tension to teamwork. In L. K. Brendtro & A. E. Ness, *Re-educating troubled youth*. New York: Aldine.

Hersey, P., & Blanchard, K. H. (1977). *Management of organizational behavior*. Englewood Cliffs, NJ: Prentice-Hall.

Lafferty, J. C., Weber, T., & Pond, A. W. (1978). *The desert survival problem II*. Plymouth, MI: Human Synergistics, Inc.

Peters, T., & Waterman, R. H. (1982). *In search of excellence*. New York: Warner Books.

8 □□□
□□□
□□□

Teamwork in Medical Settings—Hospitals, Clinics, and Communities

Maité deLamerens-Pratt and Gerald S. Golden

PHYSICIANS AND TEAMS

Physicians are most likely to work with teams in the hospital setting. Almost all professionals are familiar with acute care hospitals that seem to be organized for the convenience of the physician as much as for the convenience of the patient. Hospitals have traditionally used a physician-leader model in which the patient is admitted to the physician's care, and the physician is in full charge of deciding on all tests, procedures, treatments, and even types of meals that the patient receives. The remainder of the hospital staff has the function of carrying out the physician's orders that lie within their sphere of competence and that are permitted by professional and ethical standards.

Team interactions are rare in the traditional physician-leader model. Communications are largely through written notes in the chart, and the physician's desires are transmitted to other professionals via written orders. Some interchange with the nursing staff may take place, but this appears to be neither expected nor required, and the interaction often is initiated by the nurse.

Changes in the structure and financing of modern medicine have affected the physician's autonomy. Patients may have their insurance needs covered by a managed care plan that provides a strong incentive for seeking the services of a participating physician. The physician may be limited in what days of the week the patient can be admitted to the hospital, the maximum duration of the hospital stay, and the necessity of obtaining a second opinion before certain surgical procedures are carried out. Justification for expensive diagnostic procedures also may have to be provided to the plan administrative staff or medical director. The majority of hospitals now have functioning quality-assurance systems that review the physician's records and notify her or him if certain "quality indicators" are not met.

Chronic care hospitals, such as rehabilitation centers, may use the physician-leader model or may have a functioning team of other health professionals with the physician as consultant. In such circumstances, the core team usually does not include the physician. The physician's services are provided sporadically, and information may be communicated to the team either in writing or by participation at team meetings. Clinics and other community-based practice environments also tend to use the physician-leader model. This is most obviously the case if the physician is in independent private practice. Other clinic settings—those serving primarily medically indigent patients or clinics within managed care plans such as health maintenance organizations (HMOs)—have been organized around a number of new models of service. Nurse practitioners can provide many primary medical services. In a number of states this requires the nominal supervision of a physician, but nurse practitioners often function as independent caregivers.

It should be apparent that physicians, by training and by the historical role they always have played, are hardly ever members of a team; and if they are, they usually participate as the leader or occasionally as the consultant. It is rare in community practice to find the physician as a functioning team member with status equal to that of other health care professionals.

MODELS OF TEAMWORK IN MEDICAL SETTINGS

Health care teams have developed over the last 40 years as a result of increased specialization and the introduction of complex techniques. The focus of these teams is on viewing a patient as a whole person rather than as a collection of symptoms (Thompson, 1986). One of the challenges of the health care system is to identify the most appropriate model for effective team functioning. This usually is based on the specific situation involved or the condition being evaluated.

Multidisciplinary Team Model

The multidisciplinary model is one of the earliest models of cooperative team functioning. It is actually grounded in the medical profession. This is due to the fact that many evaluation clinics and early intervention programs for children with severe disabilities were based in medical centers (Beller, 1979; Denhoff, 1981; Haring & Hutchinson, 1982). Review of the medical literature reveals that the terms multidisciplinary and interdisciplinary are often used interchangeably with little regard to the actual team process (Haring & Hutchinson, 1982; Schmitt, 1982). Despite terminology, most medical teams actually employ a multidisciplinary model of team functioning where evaluation and treatment are provided by a varied group of professionals independently addressing a specific situation. This model has been employed in the hospital, clinic, and community settings. In most cases, these teams are physician directed.

Examples of the multidisciplinary process include teams involved in the treatment and rehabilitation of stroke or heart attack patients admitted to an Intensive Care Unit (Kasuya & Holm, 1986; Messin, 1978). Multidisciplinary clinics include those involved with the evaluation and treatment of menopausal disorders; chronic back pain; craniofacial anomalies; inborn errors of metabolism; and other chronic or catastrophic diseases such as muscular dystrophy, cancer, or spina bifida (Birkenfeld & Kase, 1991; Hazard, Bendix, & Fenwick, 1991).

Acquired immune deficiency syndrome (AIDS) is an example of a complex medical, social, and ethical condition that does not really fit into the traditional system of health care (Volberding, 1989). Physicians who commit themselves to the care of a patient with AIDS must be educated generalists. They must be able to assemble a team of physicians and supportive personnel ready to deal in a coordinated fashion with a wide spectrum of conditions.

At San Francisco General Hospital, a multidisciplinary team runs the AIDS-dedicated inpatient units and outpatient clinics. This system combines a team of generalists specially trained in AIDS management with added support from pertinent subspecialties—hematology, oncology, and infectious disease. The multidisciplinary approach also has been used in the care of these patients by groups known as the Shanti Project in San Francisco, the Howard Brown Memorial Clinic in Chicago, and the Gay Men's Health Crisis Center in New York City (Sadovsky, 1991). These groups provide a full range of supportive services designed to complement the work of the doctor. This includes peer crisis intervention, a "buddy" system to assist patients with daily chores, and recreational stimulation and stress-reduction activities. This is an example of how the physician interfaces with several other professions to optimize supportive services for a patient.

Another example of a multidisciplinary team focuses on behavioral changes in eating, exercise, and enhancement of healthy lifestyles. The team, made up of a nurse specialist, a dietitian, a behavior specialist, and an exercise specialist, conducts the clinic in the school under the guidance of a physician (Johnson, Nicklas, Arbeit, Harsha, Molt, Hunter, Wattigney, & Berenson, 1991). There are numerous reports in the literature describing the multidisciplinary model for nutrition assessment (Hamaoui & Nichols, 1993). Traditionally this has been a function of the dietitian in clinical practice. With recent documentation of the substantial incidence of malnutrition in hospitals, the need for a more comprehensive nutritional assessment has become apparent (Jensen & Dudrick, 1981).

A multidisciplinary nutrition assessment has been implemented at Hermann Hospital and the University of Texas at Houston. A nutritional assessment is ordered by the attending physician and communicated to the department of dietetics. Within 12 hours, the nutrition technician submits a standard order set to the medical record and transcribes appropriate orders that are later signed by the doctor. Nutrition technicians do anthropometric measurement They consult with the physician's orders to avoid duplication of laboratory tests. They also complete the nutritional assessment laboratory tests required. Nurses are in charge of monitoring oral intake as well as output. Hyperalimentation nurses administer the skin test recall antigens. The secretarial coordinator tabulates the appropriate data. The physician countersigns all profiles and notes the effects of the disease, procedures, and medications used in therapy. This individual is usually a surgeon following postoperative patients. The clinical nutrition specialist assesses individual nutrient needs, develops nutritional care plans, evaluates the effect of nutritional therapy, and interprets the data along with the physician.

The disciplines involved in nutrition support teams may vary between centers (Hamaoui & Nichols, 1993). Other models of nutritional assessment employ teams consisting of a physician, dietitian, pharmacist, and nurse. Like many hospital-based multidisciplinary teams, the physician has overall responsibility for the patient. The therapy is doctor directed and supervised like the treatment of any other disease. The unique role of the physician involved in nutrition assessment requires knowledge about metabolism in health and in disease. The physician performs a history and physical examination and obtains appropriate laboratory tests and medical consultations to aid in diagnosing the cause of malnutrition. He or she then recommends treatment after appropriate consultation with the dietitian, pharmacist, and nurse.

Medicare and Medicaid are promoting comprehensive services for geriatric patients involving a team of a nurse, a physical therapist, a home health assistant, a speech therapist, and others. This multidisciplinary team structure depends on physician referral. Unfortunately the patient's primary physician often is isolated from the team because he or she is not employed by the agency employing the rest of the team (Penznecker & Paquin, 1982).

Potential Difficulties

The multidisciplinary model often has drawbacks if team functioning is not carefully monitored. Out in the community, the process can lack coordination as each discipline acts independently, affected little by the others' contributions. The leader of the team by default would be the physician who first saw the patient, and the other team members would be the individuals consulted to aid in the evaluation and care of the patient. Information usually is not synthesized by the group and thus care can be fragmented. The lack of consultation between members may result in leaving those team members charged with implementing the recommendations to resolve conflicts of opinions between the professionals on their own. Typically one member collates all the information and provides interpretation to the family. This can prove disadvantageous as the person responsible for collating and interpreting the reports may place more emphasis on the information he or she collected (Haring & Hutchinson, 1982, Fiscus & Mandell, 1983).

Interdisciplinary Team Model

During the revolution in human services seen in the 1960s and 1970s, attempts to provide adequate management of families with multiply handicapped children brought about the implementation of the interdisciplinary team. As many as 15 to 20 percent of infants and children have some form of developmental disability (Urbano, Farness, Lynch, Bener, Rothberg, & Gardner, 1984). The child with a developmental disorder usually presents a spectrum of problems requiring evaluation by more than one discipline. Federal legislation creating University Affiliated Programs (P.L. 88–164—the Mental Retardation and Community Health Centers Construction Act of 1963) was instrumental in establishing this interdisciplinary process as a model of optimal care for children with developmental disabilities. In addition to research and the provision of services, the mandates for these centers were to train medical and allied health professionals in the interdisciplinary team process.

In contrast to the multidisciplinary team, the interdisciplinary team requires group synthesis. After independent evaluations, the various professionals convene to compare data, review findings, and arrive at mutually agreed on recommendations for care and management. This is truly an optimal process for the assessment of developmental disabilities (Urbano et al., 1984). Although each team member has expertise in her or his own discipline, she or he is familiar with that of the others. For this process to work, team members must speak a common language, must have the ability to listen, and must be flexible in their interactions with the team (Dietrich & Dietrich, 1979).

The assessment of developmental disabilities at the Boling Center for Developmental Disabilities at the University of Tennessee Medical Center provides a model of a working interdisciplinary team. Referrals are received at the center from various sources, including schools, public health clinics, private physicians, and mental health clinics. Self-referrals from parents and patients are also accepted. The admissions committee, which is made up of members representing the various disciplines, including pediatrics, reviews each application. Because developmental disabilities are an extremely complex and heterogeneous group of disorders, the choice of team members to involve in the interdisciplinary process is individualized for each child. While team members have expertise in different fields, each individual has been trained in the interdisciplinary process, which optimizes team communication.

In almost all cases, the developmental pediatrician takes part in the team assessment. The role of the pediatrician involves identifying any organic disease process and determining possible etiologies for the presenting condition. This is achieved by history taking, physical examination, neurodevelopmental testing, and obtaining any pertinent laboratory tests. The psychologist also is involved in almost all cases and evaluates the child's cognitive and behavioral functioning through interviews, standardized psychometric instruments, and behavioral assessments. The audiologist's and the speech pathologist's evaluations of communication skills add invaluable information. The social worker provides psychosocial assessment of the child and his or her family relationships.

On the day of the evaluation, the child and parents are seen independently by each discipline. Some centers employ an alternate model where several disciplines are involved in a general intake period that is moderated by a service coordinator. After the intake is completed, the team then disperses for individual formal evaluations. Because this evaluation clinic is a training experience for several disciplines, individual evaluations usually are performed in a room with a one-way window. This affords the other disciplines the opportunity to observe all evaluations without overwhelming the family by having several individuals in the same room. At the end of the day, the individuals involved convene in a staffing conference. It is this meeting that provides the greatest opportunity for communication and exchange of information among the professionals. Since no single developmental problem pertains exclusively to one discipline, without question the views of all team members are equally valued.

Because of the scope and complexity of health care needs of geriatric patients, the interdisciplinary team approach has recently become popular with this group of patients (Schmitt, Farrell, & Heinemann, 1988). In acute care settings, patients may be admitted to geriatric evaluation units (GEUs) that employ a team approach for comprehensive evaluation and treatment. During daily rounds involving all members, the team discusses each patient's progress and often makes recommendations regarding long-term care (Barker, Williams, Zimmer, Van Buren, Vincent, & Pickrel, 1985; Campion, Jett, & Berkman, 1983).

The Veterans Administration utilizes an interdisciplinary team that is involved in comprehensive evaluation and treatment of patients admitted to their Ambulatory Care Center (Rubenstein, Wieland, English,

Josephson, Sayre, & Abrass, 1984). Some geriatric interdisciplinary teams are involved in community settings that provide services through home health plans (Katz, Halstead, & Wierenga, 1975). Although the cost of the interdisciplinary process may initially be higher because of ongoing services, in the long run, the expense is less because several hospital admissions can be avoided.

Transdisciplinary Team Model

The use of transdisciplinary teams is rarely described in the medical literature. This approach, described by Hutchinson (1976) and exemplified in the special education system, emphasizes a sharing of team responsibilities. A manager coordinates the activities of the team professionals and often carries out the recommendations of the team with their full support. Members teach each other both knowledge and skills from their respective disciplines, which are believed to aid in team decision making (Russell, 1988). Examples include the occupational therapist or psychologist who instructs a teacher regarding specific behavior management or exercise routines (Fiscus & Mandell, 1983).

Medical practice, however, is usually problem or diagnosis oriented, which makes the application of this model difficult. Physicians have extensive training and experience that allow them to interview and examine a patient and then decide on assessment measures to identify a diagnosis. This expertise is difficult to pass on to another individual with the idea that these skills can be reduplicated. Certainly there are instances where other health professionals carry out some of the physician's responsibilities. But these individuals usually have been trained and have licensure to perform these tasks. An example is the physician's assistant who performs the initial history and physical examination or writes routine admission or postoperative orders. Several specialties employ clinical nurse specialists or licensed nurse practitioners to help with caseloads. For instance, a clinical nurse specialist can do initial psychiatric assessments, monitor blood pressure medications, see patients in follow-up after a fracture, or perform well-child check-ups. This individual and the medical doctor with whom he or she works can be thought of as a transdisciplinary team, but the doctor is usually legally accountable for the health professionals' actions. Again, the clinical specialist requires a license to perform these functions and to write prescriptions for specific medications.

Another example of a transdisciplinary team is an infant assessment clinic where a pediatrician, nurse, occupational therapist, and nutritionist conduct a joint evaluation to be able to formulate program recommendations. The goal of working together in the evaluation is to allow team members to instruct each other in the knowledge and skills of their respective disciplines to such a degree that each may function adequately in the other's role when necessary (Hart, 1977). While any of the team members may know or learn the specifics of medical history taking, a complete physical exam, including a neurological exam, is not logistically a transdisciplinary task. In the same vein, there are other skills for which the physician is not trained that are better left to other disciplines such as psychometric assessments.

ROLES OF TEAM MEMBERS

Literature discussing modern teamwork in the health professions identifies three specific roles required of its team members (Brill, 1976). The role of specialist is based on knowledge and skill. The leadership role depends on the team structure (multi-, inter-, or transdisciplinary) and the personalities of the team members. The role of the service coordinator relates to the consumer and allows for integration of the total team effort. This individual provides an essential link in an ongoing relationship with the client that enables the client to make maximum use of the services available.

The physician involved in a team evaluation may be required to assume one or more of these three roles. Most often, the physician's role is that of specialist, working in association with other discipline specialists. When discussing the role of the specialist, one can see that one of the problems in team functioning may involve a lack of role definition. Several roles may overlap. Continuous ongoing communication and role negotiation are needed.

An effective team allows for flexibility in roles, providing the opportunity to use the unique talents of each team member without regard to specialty. This adaptability can be anxiety provoking if the individuals involved are not trained in the team approach. In the interdisciplinary team process, training of team members in ongoing role negotiation helps to avoid conflict.

In the multidisciplinary process, role definitions may be poorly communicated because of the lack of proximity among the team members; this may result in conflict. The physician evaluating a patient may decide on a differential diagnosis and discuss this with the patient. The physician may then refer the patient to other specialists for further evaluation to delineate the possible diagnoses. Other specialists may take it on themselves to assume care of the patient without collaborating with the patient's original physician. Patients may become confused if assessments are duplicated or findings are contradictory.

In the transdisciplinary process, the overlap in special abilities may prove useful, for example, in the case of a cardiopulmonary resuscitation (CPR) team on call for emergencies. If one member is missing, usually the other members have sufficient training to perform the necessary procedures.

THE PHYSICIAN AND TEAM LEADERSHIP

Before discussing the physician in the role of the team leader, the various functions of a leader should be reviewed. For the purpose of clarification, the term *team leader* will describe that individual responsible for the coordination of the evaluation process, the integration of findings, or long-term management and coordination of services.

There are various models of leaders, i.e., coordinator, authoritarian figure, or supervisor (Brill, 1976). Responsibilities may vary from managing and arranging meetings, providing liaison with host institutions, and interpreting the work of the team, to working on policies and problems. This individual may chair team meetings, keep time notices during discussions, keep discussions focused, clarify, summarize, and support. This individual may assess and evaluate the work done, the team members themselves, or the overall team process. Although the leader does not perform all of the above roles, he or she is responsible for delegating these jobs. Depending on the type of team process in question and the type of situation involved, the physician may be responsible for any of these functions.

Brill (1976) describes three ways in which any team leader (including a physician) can be assigned: designated, emergent, and situational. The designated leader is selected by the organization or the team. Usually this role is clearly defined. It may involve the specialist role, or it may be purely an administrative position. Sometimes conflict may arise between the roles of the collegial specialists and the administrative authority. The natural or emergent leader arises during the team process.

There may be a designated and emergent leader at the same time. Smooth collaboration is important to effective team functioning. If not, when conflict arises, the team will split. The emergent leader often acts as the dissatisfied enabler of change, usually one of the specialists. For example, the member with the greatest skill and knowledge in a particular area will provide leadership in that effort. This specialized leadership does not encompass the total range of functions for which ongoing responsibility is needed, but it does have a legitimate place in teamwork and is increasingly used as the team matures and makes use of all its members' capacities. Effective team members can accept and work with the fact that the leadership role will move from person to person according to the expertise needed to deal with the particular matter under consideration.

Multidisciplinary Team Leadership

In the multidisciplinary team process, the physician who first sees the patient often assumes the leadership role in a team evaluation and then decides on the need for other specialty consultations. P.L. 99–457, Part H of the Individuals with Disabilities Act, emphasizes prevention and early intervention of developmental disabilities. This requires the cooperation of medical, educational, and therapeutic early intervention services for infants and young children. Children eligible for services under P.L. 99–457 often require a variety of medical specialists, each making a unique and valuable contribution. It is vital, however, that someone assume responsibility for holistic care of these children, coordinate the multiple aspects of their highly specialized treatment, and assist the family with long-range planning (Brewer, McPherson, Magrab, & Hutchins, 1989). Private medical doctors, serving as medical "homes" for children, are in a unique position to respond to their special needs. This physician is an important part of the team, providing leadership in terms of supervision, medical authority, and coordination of services. Through the medical home, specialty care will be viewed in the context of the family, the community, and the child's developmental stage since the physician is familiar with the family over time.

Interdisciplinary Team Leadership

An effective and successful interdisciplinary evaluation relies on the presence of a leader who can unite the team to a common plan of action. This person must be attuned to the interactions within the group, the personality traits of the members, as well as the ultimate needs of the client being evaluated. Sensitivity to the way the team approaches a problem allows the leader to better facilitate the decision-making process. The team leader's responsibilities include dealing with agreement among the members by helping to identify causes of conflict, offering feedback when some members dominate the interactions or show lack of participation, and assuring efficient use of time during staffing conferences.

The developmental pediatrician involved in the interdisciplinary evaluation of a child with a developmental delay often acts as the team leader. In this situation, the developmental pediatrician's specialty training provides the ability to cross over between medical and nonmedical areas with a greater understanding of the complexity of the spectrum of developmental disabilities. With this knowledge, this individual is capable of communicating with other professionals and parents helping them to understand the special needs of the child.

The physician may be designated as team leader. Often the institutions providing interdisciplinary evaluations are funded by training grants. These grants require that trainees of all disciplines be instructed in the interdisciplinary process. This includes observation of other disciplines, including medicine, and acting as team leader.

The physician may emerge as the team leader because of the findings of the case. It is not uncommon that a medical condition is thought to be directly associated with the developmental disorder and thus may be the primary reason for evaluation, e.g., Down syndrome, cerebral palsy, attention deficit hyperactivity disorder, genetic syndromes, or inborn errors of metabolism. At times an unsuspected medical condition may be identified during the evaluation, such as failure to thrive or an abnormal neurologic finding, which may or may not be a contributing factor to the disability but which may need further evaluation. The physician might then assume the role of interpreting recommendations to the family and assuring follow-up. The quality of work accomplished by the team is heavily dependent on the communication skills and decision-making abilities of the participants.

TEAMWORK PROCESSES

The success of any team process is influenced by a number of factors. While the contributions and expertise that each professional brings to the group are invaluable, the quality of the final product is influenced by the leadership provided to the group, the communication skills of the members, the decision-making process, and ultimately the team's accountability for its actions.

In the *multidisciplinary process*, the design and implementation of treatment strategies depend on the personalities and working styles of the team members. The professionals involved are often in different locations so that information must be exchanged via phone contact or written reports. This causes a time delay. Without a team conference, some members may miss out on information obtained by another discipline. Decisions may be more independent of other team member's findings. The client's problems may be addressed in a disjointed manner, which may lead to poor patient compliance. Out in the community, primary care physicians provide a medical home for children with special health care needs, working in collaboration with several other professionals. Because of their close proximity to the patient, primary care providers are an ideal choice for service coordinator to ensure patient compliance. Unfortunately this can be a difficult role for physicians because of time constraints, lack of reimbursement, and limited knowledge about services available.

The *interdisciplinary process* affords the greatest opportunity for each professional to share her or his findings. The decision-making process occurs in an atmosphere of openness and respect. The results are discussed with the client's ultimate well-being in mind. Recommendations are mutually agreed on. Although one individual acts as team coordinator, the opinions of all participants are equally considered. Several examples of physician involvement in the interdisciplinary team have already been mentioned. Some overlap of observations and ideas is to be expected among team members. This redundancy protects against arbitrary decisions or the pursuit of vested interests by an individual team member. Disagreements need to be dealt with in a positive manner, taking into consideration the personalities of the members involved. The team leader must be sensitive to the possible causes of conflict so as to facilitate the team's interactions and to allow for effective problem solving.

Team Accountability

Also impacting on the overall success of the evaluation process is the means by which a team accounts for its actions, legally and professionally. Because each discipline is so specialized, it often is difficult to find one person who can provide the evaluation and instruction of team supervision. Single disciplines award autonomy to their students after sufficient training by conveying licensure. When involved in a team process, it is expected that each member is capable of a degree of autonomous practice in fulfilling the role for which he or she is employed. Through continued teaching and learning, each team member should keep up to date on individual skills. This is true not only in the context of each individual specialty but also in the process of teaming. Increasingly, the instruction of supervision in the modern human service teams is being performed by the teams themselves through the outside use of consultants and workshops (Brill, 1976).

In summary, the evaluation of any individual with multiple problems may be optimized by using a team approach depending on the type of team used. Increasing physician involvement requires training in the team process. Careful choice of a team leader and open communication among team members enhances the decision-making process. Team accountability is enhanced through continued teaching and learning, which ultimately ensure an effective evaluation and intervention process.

TYPICAL PROBLEMS WITH TEAMS IN MEDICAL SETTINGS

The most common problem that arises when a physician is a member of a team is the perception of a hierarchy of authority. Although training of physicians is largely limited to medical issues, team members often believe the physician has a broader scope of knowledge and is able to integrate material in a way that cannot be done by other members. This perception is reinforced if the client's problems involve complicated or highly technical medical issues. Team members may believe that the physician is able to provide the family with an adequate summary of the psychosocial and psychometric data as well as information concerning the biological medical issues.

This perception of a hierarchy of authority also may impinge on the choice of a team leader and a case manager, as well as the assignment of responsibility for client follow-up. The same perceptions of inadequate understanding of the medical issues inhibit other professionals from taking a leadership role when, in fact, the medical condition is usually secondary and the functional limitations in nonmedical spheres are the source of the client's disability and will be the focus of treatment and follow-up.

The delegation of excessive responsibility to the physician does not derive solely from the perceptions of other professionals. Most medical training takes place in acute care hospitals and community-based outpatient clinics where a physician-leader model is the dominant mode. Few physicians receive training in group process or team collaboration unless they specifically plan to enter a field in which these models are used. Developmental pediatrics and rehabilitation medicine are among the few specialties in which physicians receive training as a team member.

POSSIBLE SOLUTIONS TO TEAM PROBLEMS

The solution to the problem of the physician needing to participate as a functioning member of the team ultimately depends on changing currently used models of practice and modifying medical education so that graduates of medical schools and residency programs understand team process and can work in such a setting. Although there is some movement in this direction in fields such as psychiatry, the physician-leader model continues to dominate both practice and medical training.

Additional solutions to the current problems include attempts to clarify authority, define responsibility, and place medical issues in the proper perspective. This last concept has already been commented on. Although the underlying etiology of many problems may derive from a medical condition, the majority of these conditions are static, and the role of medical treatment is limited. Having the team focus on the impairment of psychosocial and psychomotor function will give all team members an equal share of the authority and an equal voice. The role of team leader would then logically devolve on the person whose professional skills most directly focus on the core issues raised by the client. It also is essential that the team leader be able to delegate to other professionals responsibility for appropriate parts of the evaluation, the formulation of a treatment plan, and the discussion of the data and recommendations with the client and family.

Clarification of responsibility raises some issues that are different from those related to clarification of authority. Each team member, including the physician, must have a clear definition of their function on the team, what their evaluation will contribute, and the limits of involvement of their discipline. The definition of function also must be associated with a clear definition of the reporting lines. It is the team leader's responsibility to maintain control over these issues.

THE FUTURE OF TEAMWORK IN MEDICAL SETTINGS

Most programs that have provided interdisciplinary evaluations through the use of large teams, consisting of professionals in many disciplines, are being forced to reconsider the cost and efficiency of this model. Mechanical issues, such as scheduling, assume inordinate importance, and it is often impossible to keep both patient and family on a rigid timetable for one or more days. The logistics of having a sufficient number of professionals in one place at one time are difficult and causes professionals to have blocks of time in which they have no specific tasks. Finally, the failure of a patient to keep an appointment can be devastating and cause a lost workday for a large number of individuals.

Another problem with the large team concept is that of the limited availability of professionals in certain disciplines. It is essential that the team and consultation time of these professionals be closely guarded. It is unrealistic to assume that they must be part of the evaluation of every client.

Two approaches are being taken to improve the efficiency and cost effectiveness of interdisciplinary teams. The first is that of a small generic team with a fixed composition. In many settings, the core disciplines involved in the developmental evaluation of a child are medicine, psychology, speech–language pathology, and social work. Once the child achieves school age, special educators join the core team, and the role of the physician diminishes unless neurologic abnormalities are clearly present or conditions such as attention deficit hyperactivity disorder or seizures are present.

A second approach is the use of specialized teams. These teams can be constructed based on either the needs of clients with specific diagnoses or the needs of clients with specific functional problems. An example of the former would be a clinic for individuals with Down syndrome. An example of a team based on specific functional problems would be a feeding disorder clinic that would serve clients with an inability to eat, chew, or swallow regardless of the underlying medical condition. The role of the physician would then be highly dependent on the nature of the client population served by the team. This role could range from minimal in a clinic for children with conduct disorders to primary in a clinic for children with inherited metabolic disorders.

Although the development of diagnosis or problem-based teams is counter to the trend toward providing generic services for individuals with disabilities, the efficiencies of time and cost and the ability of professionals in all disciplines to develop a specific and detailed body of knowledge make these teams worthwhile. General medical needs still would be met in the generic health care system.

REFERENCES

Barker, W. H., Williams, T. F., Zimmer, J. G., Van Buren, C., Vincent, S. T., & Pickrel, S. G. (1985). Geriatric consultation teams in acute hospitals: Impact on back-up of elderly patients. *Journal of the American Geriatric Society*, 33, 422-428.

Beller, E. K. (1979). Early intervention programs. In J. D. Osofsky (Ed.), *Handbook of infant development* (pp. 852-894). New York: Wiley.

Birkenfeld, A., & Kase, N. (1991). Menopause medicine: Current treatment options and trends. *Comprehensive Therapy*, 17(7), 36-45.

Brewer, E. J., McPherson, M., Magrab, P. R., & Hutchins, V. L. (1989). Family-centered, community-based, coordinated care for children with special health care needs. *Pediatrics*, 83, 1055-1060.

Brill, N. I. (1976). *Teamwork: Working together in the human services*. New York: Lippincott.

Campion, E. W., Jette, A., & Berkman, B. (1983). An interdisciplinary geriatric consultation service: A controlled trial. *Journal of the American Geriatric Society*, 31, 792-796.

Denhoff, E. (1981). Current status of infant stimulation or enrichment programs for children with developmental disabilities. *Pediatrics*, 67, 32-37.

Dietrich, A. P., & Dietrich, W. L. (1979). Educational evaluation of the learning disabled child. In M. I. Gottlieb, P. W. Zinkus, & L. J. Bradford (Eds.), *Current issues in developmental pediatrics: The learning disabled child* (pp. 399-412). New York: Grune & Stratton.

Fiscus, E. D., & Mandell, C. J. (1983). *Developing individualized education programs*. St. Paul, MN: West Publishing.

Haring, N. G., & Hutchinson, T. A. (1982). Serving exceptional individuals: Trends and issues. In N. G. Haring (Ed.), *Exceptional children and youth*. Columbus, OH: Merrill.

Hart, V. (1977). The use of many disciplines with the severely and profoundly handicapped. In E. Sontag, J. Smith, & N. Certo (Eds.), *Educational programming for the severely and profoundly handicapped* (pp. 391-396). Reston, VA: Council for Exceptional Children.

Hamaoi, E., & Nichols, L. O. (1993). The nutrition support team organization and dynamics. In J. L. Rombeau & M. D. Caldwell (Eds.), *Clinical parenteral nutrition* (Vol. 2) (pp. 284-310). Philadelphia: Saunders.

Hazard, R. G., Bendix, A., & Fenwick, J. W. (1991). Disability exaggeration as a predictor of functional restoration outcomes for patients with chronic low-back pain. *Spine, 16,* 1062-1067.

Hutchinson, D. (1976). *A model for transdisciplinary staff development* (Technical Report No. 8). New York: United Cerebral Palsy Association.

Jensen, T., & Dudrick, S. J. (1981). Implementation of a multidisciplinary nutritional assessment program. *Journal of the American Dietetic Association, 79,* 258-266.

Johnson, C. C., Nicklas, T. A., Arbeit, M. L., Harsha, D. W., Molt, D. S., Hunter, S. M., Wattigney, W., & Berenson, G. S. (1991). Cardiovascular intervention for high risk families: The heart smart program. *Southern Medical Journal, 84,* 1305-1312.

Kasuya, A., & Holm, K. (1986). Pharmacologic approach to ischemic stroke management. *Nursing Clinics of North America, 21,* 289-296.

Katz, S., Halstead, L., & Wierenga, M. (1975). A medical perspective on team care. In S. Sherwood (Ed.), *Long-term care: A handbook for researchers, planners and providers* (pp. 213-252). New York: Spectrum.

Messin, R. (1978). Myocardial infarction rehabilitation in 1990. *Acta Cardiologica, 45*(2), 95-99.

Peznecker, B. L., & Paquin, R. (1982). Implementing interdisciplinary team practice in home-care of geriatric clients. *Journal of Gerontological Nursing, 8,* 504-508.

Rubenstein, L. Z., Wieland, G. D., English, P., Josephson, K., Sayre, J. A., &

Abrass, I. B. (1984). The Sepulveda VA geriatric evaluation unit: Data on four-year outcomes and predictors of improved patient outcomes. *Journal of the American Geriatric Society, 32,* 503-512.

Russell, S. C. (1988). Challenges to effective team functioning: Multi-, inter-, trans-disciplinary models. In *Proceedings of the Tenth Annual Interdisciplinary Health Care Team Conference* (pp. 38-45). Bowling Green, OH: College of Health and Human Services, Bowling Green University.

Sadovsky, R. (1991). Psychosocial issues in symptomatic HIV infections. *AFP, 44,* 2065-2072.

Schmitt, M. H. (1982). Research and evaluation on health care teams: How to shoot at a moving target, Part III, Central issues in successful team research efforts. In J. E. Bachman (Ed.), *Interdisciplinary health care: Proceedings of the third annual interdisciplinary team care conference* (pp. 215-220). Kalamazoo, MI: Center for Human Services, Western Michigan University.

Schmitt, M. H., Farrell, M. P., & Heinemann, G. D. (1988). Conceptual and methodologic problems in studying the effects of interdisciplinary geriatric teams. *The Gerontologist, 28,* 753-764.

Thompson, T. (1986). *Communication for health professionals.* New York: Harper & Row.

Urbano, R. C., Farness, S. R., Lynch, E. W., Bender, M., Rothberg, J. M., & Gardner, T. P. (1984). Interdisciplinary evaluation: Types of children referred to UAF clinics and hospitals. *Mental Retardation, 22,* 117-120.

Volberding, P. A. (1989). Supporting the health care team in caring for patients with AIDS. *Journal of the American Medical Association, 261,* 747-748.

9

Community Services and Supports for Persons with Disabilities

Virginia J. Williams and
Tawara D. Taylor

       The deinstitutionalization movement initiated in the 1970s has prompted states across the country to close their large congregate care facilities in favor of a variety of community living alternatives and other support services for people with disabilities. States and communities are currently grappling with the many issues and dilemmas of developing new service delivery systems and approaches for community living that are radically opposed to core principles and established practices in the field. Today marks an era characterized by global, sweeping change as people with disabilities are asserting their right to be valued and included members of this society. There must be a balancing of political, professional, community, legal, and ethical needs in bringing community-based alternatives into existence for persons with disabilities. This represents a formidable challenge for all groups involved. Community living and support systems, therefore, must create a network of comprehensive, integrated, and effective services for all people with disabilities. This chapter will discuss emerging trends in community living and support services for people with disabilities and the models of teamwork that have been developed to provide these services in various settings.

In the past, federal funding to support community-based services was more restrictive than today. Within the past 10 years, however, federal legislation has been enacted or amended to allow for more flexibility in funding community-based services to meet the demands of consumers, families, and advocacy groups. Examples of such legislation include:

1. Title XIX of the Social Security Act Amendments, 1965, which authorized Medicaid;
2. Supplemental Security Income (SSI) (1972);
3. The Vocational Rehabilitation Act (1973);
4. Americans with Disabilities Act (1990);
5. Individuals with Disabilities Education Act (IDEA) (1990); and
6. Community Supported Living Arrangements (1990).

These legislative mandates have created much needed options in the way people with disabilities live and receive services and supports in the community. States are in varying stages of adapting and implementing programs and other service options to transition from institutional to community-based service delivery systems.

The 1990s ushered in a vast array of service and support options for people with disabilities living in their respective communities. Traditionally community-based services have provided for health care, employment, vocational training, respite/crisis intervention, transportation, and recreation. Although these services may have been physically located in community settings, they were indeed segregated and not embraced as a part of mainstream community life. New trends are emerging that recognize the need for community services and supports to be fully integrated, consumer directed, flexible, cost efficient, and effective. For the purposes of this chapter, community services and supports are defined as all resources (fiscal, human, material) that persons with disabilities prefer and need to live, work, and be fully included into their chosen communities.

Current thinking and research in the field support the philosophy that all people with disabilities, regardless of level of severity, can live in the community and be fully included and valued in all aspects of community life. "It is equally clear that in general when compared with institutionalized persons, people living in community settings have substantially better integrated and more typical life experiences" (Hill, Lakin, Bruininks, Amado, Anderson, & Copher, 1989, p. 5).

This philosophy is not limited to residential settings. It is emerging as state-of-the-art practice in vocational settings as well. As Lyn Drucker wrote: "The workshops of today are rapidly becoming a dead-end placement for most persons with mental retardation regardless of their functioning level. It is critical to integrate persons so that they can learn real work skills in a real work environment" (Taylor, Racino, Knoll, & Lutfiyya, 1987, p. 37). There are several jurisdictions in the country that have been successful in putting this philosophy into practice. In 1991, the state of New Hampshire closed its institutions and thereby established a totally community-based system of care and support for persons with mental retardation. The Macomb–Oakland region in Michigan and Madison, Wisconsin, have been cited as exemplary models of community inclusion for people with disabilities. Most recently the District of Columbia, with the closure of its institution, has joined New Hampshire; it is the second jurisdiction in the country to convert to a totally community-based system of service delivery.

Best practices in community living and support services for people with disabilities incorporate the following principles:

- *Best practices are flexible.* Community services and supports recognize and respond to changing needs and preferences of consumers/families by creating innovative options for integrated service delivery.
- *Best practices are consumer directed.* Community services and supports must respect consumers and families basic rights of self-determination and autonomy.
- *Best practices are state-of-the-art.* Community services and supports should reflect the most recent approaches, technologies, and philosophies based on proven research and advances in the field.
- *Best practices are culturally competent.* Community services and supports must embrace the diversity among people who comprise American society today.

These principles serve as a foundation for building a comprehensive community-based system of services and supports for people with disabilities and their families that is accessible, accountable, and fair.

The 1990 census revealed a significant increase in culturally diverse populations in the United States. Due to changing demographics in the United States, there has been recent emphasis placed on cultural diversity in education, social services, and health care delivery systems. It is imperative that teams in the helping professions have the knowledge, skills, and sensitivity to provide services and supports to persons with disabilities and their families from diverse cultural and ethnic heritages.

The following definition of cultural competence was selected from Isaacs and Benjamin (1991), *Towards a Culturally Competent System of Care*:

> The word *culture* is used because it implies the integrated pattern of human behavior that includes thoughts, communications, actions, customs, beliefs, values, and institutions of a racial, ethnic, religious, or social group. The word competence is used because it implies having the capacity to function in a particular way.
>
> Thus, *cultural competence* is defined as a set of congruent behaviors, attitudes, and policies that come together in a system, agency, or amongst professionals and enables that system, agency, or those professionals to work effectively in cross-cultural situations.
>
> According to the authors, five essential elements contribute to a system's institutions, or agency's ability to become more culturally competent. The culturally competent system would: (1) value diversity, (2) have the capacity of cultural self-assessment, (3) be conscious of the dynamics inherent when cultures interact, (4) have institutionalized cultural knowledge, and (5) have developed adaptations to service delivery reflecting an understanding of cultural diversity. Further these five elements would be manifested at every level of an organization—policymaking, administrative, and practice levels— and would be reflected in its attitudes, structures, policies, and services. (pp. 15–16)

MODELS OF TEAMWORK IN COMMUNITY SERVICES AND SUPPORTS

Providers of community services and supports face a myriad of problems in their attempts to deliver services to people with disabilities. Because people with disabilities have such diverse needs, services and supports are frequently required from multiple agencies with varying and often conflicting federal, state, and local mandates. In the field today there are two primary issues that span the entire scope of community living and support services for people with disabilities. These issues, the result of fiscal constraints, limited resources, and changing paradigms, are: (1) how to promote resource sharing at all levels through collaboration, and (2) how to shift from a systems-based model to an individualized or person-centered model. This chapter will present two models of team-work—the community collaborative team and the community member-ship team—which will exemplify how these issues can be addressed to establish and maintain service delivery systems that are both compre-hensive and flexible and allow for replication.

Community Collaborative Team Model

Collaboration among all sectors of the community is essen-tial to ensure that people with disabilities receive the full complement of resources and supports necessary to live productive and meaningful lives. In the interest of the delivery of services and supports that are compre-hensive, efficient, and cost effective, communities must pool existing resources to provide creative and flexible options for people with disabil-ities and their families. To affect change in existing systems or to create new ones, a community collaborative team model may be established.

Melaville and Blank (1991) describe collaboration at the systems level as follows:

> Collaborative ventures at the system level are empowered—politically, by virtue of their members' collective "clout," or legally, by the state or other entity—to negotiate, as well as to advocate for programs and policies leading to more comprehensive service delivery. (p. 17)

This team should have diverse representation from consumers/fami-lies, business, advocacy groups, both public and private service providers, policy-makers, and interested others within communities. Community collaborative teams must have the authority of their local jurisdictions to make decisions on how to allocate existing resources, leverage additional resources, and identify and utilize naturally occurring resources in their respective geographic locales. Additionally, community collaborative teams can affect policy and legislation that allow for the incorporation of best practices into the delivery of services and supports.

An example of a successful model of a community collaborative team can be seen in the District of Columbia. The District of Columbia's insti-tution for persons with mental retardation and other developmental dis-abilities was initially court ordered to close in 1978. Continuing litigation resulted in a final court order that the institution permanently close by

October 1, 1991. The need to establish community-based services and supports for the remaining 250 residents of the institution quickly became evident to the public and private sector alike.

The District of Columbia is somewhat unique when compared to other states in that all community-based residential services are provided by the private sector. Thus, the District government realized its inability to comply with the court order without establishing a community collaborative team.

The D.C. Coalition for Persons with Mental Retardation and Developmental Disabilities was formed in 1988. This coalition cemented a formal agreement between numerous organizations representative of the interests of the disabilities community in the District. Some 20 member agencies belong to this coalition and present a strong and united voice that advocates for persons with disabilities. This coalition has been successful in effecting systems change by (1) impacting on the District's Medicaid reimbursement procedures, (2) influencing the District's budget process and appropriated funds for disabilities programs and services, (3) supporting a citywide training initiative to improve the quality of services provision, and (4) developing and disseminating a position paper to regulate the size of residential programs in the District.

The coalition and the District government worked collaboratively to transition 250 individuals to community-based residential settings in an 18-month period. The effort included expediting building and construction permits, licensing procedures, and zoning variances to accommodate additional homes in neighborhoods. Start-up costs were made available to coalition members to hasten program development. Lastly, individual plans were developed for each person who remained at the institution to facilitate successful transition to newly established homes in the community. When confronted with the most challenging tasks, this community collaborative team model clearly documents that "collective clout" can achieve a common goal.

Community Membership Team Model

Community living and support services should be viewed by the function they provide rather than by agency or source of funding. Policies and procedures must be modified or redefined to break down barriers that hinder innovative approaches to supporting individualized and integrated services and supports to people with disabilities. The provision of community services and supports is based on the strengths and needs of the consumer or family rather than attempts to fit the consumer/family into available programs or service delivery models. To accomplish collaboration at this level, a community membership team model may be adopted. Melaville and Blank (1991) describe collaboration at the service delivery level as follows:

> Instead of focusing on their individual agendas, collaborative partnerships establish common goals. In order to address problems that lie beyond any single agency's exclusive purview, but which concern them all, partners agree to pool resources, jointly plan, implement, and evaluate new services and procedures, and delegate individual responsibility for the outcomes of their joint efforts. (p. 16)

The community membership team model supports the concept that people with disabilities, regardless of severity, will lead lives that allow for work, recreation, and inclusion as valued members of their communities.

Within the community membership team model, there are a variety of models of teamwork needed to support a comprehensive and committed community service delivery system for individuals with disabilities. These models will vary according to locale and specific setting. A model designed to support an individual living in a community residential facility will not be the same as a model for someone living in their natural home. Teams must be designed in support of the individual as opposed to designed to promote or support a system. The following sections discuss functioning community membership team models in three different settings: (1) an adult dependent living in his natural home, (2) an adult living independently, and (3) an adult living in a supported residence.

Team 1: An Adult Dependent Living in His Natural Home

John J. is 35 and has multiple severe disabilities. His family agreed that he will live at home despite the severity of his disabilities. His parents believe the natural home setting provides the best opportunity for growth for their son. The team that provides his care has several members. John J.'s parents are the designated team leaders with ample support from a case manager from the state Bureau of Developmental Services. Other members of the team include John J.'s health care providers, a nurse from the Visiting Nurses Association, his primary care physician, a member of a local community volunteer group, and a habilitation counselor from a private non profit organization.

John J.'s habilitation counselor convenes an annual meeting to discuss the past year's accomplishments and to plan for the upcoming year. His parents, health care provider, and case manager are usually in attendance. The issue with which the team is grappling this year is long-range planning for John J.'s continuing supports in the event of his parents' death or if they are no longer able to provide for his care. If concerns arise during the year that warrant a team meeting, either John J.'s parents or his case manager will convene a meeting or negotiate matters through telephone conferences.

John J.'s parents share equal partnerships with other professionals on the team. Team members provide specific knowledge and skills. However, John J.'s parents, as the team leaders, are free to make ultimate decisions about his care according to their own values and beliefs. John J. is unable to make major decisions about his habilitation, health care, or finances. However, he is encouraged to make choices in many aspects of his daily life among equally desirable alternatives. This team approach illustrates the practice of consumer-directed services.

Team 2: An Adult Living Independently

Rose B. is 27 and resides in a ground floor apartment complex. She is dependent on a wheelchair as her primary means of mobility. She is employed as a computer operator. Rose B. assumes leadership in coordinating the care and supports she needs to live independently. Other members of the team include personal assistants from the local United Cerebral Palsy Association, a physical therapist in private practice, a neighbor who is a close personal friend, and a case manager from the state Vocational Rehabilitation Administration.

Rose B. is the team leader. She is fully aware of her strengths and needs and uses team members to assist her in accessing services and providing only those supports necessary for her independence. Rose B. uses public transportation to travel to and from work. She encountered difficulty with the Regional Transit Authority ensuring routine availability of an accessible vehicle with a wheelchair lift. Rose B. convened a meeting with appropriate team members to discuss strategies to assist her in advocating for reliable and accessible public transportation services in her community. This approach illustrates the practices of needs-based and consumer-directed supports.

Team 3: An Adult Living in a Supported Residence

Bobby T. is 45 and resides with one other adult in a newly renovated condominium. He and his housemate chose to live with one another prior to a recent move from a state institution. The home is one of several owned by the state government that can be purchased through a first-time home ownership program. Support services to Bobby T. and his housemate are provided through a contract with a community agency funded by the state.

This community agency is a grass roots organization that has a long history of involvement and advocacy for people with disabilities. Its most recent initiative was to assist persons with severe disabilities to find permanent housing and coordinate support services necessary for them to live as independently as possible.

The agency also is responsible for selecting and assigning a case manager and counselors to assist Bobby in his transition from the institution to the community. Bobby T. is a vocal member of his team, headed by a senior counselor, which includes his brother who has always been actively involved in his life. The team meets monthly. Issues of primary importance that the team has identified are finding employment for Bobby T., assisting him with access to public transportation, and managing the many household responsibilities associated with his new home. This team illustrates an emerging thrust to separate housing from the delivery of services. It also supports the concept of home ownership for people with disabilities.

Analysis and Discussion

In all the teams described, we see the use of natural and existing supports. John J. is himself a volunteer with the local humane society. With the assistance of a volunteer, he helps provide care to animals at an animal shelter. Rose B. has close personal friends and neighbors with whom she enjoys recreational and leisure pursuits. Bobby T. visits with his brother on weekends and holidays and participates fully in regular family routines. These community membership team models allow for flexible lifestyles that promote full community inclusion of persons with disabilities.

Each team model represents a different approach to the provision of community services and supports. These community membership team models represent emerging trends and best practices in the field, including: (1) consumer-directed services; (2) needs-based, individualized, and integrated services; (3) use of natural and existing supports; (4) separation of housing from the delivery of services; and (5) potential for home ownership.

In the three community membership team models presented, services and supports are mandated by the needs and preferences of the consumer/family as opposed to the dictates of a system. Policies and funding sources in these respective communities have allowed for individualization, choice, and a least-intrusive approach to community living.

Leadership in these community membership team models varied according to the setting and membership varied based on individual needs and preferences. Each community membership team model functioned differently; however, there are basic fundamental principles and practices inherent in any functioning team. Leadership, communication, decision making, and accountability are essential elements of a functioning team. The following section is devoted to these fundamental principles and practices, typical problems inherent in functioning teams, and some possible solutions.

ISSUES AND PROBLEMS IN TEAM FUNCTIONING

Team Leadership

The disabilities field is fraught with politicalization, special interest groups, fads, and entrenched traditionalism. The challenge of effective leadership is to unite team members in a shared vision and create the environment needed to allow the vision to become reality. This may seem like a formidable task given the differing issues representative of the disabilities movement. However, there is a common thread that links all members of the disabilities community. An effective leader will recognize the strengths of these common interests that allow team members to remain committed to the shared vision. Melaville and Blank (1991), authors of *What It Takes*, describe effective leadership as follows:

The quality of leadership greatly influences the process of agreeing on a common goal and negotiating a practical vision. Effective leaders press each side to understand their partners' point of view and the way they perceive the issues and problems at hand. Leaders generate alternative solutions and pursue, from the many interests identified, those that constitute common ground. A leader's ability to keep participants focused on goals prevents individual interests from derailing the initiative during the difficult process of determining how shared goals will be met and encourages partners to contribute to the full extent of their abilities. A leader focuses not only on the internal process of the group, but represents its goals and interests to the community at large and cultivates potential allies. (p. 25)

Challenges that leaders of community collaborative teams and community membership teams may encounter include:

- Establishing and maintaining trust among team members when there has been a history of adversarial relationships;
- Effectively and equitably sharing limited resources among competing needs;
- Affecting change in federal, state, and local policies that hinder full access to services and supports across disability groups;
- Assigning roles and responsibilities that ensure all team members' individual contributions are valued and respected; and
- Maintaining working relationships among team members despite turnover in personnel.

Some Possible Solutions to Leadership Issues

It is a difficult task to bring about solutions to problems that exist in service delivery systems that have been inherent in those systems for decades. When these systems are challenged to shift to a team partnership or community approach, the task is even greater.

The mission and goals of any functioning team must be clearly established. The team leader can play a critical role in bringing this about. The process by which a community team reaches the mission statement can be as important as the mission itself. First, all members of the community team must reach consensus on the mission. The team leader may have to facilitate negotiation and compromise to accomplish this feat. Second, the mission should include a statement reflecting intended outcomes as this encourages a shared vision. "The mission serves as the overall guiding direction for the team's efforts. It is the link between the statement of beliefs and the subsequent activities engaged in by the team" (Magrab, Elder, Kazuk, Pelosi, & Weigerink, 1981, p. 18).

Overcoming Territoriality

Dispelling territoriality and turfism is a tremendous task for the leader of any community team. State agencies, private agencies, and consumer/advocacy groups have not always developed partnerships of trust. The team leader must bring all involved parties to the table and ensure them of equal standing and mutual respect in their collaborative endeavors. The team leader assists the community team in the identification of gaps in services, overlapping services, and review of legislative or regulatory mandates of agencies to eliminate conflicting commitments. In a trusting environment, agencies and consumer groups will be more apt to cross traditional boundaries because the benefits of mutual collaboration outweigh the limitations inherent in a single approach. Collaboration enables providers to get as much mileage as possible out of available resources and to improve the quality and range of services (Melaville & Blank, 1991).

Sharing Resources Through Interagency Agreements

Encouraging the pooling and sharing of limited resources in a time when many special interest groups are competing for the same dollars is more than a challenge for any team leader. Community team members must commit resources of all kinds to assist in team growth and the development toward a comprehensive system of supports for persons with disabilities. Committed resources may consist of fiscal supports, shared staff time and expertise, in-kind contributions, volunteers, and shared physical space and equipment. The goal in resource sharing is to make the commitments permanent, not short lived, based on team membership or other administrative or political changes. The team leader should facilitate the establishment of binding interagency agreements. The team leader also should develop awareness and promote partnerships with individuals and organizations outside of the disabilities movement to foster a broader base for community inclusion.

Changing Policies

Community teams must influence policy decisions that hinder access to services across disability groups. Community team leaders can expand the scope of their involvement by participating and encouraging other team members to participate on local, state, and regional boards that impact policy. This may involve extensive advocacy to amend legislation or the development of new legislation that promotes best policy and practices in the provision of services and supports to people with disabilities.

Using Power Fairly and Effectively

Lastly, the team leader has primary responsibility for ensuring that the process of establishing and assigning roles for each community team member is fair and just. Nurturing leadership is as important as leadership itself. The team leader must have the ability to exercise power when needed, broker power among all team members, and use the collective clout of the community team to wield influence in its local surroundings and in the society at large.

The team leader must be particularly sensitive to human factors that are always present in all aspects of a functioning team.

> Problems in team life can subvert the accomplishment of important tasks. Lack of responsibility, feelings of apathy and impotence, and competitiveness on the part of members can fragment and diffuse the energy of the group towards integration of group and personal goals. Individual members' relationship to control over the process of the team may also create problems for the team. Hostility and rebellion on the part of group members can prevent the group from achieving problem solving and mutual reliance. (Magrab et al., 1981, p. 25)

The team leader must create an atmosphere based on openness, mutual respect, and trust. Such an atmosphere will mitigate human factors that can hinder team functioning.

Problems in Team Communication

Effective communication among team members is essential. Communication must be respectful, timely, clear, and concise. The team leader can be instrumental in setting the tone for communication among team members. "Every leader ought to know how to paraphrase, summarize, express feelings, disclose personal information, admit mistakes, respond nondefensively, ask for clarification, solicit different views and so on" (Kouzes & Posner, 1990, p. 181). These behaviors promote an atmosphere in which effective communication is encouraged and valued among all team members.

There are a number of communication problems facing community teams. Some are at the interpersonal level while others are at the systems level. An example of a typical systems communication problem is that different terminology and language are used from agency to agency to refer to people with disabilities and the services they require. Another emerging problem confronting community teams, which spans both the interpersonal and systems level, is communication with the increasing number of individuals from diverse cultures who do not speak English as a first language. A particularly challenging problem is the establishment and maintenance of a system that utilizes all modes of advanced communication technologies and ensures full access by all team members.

Some Possible Solutions to Team Communication Problems

Building effective communication systems for community teams serving the broad range of persons with disabilities is a herculean task. Service delivery and support systems, guided by agency-specific regulations and eligibility criteria, have differing language and terminology to describe the populations they serve. A set of common terms, criteria, or definitions accepted by community team members would break down this barrier. Cross-training of staff in participating agencies will eliminate conflict in the use of different terminology.

The changing demographics of the American population presents an even greater challenge to effective communication at the systems and interpersonal levels. According to the U.S. Census Bureau, over the last decade the number of Asian Americans more than doubled and the Latino/Hispanic population grew by more than 50 percent (Isaacs & Benjamin, 1991). Community team members need to be knowledgeable about the cultural diversity of persons with disabilities in their respective locales. Providers of community services and supports must develop modes of communication that reach groups whose first language is not English. A communication system based only on the language of the majority of the population is a barrier to full access to services. To mitigate the effects of this barrier to service delivery, agencies should hire multilingual staff, use volunteers as translators, disseminate multilingual publications, and modify telecommunication systems.

Technology and state-of-the-art modes of communication can assist community team members in sharing information in a timely and efficient manner. Community team members should have access to the same information. This fosters trust among team members as all feel equally important and valued. The community team needs to maintain current information and mandates of new or changing federal, state, and local policies impacting on the delivery of community services and supports to persons with disabilities. The communication system must allow for the sharing of such information among community team members and their constituents.

Problems in Team Decision Making

When presented with varying and conflicting opinions, making a decision is a most difficult task; community teams are faced with this on a regular basis. Effective decision making is critical to facilitate optimum functioning of any team. All team members have a responsibility to participate in the decision-making process and may play different roles. "Teams that are effective usually have members who can fill a diversity of roles. Members must feel as if they contribute something that is essential to the decision-making process to maintain their commitment" (Magrab et al., 1981, p. 33).

Problems arise when there is no established framework in which team decisions are reached or when there are poor procedures for decision making. Problems also may arise in the decision-making process when a lack of respect and trust is felt among team members. As a result, team members' behaviors may be characterized by hostility, impatience, apathy, and lack of cooperation. Such behaviors will impede the progress of any team.

Some Possible Solutions to Team Decision Making

The decision-making process of a team solicits the collective views, ideas, and philosophies of all team members. To ensure that all team members are fully included, teams need to periodically assess their decision-making processes. A strategy for assessing team decision making is presented by Magrab et al. (1981) in *Developing a Community Team.* The following questions can assist teams in accomplishing this task.

1. Is the atmosphere of the community team conducive to your active participation on the team?
2. What is the level of commitment of team members to the mission of the community team?
3. What is the level of trust and respect among team members?
4. Do most members participate in important decisions? Which members get left out? Why?
5. To what extent are members satisfied with the process and outcomes of the problem-solving approach of the community team?
6. To what extent are you as a group member maximizing your potential to contribute to the decision-making process? (p. 33)

Team members must determine the method by which decisions are made and the roles different members may assume. These roles can be interchangeable and may include giving or seeking suggestions, soliciting information or opinions, summarizing ideas for the group, or coordinating follow-up activities for decisions agreed on by the team. In the event of a conflict, some members may play the role of mediator. All roles are crucial to the decision-making process.

Problems in Team Accountability

Accountability in the human service field has been slow in coming and even slower in the disabilities movement. Historically, accountability has taken the form of responding to mandated federal, state, and local regulations and has been largely punitive in nature. The move away from institutional systems of care to community living and individualized systems of services and supports demands an effective and reliable system of accountability that fully assesses the following: (1) the outcomes of the various services delivered, (2) the quality of the services delivered, (3) consumer/family satisfaction with services delivered, and (4) overall cost effectiveness. Components of an effective system of accountability include timely documentation, monitoring, and evaluation of service delivery. A number of problems related to accountability are encountered by a collaborative community team model and a community membership team model at the policy and the direct services levels. These problems may include:

- Meeting federal and state regulations, guidelines, or standards that may be rigid and simultaneously develop new service and support options that are flexible and creative;
- Ensuring that funds for community services and supports are expended appropriately and responsibly;
- Designing and implementing procedures for evaluating the outcomes compared to the costs of community services and supports;
- Involving consumers/families, advocates, providers of service and supports and interested others in ensuring quality services are delivered; and
- Ensuring that community services and supports delivered in the natural home setting are accountable without being intrusive to the consumer/family.

Some Possible Solutions to Team Accountability

Systems of accountability for community services and supports for people with disabilities must undergo radical change during this decade. Community teams will be challenged to develop new systems of accountability that place less emphasis and resources on facility mandates.

The optimum residential settings for persons with disabilities are homes. The level of accountability—documentation, monitoring, and evaluation of services—necessary in a home should be minimally intrusive to the consumer/family. However, this does not negate the need for ensuring that both quality services are indeed delivered and vulnerable consumers/families are protected.

Increased emphasis must be placed on assessing consumer/family satisfaction with the services and supports they receive. This has been a long-neglected area as people with disabilities had to settle for the services that were available. Changing the paradigm from institutional systems of care to individualized and person-centered modes of service delivery and supports dictates that different standards be developed. Accountability systems will need to redesign procedures that measure quality of services delivered and outcomes for consumers and families. At the systems level, Taylor et al. (1987) propose development and funding of a community-monitoring group consisting of parents, consumers, and interested citizens to look at quality-of-life issues in existing community homes. At the direct service level, if consumers and families are given the choice and power to select their own services, invariably individuals and agencies providing mediocre or inferior services will be eliminated.

Cost efficiency will be an important component of newly developed systems of accountability. Kaiser and McWharton (1990) (p. 235) comment:

> There is considerable pressure to earmark funds for specific programs and to write legislation that clearly delimits use of funding. While the pressures are understandable in times of limited resources, they may mitigate against the design of flexible programs to serve persons with a range of disabilities in individualized appropriate ways.

Taylor et al. (1987) suggest establishing self-advocacy initiatives that would include fiscal support for independent advisors for people with disabilities and their families. It is through such advocacy efforts that consumers and families can wield influence, affect change, and ensure accountability at the local and state levels that funding options remain flexible.

To examine cost efficiency in service provision further, communities can conduct surveys of existing services to identify the needs and gaps in these service delivery systems. In times of fiscal restraint, it is essential that duplication and underutilization of services be eliminated. To assist in this effort, communities may develop cluster groups consisting of area service providers, parents, consumers, and interested citizens to review proposed services.

THE FUTURE OF TEAMWORK IN THE DISABILITIES FIELD

All people with disabilities, regardless of level of severity, can live in the community and be fully included and valued in all aspects of community life. If this vision is to be accomplished, cooperation and collaboration among the helping professions are mandatory. "In order to transform our current system and change institutional dimensions that foster single issue, crisis-oriented services, agencies must make substantial changes in the ways they have traditionally done business" (Melaville & Blank, 1991, p. 15).

Team building is not a new phenomenon of the helping professions in the disabilities field. The future of these teams, however, is dependent on successful expansion outside of the field to establish collaborative relationships with broader segments of society. Collaboration is the key to the future of teamwork in the disabilities field.

Community teams must continue to be advocates, change agents, policy-makers, and power brokers for the ever-changing needs and demands of persons with disabilities and their families. Community teams must assume leadership in closing the gaps between most recent and proven best practices and existing policies and regulations that often lag far behind. In the future, community teams must influence policy to ensure that adequate levels of funding and resources remain available to provide for the myriad of services and supports needed to promote optimum quality of life for persons with disabilities.

Community teams must assume accountability for ensuring fiscal resources are utilized efficiently, are not duplicative, and are equitably distributed among urban and rural settings in their respective jurisdictions. Community teams must be proactive by anticipating needs. The future will depend on visionary and strategic planning if community teams are to succeed in ensuring full inclusion and comprehensive services and supports to persons with disabilities and their families.

REFERENCES

Hill, B. K., Lakin, C. K., Bruininks, R. H., Amado, A. N., Anderson, D. J., & Copher, J. I. (1989). *Living in the community: A comparative study of foster homes and small group homes for people with mental retardation.* Minneapolis, MN: University of Minnesota.

Isaacs, M., & Benjamin, M. (1991). *Towards a culturally competent system of care, Vol. II, Monograph.* Washington, DC: Georgetown University Child Development Center.

Kaiser, A. D., & McWhorter, C. M. (1990). Contemporary policy and best practice. In A. P. Kaiser & McWhorter (Eds.), *Preparing personnel to work with persons with severe disabilities.* Baltimore: Paul H. Brookes.

Kouzes, J. M., & Posner, B. Z. (1990). *The leadership challenge.* San Francisco: Jossey-Bass.

Magrab, P., Edler, J., Kazuk, E., Wiegerink, R., & Pelosi, J. (1981). *Developing a community team*. Washington, DC: Georgetown University Child Development Center.

Melaville, A., & Blank, M. (1991). *What it takes: Structuring interagency partnerships to connect children and families with comprehensive services*. Washington, DC: Education and Human Services Consortium.

Taylor, S. J., Racino, J. A., Knoll, J. A., & Lutfiyya, Z. (1987). *The nonrestrictive environment: On community integration for people with the most severe disabilities*. Syracuse, NY: The Human Policy Press.

10 □□□
□□□
□□□

Teamwork in Programs for Older Persons

Judith A. Hernan

INTRODUCTION

Need for Interdisciplinary Teams

The following example of an older person's health problems and losses may appear to be both negative and exaggerated, but it is not an unusual situation for health care professionals to encounter. Older adults' chronic illnesses often coexist with and directly affect many other changes related to the aging process.

Mrs. J., a 75-year-old diabetic widow who lives alone, has begun treatment of ulcerated areas on her legs due to impaired blood circulation. Her decreased mobility related to this treatment (such as elevation of her legs) is causing significant stiffness of her arthritic hips. The longer the decreased mobility continues, the greater impact it will have on her ability to care for herself.

Mrs. J. has been preparing and injecting insulin to control her diabetes, but aging changes in her eyes, as well as visual changes caused by the diabetes, have made it increasingly difficult for her to do this accurately. Because of her visual and mobility deficits, there is also a potential for social isolation, which may lead to emotional and psychological problems.

Another chronic illness, congestive heart failure, is being treated with a digitalis preparation. Aging changes in Mrs. J.'s body, however, create a distinct risk for drug toxicity. This may cause disorientation or visual blurring, thus complicating her health status further. Compliance with dietary treatment of her illnesses also is affected by impaired mobility, inability to read food labels clearly, and her limited finances.

Mrs. J. owns her home, but the two-story structure has no first floor bathroom. A son and his wife who live nearby have attempted to help Mrs. J., but full-time jobs and other family pressures impede their efforts. They express deep concern regarding Mrs. J.'s situation but expect that total physical and mental decline will be the only eventual outcome.

Because Mrs. J. is experiencing numerous and varied physical and psychosocial assaults, the treatment of her ulcerated legs must take the impact of all these factors into account. Therefore, how can any one health care discipline possibly meet this person's complex array of physical, emotional, and psychological needs?

If Mrs. J. is hospitalized, her length of stay will be limited because of the Medicare prospective payment system with which hospitals must comply. Because there are reimbursement ceilings for specific diagnoses, hospitals have a financial incentive to limit a person's stay as much as possible. During Mrs. J.'s possibly brief hospitalization, she would be approached, examined, and questioned by physicians, nurses, social worker, dietitian, physical therapist, and members of other health care disciplines. Her resulting treatment plan may be either fragmented, incomplete, or characterized by overlap and duplication of services.

When she is discharged from the hospital, a home health agency may expand Mrs. J.'s services in a more comprehensive manner, but a true interdisciplinary effort may be restricted by time, resources, and the limited or nonexistent availability of a physician as part of a functioning team. If she is admitted to a nursing facility on a short- or long-term basis, the same need to view Mrs. J. from the perspective of various disciplines would exist. But could that nursing home provide a collaborative, restorative approach to her care, or would her treatment continue to be fragmented?

Basis and Rationale for a Team Approach

The popular rationale for utilizing the interdisciplinary team approach to patient care can be applied to many age groups and situations. One of the primary arguments for interdisciplinary care addresses the need for treating the "whole person" instead of having a fragmented focus. Other reasons include preventing duplication of services, providing an efficient method of service delivery, and ensuring prompt access to the expertise of more than one health care discipline. The overriding emphasis is on interdependence of team members, for the collaborative effort and product of the whole team are greater than the sum of each member's individual contribution.

On the basis of this rationale, it is apparent that interdisciplinary teamwork for many health care recipients may indeed be a desirable model. But for an older population, the need for such an approach is even more emphatic, as illustrated by the example of Mrs. J. Treating the whole person takes on added complexity in aging, requiring the expertise and perspectives of various health care disciplines to work collaboratively. This is because an older adult's "primary" illness rarely exists in isolation. Unlike the acute illnesses of many younger persons, several other health problems, usually chronic in nature, may be superimposed onto the older individual's current problem, thus complicating and broadening the scope of treatment (Steinberg, 1983; Reilly, 1990).

Coexisting with these multiple problems, and further affecting health care delivery, are age-related factors that may include psychological, social, cultural, economic, and other issues. As Shepard, Yeo, and McGann (1985) state:

> The elderly population does not fit well into a disease-oriented, acute model of health care provision. . . . Patients and their families who must live with long-term illness and disability are likely to develop social and psychological problems. . . . Interdisciplinary health care provision requires health care professionals who understand the presence and interrelatedness of these problems. . . . (p. 300)

Other authors echo this view, recommending an interdisciplinary team model to meet the multiple needs of older persons (Croen, Hamermann, & Goetzel, 1984; Whall & Conklin, 1985). Participation on a geriatric team also has been viewed as a worthwhile experience, marked by "the enthusiasm of team members, the positive approach to solving difficult problems, and the sharing of responsibilities in decision making" (Thompson, Rhyne, Stratton, & Franklin, 1988, p. 797).

Adding great relevance to the need for an interdisciplinary approach is the rapidly increasing number of older people, many of whom will enter the health care system. "With our elderly population steadily increasing, an exploration of how an interdisciplinary approach can provide a legitimate and effective base for programs on geriatric care takes on new importance. . . . The potential for team practice in geriatrics is enormous" (Bottom, 1980, pp. 106–107).

Other Models of Care

The traditional model of health care may involve the physician as the initial or possibly only contact person in spite of the existence of multilevel problems. A related model, as illustrated in the example of Mrs. J., tends to expand this physician/patient dyad but remains fragmented in its approach. The physician sees the patient initially, and in turn the person is questioned and assessed by a parade of health care professionals each of whom develops treatment approaches independently. These professionals may never meet to discuss goals and plans of care or to collaborate in any way. Their efforts, therefore, might be characterized by overlap, duplication of services, competition, lack of coordination of services, and a sense of territoriality that ignores the need for diverse professional perspectives.

The older person, at a disadvantage, thus may be faced with the time-consuming process of trying to arrange or remember multiple appointments and sort out various sets of instructions from individual disciplines. For many frail older persons this process can be an overwhelming aggravation and perhaps an impossible endeavor. For the hospitalized or institutionalized older person, even the answering of repetitious questions asked by one health care discipline after another can be exhausting, annoying, and confusing.

KEY ELEMENTS FOR TEAMWORK

Functional Assessment of Older Adults

Perhaps one of the most critical ingredients in the care of older persons, and one that seems to demand an interdisciplinary effort, is that of functional assessment, or an identification of a person's ability to perform activities of daily living. The immense impact that illness can have on a person's self-care and independence is illustrated in the example of Mrs. J. For a given illness or problem, however, there is no set pattern of how it affects each older individual's physical and mental functioning in day-to-day living (Eastman, 1983; Rowe, 1985).

The effect of illness or aging on functional ability varies greatly from person to person. It is the interdisciplinary team's responsibility to assess this functional response and then provide a comprehensive, realistic plan of care based on that particular individual's strengths, abilities, and needs (Tsukada, 1990). Using a functional approach to care is in direct contrast to a *medical model*, which tends to focus narrowly on medical treatment of an illness rather than including the many other ramifications. A medical model clearly is not sufficient or broad enough to meet the many needs of an older population (Rameizl, 1984). It is the interdisciplinary team approach that moves away from a narrow focus toward a comprehensive model of care, which can be facilitated through the team's use of functional assessment instruments (assessment forms) such as those described by Rameizl (1984) or Kane and Kane (1983).

An example is the CADET instrument described by Rameizl. It provides a model of assessing and scoring an individual's abilities related to communication, ambulation, daily living activities, elimination, and transfer. Such an instrument is best used together with a mental status examination that assesses orientation, reasoning, judgment, memory, and other aspects of mental health. In this author's experience in several long-term care settings, including that of a continuing care retirement community, the use of instruments such as the CADET provides valuable insight as well as a basis from which any change in the older person can be measured.

Attitudes Toward Aging

Inherent in the interdisciplinary model of care is the issue of attitudes about aging and care of older adults. Are team members proponents of "custodial" care only, or do they believe that improvement and rehabilitation of older persons may be achievable goals? Do the elderly and their families expect illness and mental decline to be irrevocable parts of aging? What myths and stereotypes about the aging process can be identified, explored, and replaced by knowledge?

Attitudes toward aging may affect, in a positive or negative manner, expectations of what can and should be done in the care of older persons (Rao, 1977; Hernan, 1984). A recognition by team members that aging

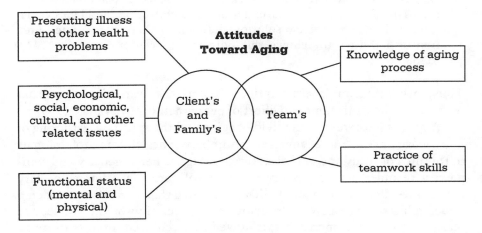

FIGURE 10.1 Components of interdisciplinary teamwork in care of older adults.

itself is not synonymous with illness promotes a positive attitude, plus a realization that older people require and deserve far more than merely a custodial level of care. Concurrent with attitudinal awareness, the team's knowledge of gerontology—the study of the aging process, geriatrics—treatment of illness in aging, and interdisciplinary teamwork skills is also a crucial factor in planning care for older persons. Figure 10-1 illustrates the interrelated factors of attitudes and educational needs that are important components of interdisciplinary teams who serve older adults.

Preparing for Teamwork

Although the treatment and prevention of multiple problems of older persons may be more effective with an interdisciplinary approach, providing this model of care may not be an easy task. The mere convening of a group of health care professionals does not in itself constitute an interdisciplinary team, especially one geared toward working with an older population (Garner, 1988).

The "team" should not be composed of professional members thrown together by chance or order, but should consist of a deliberately selected group of health workers who bring complementary knowledge, skill, and expertise to the situation. Patient care is approached by team members on the basis of joint problem formulation, data collection, problem evaluation, goal setting, problem solution, outcome prediction, and determination of activities to achieve this outcome. (Given & Simmons, 1977, p. 168)

Thus, becoming an interdisciplinary team is a learned process that requires the commitment and effort of every member (Mariano, 1989).

A growing interest in the field of aging and the resultant gathering of knowledge have attracted increasing numbers of health care professionals to this area of study and practice. Recognizing the heterogeneity and complexity of older persons, many members of geriatric interdisciplinary teams have discovered great challenge in a field that was once considered undesirable or nonexistent. In addition, appreciation of the concept of teamwork has been increasing, followed by a renewed interest in interdisciplinary team training and development strategies such as those described by Rubin, Plotnick, and Fry (1975), Dyer (1977), Johnson and Johnson (1982), and Thompson et al. (1988).

It becomes crucial, then, that a team which serves older adults must secure or update knowledge of aging and of the many issues that surround this developmental process, as well as learn and apply the skills necessary for working collaboratively with other disciplines. It is the integration of these two factors that provides the key to interdisciplinary team care of older people.

It is important to note, however, that many aspiring interdisciplinary teams, in spite of a resurgence of interest in teamwork, do not have adequate training for this undertaking. This deficit often reaches back to their preprofessional educational programs, wherein the concept of collaboration with other disciplines may not have been addressed or encouraged (Given & Simmons, 1977). The roots of territoriality may sprout and take hold during this phase and eventually result in a limited approach to care that may be at the expense of the person receiving the care (Bufford & Kindig, 1974). A parallel to this educational gap is the paucity of courses on aging offered in many academic programs. Although such courses are becoming more prevalent, it is still unlikely that all geriatric team members will have had formal education in aging, and quite probable that an interdisciplinary approach may be new to some team members.

Components of Teamwork Education

In an attempt to meet the need for education in aging, many workshops or continuing education seminars are currently being offered for practicing health care professionals, often from an interdisciplinary perspective. There is also a growing effort to implement innovative team programs within some health care facilities. A major program for both practicing professionals and graduate students in health care, focusing on the integration of teamwork skills and the practice of geriatrics, is prominent at a number of Veterans Affairs medical centers across the country. This effective program provides advanced students with the education and experience needed to function as contributing members of a geriatric interdisciplinary team.

Although an introduction to interdisciplinary teamwork skills may also be a useful addition to the curricula of undergraduate or basic professional programs, beginning students may not be ready to incorporate the concept of interdisciplinary collaboration into their early clinical practice. As Ducanis and Golin (1979) state:

> It may well be that students are not ready to profit fully from an interdisciplinary team experience until they have developed sufficient clinical or professional skills to have some degree of confidence in their identities and abilities. Only then can they truly represent their profession to other members of the team so that all can learn from each other. (p. 161)

In other words, it is important that students first have an opportunity to develop a firm identity within their own professions. Only then can one have the openness and security to accept and respond to the challenge that interdisciplinary teamwork creates and fosters.

Because the inclusion of team training in the early levels of professional education may be questionable and because many practicing professionals also are not versed in this concept, there may be considerable merit in offering such training through a continuing education model. Besides the study of aging, interdisciplinary team programs or seminars might include teamwork skills such as role clarification, decision making, problem solving, and conflict management. All are highly relevant to well-functioning geriatric teams, for "the value of the individual to the team is based on his contributions to the problem-solving effort" (Feiger & Schmitt, 1979, p. 218). By participating in such programs, team members who have limited academic preparation in the field of aging may increase their recognition that the complex needs of older adults require not only discipline-specific knowledge, but the combined expertise of many health care disciplines.

Other educational programs that have addressed the provision of interdisciplinary care have been reviewed by Shepard, Yeo, and McGann (1985), who compiled a list of 10 components of successful interdisciplinary education gleaned from their study of many existing programs. These concepts help provide an educational guideline and rationale for determining "which students to include at what levels of education and which topics should be taught and by whom" (p. 297). The successful components of interdisciplinary education have been identified as follows:

1. Emphasis on clinical science content;
2. Real or simulated clinical experiences;
3. Students with established professional identities;
4. Complex and thought-provoking materials;
5. Educators from many health care disciplines;
6. Interdisciplinary team experience;
7. Exposure to real-life problems related to finance and health care regulations;
8. Short, interspersed educational experiences;
9. Student peer teaching; and
10. Course scheduling responsive to student needs.

Although directed toward academic interdisciplinary programs, the components offer a worthwhile framework for the teaching of interdisciplinary teamwork to both advanced students and seasoned health care professionals.

DESCRIPTION OF A FUNCTIONING TEAM

Team Task Performance

To illustrate the functioning of an interdisciplinary geriatric team that is committed to team care and experienced in its application, the following example based on the collective observations and experiences of this author in a long-term care setting is offered. Following this illustration is a description of this team's efforts to support and nurture its members through various team maintenance behaviors, as well as the identification of several underlying problems and issues the team faces in this health care setting.

Composition and Leadership

At 9 A.M., the weekly meeting time set by this team, the members enter the conference room of a continuing care retirement community that includes a long-term care nursing facility. The team is composed of nurses (including a gerontological nurse practitioner), a physician (on a limited basis), social workers, a dietitian, an occupational and/or physical therapist, and a recreation therapist. Administrative or supervisory personnel may be present as functioning or "ex officio" team members. This team also has chosen to include a member of the retirement community's housekeeping staff, because the nature of her job keeps her in close contact with all older adults (referred to as "residents") in this community. Because physician representation is not possible for the entire meeting, the agenda is constructed so that residents most in need of physician intervention are discussed first. The presence of the nurse practitioner throughout the meeting also contributes to the medical component of team decision making.

There is a chairperson for the meeting, whose job it is to keep people on track, facilitate discussion, and pace the meeting so that all agenda items can be covered in the allotted time frame. All health professional team members take a turn, for a month at a time, in the chairperson role. Other than the aforementioned functions of this role, the chairperson has no more authority on the team than any other member. The recording of team minutes also is conducted on a rotating basis, with each member filling this role a month at a time. The chairperson and minute-recorder are never the same person.

Communication among Team Members

As the meeting unfolds, various topics are addressed such as concerns regarding new admissions or current residents, plans for discharge back to the independent living component of the retirement community, identification and discussion of problems, and decisions regarding plans of care. The need for possible transfer to a higher level of care is also addressed for residents whose functional status—ability to care for oneself—is becoming impaired. These are the main "tasks" of this particular geriatric interdisciplinary team, with a clear focus on a functional model of care instead of a disease-oriented medical model approach. Full participation of team members tends to be the norm, with the recognition of each discipline's specific expertise for certain health care problems and situations. Information is given, opinions are requested, points of discussion are clarified and expanded, and the decision-making process is guided by the chairperson or another team member to a consensus rather than majority rule.

It is the nature of various health care disciplines to develop certain terminology, abbreviations, and acronyms specific to their field of practice. During the team meetings, however, the use of discipline-specific jargon is kept to a minimum so the level of understanding can remain high between and among all members. Slipping back into "jargonese" usually generates good-natured reminders from fellow team members. A less-than-committed team may tend to overlook the communication barrier that the use of jargon can create, to the detriment of clear understanding and ultimately to resident care (Croen et al., 1984).

Team Decision Making

As resident care problems are identified by the team, they are broken down into specific components instead of being addressed generally. This narrowing of focus sets the tone for brainstorming of solutions by team members. Because it is this team's norm to avoid dismissing any ideas that may be presented, a free-flowing type of communication and comfort level result. Because team members express trust that they can be open with each other, collaborative decision making is facilitated and the maintenance of the team is enhanced.

In developing a framework for planning resident care, the team explores many issues relevant to older persons such as coping abilities, loss, family involvement, potential for problems related to change in environment, and risk for injury or drug toxicity. The individual's strengths are considered by the team as prime elements in developing realistic, rehabilitation-oriented plans of care. Also of prime importance is a functional instead of medical model approach to care of older adults, as described previously. The functional approach tends to provide a common language, identifying for all team members how a particular illness, situation, or the aging process itself affect an individual resident's everyday living skills.

Communication with the Older Person

Although team members work closely with family members as well as the residents themselves, the team has chosen not to include the resident or family in the regular weekly meeting. Instead, to reduce

the possible anxiety that appearing before the team may cause, the resident and/or family may be present at smaller care plan meetings held during the week as appropriate or necessary. In a smaller group setting, it is
also easier for a hearing-impaired resident to participate.

When a resident is present at any meeting, he or she is addressed in a
clear, low tone of voice by the person in closest proximity, thus taking
the changes in hearing ability experienced by many older persons into
consideration. Residents also are addressed in a manner that helps maintain their dignity and individuality such as using the name "Mr. Smith"
instead of "Joe" during the conversation or assessment process.

Team Accountability

This team has worked together for several years, developing
from beginning stages to its present high level of interdisciplinary functioning. Although weekly activities and other meetings vary for each
member, the resident care team meeting described here, called "resident
review," is a stable weekly event. Because of the importance placed on this
ongoing component of the entire retirement community, the accountability of team members is well understood and taken seriously.

This accountability is most evident by the follow-through provided to
residents as a result of team decision making. Each member fulfills her or
his individual responsibility to reach the common goal for resident care
agreed to at the team meeting. The effectiveness of each action or resident treatment is discussed, evaluated, and amended as needed during
subsequent team meetings. Also contributing to team accountability is
each discipline's ongoing quality-assurance program, which extends into
team level functioning. If a resident, such as the earlier example of Mrs. J.,
was the focus of this team, her many needs would be discussed not only
by a specific discipline, but by a group of individuals whose collective
knowledge about Mrs. J. would promote the best care possible.

Team Maintenance Behaviors

The team is aware that task performance is an important
component of its responsibility but also knows that the maintenance
function of the team itself is vital. Therefore, as an example of team
maintenance behaviors, members express their appreciation for another's
good report or idea openly. When conflict regarding plans of care arises,
the problem tends to be addressed openly through skillful communica-

tion methods. Conflict is accepted, with the understanding of team members that the problem might not be resolved by the team, but often can be managed by further exploring issues and options. If there is a conflict regarding professional role ambiguity, or "who does what," it is a common practice for team members to identify possible areas of overlap so negotiation can resolve the question. In this way costly and time-consuming duplication of services is minimized or eliminated, and the resident receiving service is spared the annoyance of several caregivers performing essentially the same function.

When a team member plans to address a potential area of conflict during a meeting, there is evidence that he or she has carefully considered the manner in which the issue should be presented. For example, a nurse with a management position wished to reintroduce the issue of a resident's discharge from the nursing facility, even though the team's consensus at a previous meeting was to provide inpatient nursing care for a while longer. This nurse consulted with the facility administrator concerning the most effective yet sensitive way to present the issue. Because the administration is supportive of and knowledgeable about interdisciplinary team maintenance, the nurse was given helpful guidance. The intent was not to "walk on communication eggshells" when presenting a potential area of conflict, but simply to speak objectively to the team in a nonaccusing manner. In this author's experience with teams, an accusatory statement, such as "You were wrong about this," can significantly damage a team's collaborative problem-solving function by interjecting the possibility that team members, forever human, may tend to respond defensively or withdraw from the discussion.

At the next meeting the topic was reintroduced skillfully as planned. The team was attentive to the nurse's concerns and responded with an open discussion of the issues. The result was an alteration in the resident's discharge plan in accordance with the concerns and ideas presented objectively and sensitively by the nurse.

This example illustrates the interdependence of open, sensitive communication, a willingness of the interdisciplinary team to consider all information and viewpoints, and an administrative climate supportive of the interdisciplinary team concept. All impact heavily on team maintenance, which in turn creates the best possible environment for successful team task performance.

Another effective strategy for team maintenance chosen by this team is the inclusion of simple refreshments at each meeting. The sharing of food and the polite act of refilling each others' coffee cups tend to help create an atmosphere of professional camaraderie that is conducive to accomplishing tasks and maintaining the team's spirit and cohesion.

Teamwork Problems and Solutions

Although this example of a geriatric interdisciplinary team is based on an actual team's behaviors, at first sight it may appear to be relatively problem free. For instance, both task and team maintenance behaviors are utilized, as is a systematic and knowledgeable approach to care of older residents. Hierarchal leadership, based on the status of members, tends to be minimal or absent, for each member recognizes the shared responsibility of leadership according to the situation and the area of expertise required at a given time. There is evidence of conflict or potential conflict, but it is addressed or managed skillfully. Plans of care are developed collaboratively.

But this team has experienced, and currently is experiencing, several problems relative to its development and functioning. It is to the team's credit that, despite barriers, it works at a high level. A firm sense of commitment to the interdisciplinary team model and to quality care of older persons may well be the impetus for continued effective functioning. The following examples of several past and current problems faced by this team may be generalized easily to many existing geriatric teams, especially those in the long-term care area.

Territoriality and Loyalty

Because some team members report to and are evaluated by their own professional discipline, it is not unusual to find a supervisor and staff member on the same team. Such situations at times tend to promote split loyalties or at least a sense of uneasiness when conflicting ideas emerge. Is the loyalty to the team or to the discipline? Where, if anywhere, should territorial lines be drawn? In collaboration with administrative personnel, the team has managed the problem by verbally identifying each discipline's recognized area of expertise, the areas of overlap between and among disciplines, and reaffirming the commitment that the outcome of team decision making is greater than the sum of its parts. The practice of shared leadership within the team is an important concept that is authorized and promoted by the retirement community's administration.

Goal Conflict

Another issue that has arisen, usually when new members join the team, is goal conflict, or what the team expects to accomplish within the realm of each discipline's role perception. At this time the team must involve all new and current members in reviewing its goals and norms, realizing that this effort is time well spent in terms of future team functioning. Although goals and norms are not meant to be inflexible, they do provide leverage or at least a point of reference when conflict arises over a goal. The team also renews its recognition that each new member brings to the team a different set of values derived from both the socialization process and from a variety of education programs. An effort to understand the values and training of other disciplines is a strong asset to interdisciplinary collaboration.

Diverse Levels of Education and Experience

Varied levels of gerontological and geriatric education and experience provide another example of problems encountered by the team described and probably by most teams who provide care to older adults. As stated previously, many academic programs have offered little content in the field of aging, partly due to the limited number of instructors who have actual experience in this comparatively new area of study. Although there has been a marked improvement in access to courses on aging, many team members have not had the time or opportunity to attend them. It follows that all members have the professional responsibility to review current literature and to avail themselves of various continuing education programs or inservice activities. To ignore or postpone this responsibility is to do a great disservice to the team and to the residents it seeks to serve. An administrative commitment to ongoing education impacts heavily on any team's effort in this regard.

External Factors Affecting Teams: Government Regulations

A final, current example of a significant problem faced by this team, as well as by other geriatric teams in long-term care, is the heavy regulatory environment in which these teams must function. The Omnibus Budget Reconciliation Act (OBRA) created many new and revised federal regulations for nursing homes that were developed in response to allegations of substandard care in some of our nation's long-term care nursing facilities (Code of Federal Regulations, 1991). The good intent of these nursing home reform laws is unquestionable, because poor care in any health care setting must be eradicated.

In the numerous nursing facilities where care is excellent, however, the functioning of teams is adversely affected by members' perceptions that the extensive paperwork required by OBRA regulations limits their time for team meetings. As members become more experienced in using the new assessment instruments required by OBRA, they may find that time management tends to improve. The installation of computers to streamline some aspects of paperwork is a solution that is being implemented in many long-term care nursing facilities. However, the problem of extensive, ever-increasing paperwork is very real in long-term care and is adding significant stress to teams that must provide high-quality services to the same population and families over long periods of time.

THE FUTURE OF TEAMWORK IN GERIATRIC LONG-TERM CARE

In long-term care settings, the creation and fostering of interdisciplinary teams may be a logical process. Both federal and state regulations for long-term care require the presence and involvement of various health care disciplines. Therefore, a number of separate health care professionals are available and possibly ripe for team development in this setting. The team approach, by its nature, tends to minimize or prevent the time-consuming duplication of effort that results from traditional methods of planning care by many individual disciplines. Because extensive government regulations necessitate a heavy load of paperwork for health professionals, a collaborative effort in the care planning process may be a time saver as well as an effective means of providing care.

The arrival of the interdisciplinary team approach has great potential in the field of aging, and particularly in the long-term care setting. With an increasing older population, especially those over the age of 85, models of care that address multiple problems in an efficient, collaborative manner must be developed, sustained, and nurtured. Great attention to the study of aging and its unique and overlapping problems needs to become an integral part of the team tasks of problem solving, decision making, and the resultant planning of care for older adults. Team members must examine their attitudes about aging and promote positive approaches to care such as fostering individual independence as much as possible.

Because more academic and continuing education programs are establishing a gerontological focus, they are paving the way for health care professionals to plan sensitive, individualized care for older persons in a team setting. If a knowledgeable geriatric team also understands the task and maintenance behaviors necessary for successful team functioning, the team's potential for planning and providing the best care possible is great.

Interdisciplinary team functioning is not automatic, and it is not an easy task or process for team members to undertake. When commitment to the team approach and to the field of aging exists concurrently, however, an integrative model arises that can fill the crucial health care needs of older persons.

REFERENCES

Bottom, W. D. (1980). Teaming up in geriatrics. *Geriatrics*, 35(10), 106-107, 110.

Bufford, J. I., & Kindig, D. (1974). Institute for team development—the next two years. In H. Wise, R. Beckhard, I. Rubin, & A. L. Kyte (Eds.), *Making health teams work* (pp. 149-159). Cambridge, MA: Ballinger.

Code of Federal Regulations. (1991). Washington, DC: U.S. Government Printing Office.

Croen, L. G., Hamermann, D., & Goetzel, R. Z. (1984). Interdisciplinary training for medical and nursing students. *Journal of the American Geriatrics Society*, 32, 56-61.

Ducanis, A. J., & Golin, A. K. (1979). *The interdisciplinary health care team: A handbook.* Rockville, MD: Aspen.

Dyer, W. G. (1977). *Team building: Issues and alternatives.* Reading, MA: Addison-Wesley.

Eastman, P. (1983). The case for functional assessment. *Geriatric Consultant*, 2(3), 26-29.

Feiger, S. M., & Schmitt, M. H. (1979). Collegiality in interdisciplinary health teams: Its measurement and its effects. *Social Science and Medicine*, 13A, 217-229.

Garner, H. G. (1988). *Helping others through teamwork.* Washington, DC: Child Welfare League of America.

Note: At the time of this writing the author was Executive Vice President of Cathedral Village, a continuing care retirement community in Philadelphia, PA.

Given, B., & Simmons, S. (1977). The interdisciplinary health care team: Fact or fiction? *Nursing Forum*, 16, 165-184.

Hernan, J. A. (1984). Exploding aging myths through retirement counseling. *Journal of Gerontological Nursing*, 10(4), 31-33.

Johnson, D. W., & Johnson, F. P. (1982). *Joining together: Group theory and group skills* (2d ed.). Englewood Cliffs, NJ: Prentice-Hall.

Kane, R. A., & Kane, R. L. (1983). *Assessing the elderly: A practical guide to measurement*. Lexington, MA: Lexington Books.

Mariano, C. (1989). The case for interdisciplinary collaboration. *Nursing Outlook*, 37, 285-288.

Rameizl, P. (1984). The case for assessment technology in long term care: The nursing perspective. *Rehabilitation Nursing*, 9(6), 29-31.

Rao, D. B. (1977). The team approach to integrated care of the elderly. *Geriatrics*, 32, 88-96.

Reilly, C. H. (1990). The geriatric consult team: Service and advocacy for elders. *Nursing Administration Quarterly*, 14(2), 21-24.

Rowe, J. W. (1985). Health care of the elderly. *New England Journal of Medicine*, 312, 827-835.

Rubin, I. M., Plovnick, M. S., & Fry, R. E. (1975). *Improving the coordination of care: A program for health team development*. Cambridge, MA: Ballinger.

Shepard, K. F., Yeo, G., & McGann, L. (1985). Successful components of interdisciplinary education. *Journal of Allied Health*, 14, 297-303.

Steinberg, F. U. (1983). Evaluation and treatment of the geriatric patient. In F. Steinberg (Ed.), *Care of the geriatric patient*. St. Louis: Mosby.

Thompson, R. F., Rhyne, R. L., Stratton, M. A., & Franklin, R. H. (1988). Using an interdisciplinary team for geriatric education in a nursing home. *Journal of Medical Education*, 63, 796-798.

Tsukada, R. A. (1990). Interdisciplinary collaboration: Teamwork in geriatrics. In C. K. Cassel, D. E. Riesenberg, L. B. Sorenson, & J. R. Walsh (Eds.), *Geriatric medicine*, 2d ed. (pp. 668-675). New York: Springer-Verlag.

Whall, A. L., & Conklin, C. (1985). Why a geropsychiatric unit? *Journal of Psychosocial Nursing*, 23(5), 23-27.

Index